Material Spirituality in Modernist Women's Writing

Material Spirituality in Modernist Women's Writing

Elizabeth Anderson

BLOOMSBURY ACADEMIC
LONDON • NEW YORK • OXFORD • NEW DELHI • SYDNEY

BLOOMSBURY ACADEMIC
Bloomsbury Publishing Plc
50 Bedford Square, London, WC1B 3DP, UK
1385 Broadway, New York, NY 10018, USA
29 Earlsfort Terrace, Dublin 2, Ireland

BLOOMSBURY, BLOOMSBURY ACADEMIC and the Diana logo are trademarks of
Bloomsbury Publishing Plc

First published in Great Britain 2020
This paperback edition published in 2021

Copyright © Sarah Elizabeth Anderson, 2020

Sarah Elizabeth Anderson has asserted her right under the Copyright, Designs and Patents
Act, 1988, to be identified as Author of this work.

For legal purposes the Acknowledgements on p. viii constitute an extension
of this copyright page.

Cover design: Eleanor Rose
Cover image © Getty Images

A catalogue record for this book is available from the British Library.

A catalog record for this book is available from the Library of Congress.

ISBN: HB: 978-1-3500-6344-0
PB: 978-1-3502-4319-4
ePDF: 978-1-3500-6345-7
eBook: 978-1-3500-6346-4

Typeset by Newgen KnowledgeWorks Pvt. Ltd., Chennai, India

To find out more about our authors and books visit www.bloomsbury.com
and sign up for our newsletters.

To Owen and Lucy
who know far more about the liveliness of things than I ever will

Contents

Acknowledgements

The early seeds of this project were sown at a seminar on objects at the Modernist Studies Association conference in Montreal in 2009. My thanks to Gabrielle Moyer for facilitating a thoughtful and generous discussion. Encouragement to consider spirituality and things in greater depth came from Heather Walton, to whom I owe a great debt of gratitude for her support as mentor, colleague and friend.

Academic work is often a solitary endeavour, but a community of friends and colleagues gathers around this work; without them, it would not have been possible. Thanks to colleagues at the Universities of Stirling and Aberdeen for fostering academic environments of good spirit. I have been so fortunate to call these places home. Particular thanks are due to Adrian Hunter and Alison Jasper for supporting me during my fellowship at Stirling. Friends and colleagues near and far have talked through difficulties, read portions of the manuscript, given me tips and texts (and distraction!) when needed: thanks to Tim Baker, Tara Beaney, Kirstie Blair, Anna Fisk, Suzanne Hobson, Jenny Hyest, Bryony Randall, Sarah Parker, Jennifer Reek, Alana Vincent, Heather Walton and Mimi Winick. The H.D. Society holds a special place in my heart for its unstinting support and collegial warmth. Special thanks to Annette Debo, Celena Kusch, Lara Vetter and Rebecca Walsh for encouraging me at numerous and diverse times and places. Helen Sword's landmark study of academic writing practices, *Air & Light & Time & Space*, reached me at a crucial stage of drafting this volume and provided just the practical support I needed. Thanks to Abby, Lauren and Shontael for being the best virtual writing group ever, for keeping me company and keeping me going. I am deeply grateful to the Bloomsbury readers whose generous and incisive comments on both the proposal and the manuscript were extremely helpful. Any remaining errors are, of course, my own. I am grateful to David Avital, Lucy Brown and Clara Herberg at Bloomsbury, for believing that sometimes the quirky books are the most interesting and who have brought this book to the light of day.

Much of the material in this book has benefited from the thoughtful engagement of colleagues at a number of conferences and research seminars. I would like to thank the organizers of the Modernist Studies Association conferences in 2013, 2016 and 2017, the International Society for Literature Religion and Culture's conference in 2016, and the 26th Annual International Conference on Virginia Woolf, for providing a platform for such exchanges. Thanks also to Judith Wolfe, Anna Fisk, Heather Walton and Suzanne Hobson for inviting me to present papers at the University of St Andrew's, the University of Glasgow and the London Modernism Seminar. This book has also benefited from discussions at a number of MSA seminars, and my thanks to Greg Erickson, Suzanne Hobson, Jenny Hyest, Roger Rothman and Mimi Winick, as organizers, as well as the participating colleagues, for scholarly conversations that were equally challenging and generous.

In 2015 I had the wonderful opportunity to work with artist Charmian Pollok to mount an exhibition at the Pathfoot Gallery, University of Stirling, inspired by the work of Mary Butts and called 'The Pebbles Were Each One Alive'. I am so grateful to Charmian, Sarah Bromage and Jane Cameron for all their work to make this possible.

I would like to thank the Carnegie Trust for the Universities of Scotland, whose support enabled me to consult the papers of H.D. and Mary Butts at the Beinecke Rare Book and Manuscript Library at Yale University, Gwendolyn Brooks' Papers at the Bancroft Library at the University of California, Berkeley and the William Morris Gallery and its archive in Walthamstow, and the Arts and Humanities Research Council for supporting an earlier visit to the Beinecke Library. Thanks to the library staff, whose unfailing professionalism and support is a gift to scholars. I wish to thank the University of Stirling, whose Impact Fellowship supported this project for several years.

Portions of Chapters One, Two and Three appeared in earlier forms in the following publications: Elizabeth Anderson, Andrew Radford and Heather Walton, eds. *Modernist Women Writers and Spirituality: A Piercing Darkness* (Palgrave Macmillan, 2016), 135–51; Jane de Gay et al., eds. *Virginia Woolf and Heritage: Selected Papers from the 26th Annual Conference on Virginia Woolf* (Clemson University Press, 2017), 102–8; 'H.D.'s Tapestry: Embroidery, William Morris and *The Sword Went Out to Sea*'. *Modernist Cultures* 12, no. 2 (2017): 226–48; 'The Consolation of Things: Domestic Objects in H.D.'s Writing from the Second World War'. *LIR Journal* 4 (2015): 167–82. I am grateful to the editors and publishers for permission to reuse this work.

I am also grateful to the following publishers for permission to reprint the quotations found herein: Excerpts from TO THE LIGHTHOUSE by Virginia Woolf. Copyright ©1927 by Houghton Mifflin Harcourt Publishing Company, renewed 1954 by Leonard Woolf. Reprinted by permission of Houghton Mifflin

Harcourt Publishing Company. All rights reserved. Additional thanks for permission to quote from *To the Lighthouse* granted by the Society of Authors as the Literary Representative of the Estate of Virginia Woolf. 'Letter to Bryher, 2 March, 1938; Letters to Bryher, 8 November, 1947; Letter to Viola Baxter Jordan, 28 April 1942; Letter to Viola Baxter Jordan, 5 September 1947?' by H.D. (Hilda Doolittle), from New Directions acting as agent, copyright © 2019 by The Schaffner Family Foundation. Reprinted by permission of New Directions Publishing Corp. Excerpts from 'Gladys, Gladiolus' and *Maud Martha Reprinted by Consent of Brooks Permissions*. I am grateful to Cynthia Walls and Pamela Williams at Brooks Permissions for their help.

This project has stretched over years that have also seen the birth of a second child, a job change and cross-country move. Without the support of family, friends and colleagues I would be considerably more frayed in body and soul; to those both near and far I offer thanks. Gratitude and gin to Rachel Smith and Meg MacDonald: you keep me going as a scholar, a mother and a person. My children have put up with this project with good grace (more or less) and bemusement for longer than they can remember. From them I have learned delight, joy and (im)patience. And finally, to James, who once again has shouldered Herculean amounts of housework, childcare and spousal moaning: Thank you, always.

I cannot mention all the innumerable objects that have supported the production of this book, but I have particular (if sometimes agonistic) attachment to my desks (at home and at work), my laptop, my PC, my community of mugs and a certain felted dandelion.

Introduction

Things had a habit of coming alive like that. Not only large substantial things like furniture but curtains and the patterns of stuff and the fringes of quilts and cushions. ... But the strangest part of this coming alive of things was what they did. They listened, they seemed to swell out with some mysterious important content, and when they were full she felt that they smiled. But it was not for her, only, their sly secret smile; they were members of a secret society and they smiled among themselves.[1]

In this passage from Katherine Mansfield's long story 'Prelude', Linda Burnell's passivity enables a connection to things that seem more lively than she, full of their own life and secret knowledges. Luminous objects abound in Mansfield's writing. Part of her colourist aesthetic is her vivid depiction of things and her continual quest to present the life that lies in, through and around them. Here we see tension between the objects' connection to the narrating subject and their resistance to connection, their inherent alterity and communion among themselves. This is a tension that runs through this book as I explore the spiritual life of things in the work of modernist women writers.

Anthropologists such as Arjun Appadurai and Daniel Miller have investigated the social life of things in their analysis of how assemblages of objects are crucial to identity formation, while Bill Brown's thing theory, in emphasizing objects' resistance to interpretation, constitutes a secret life of things.[2] My work hovers between these two views. I am interested in the relationship between subjects and objects, that is, where the boundaries between the two erode, where material objects provoke intersubjectivity, and the ethical and aesthetic implications of the meeting, meshing and differences of subjects and objects. Yet I am also concerned with how material things (natural, handcrafted or manufactured) remain irreducibly other, and where this radical alterity may be an instantiation of the sacred.[3] This introduction charts the different fields of scholarship that inform this study: the significance of both religion and materiality in modernist studies; the place of materiality in theology and religious studies and new materialist theoretical models. While this diversity represents a complex scholarly map, my work on the spiritual life of things in modernist women's writing draws them together in dialogue with recent work on (re)enchantment. Finally, I address my choice of authors and give an outline of the book's five chapters.

Things in process and things in place

The liveliness of things means that they are in process, they move through space and are dynamic as well as ongoing. The differences of the authors under consideration (particularly on the spectrum of belief/unbelief and their individual locations with respect to race, economics, war and domestic relations) lead to different manifestations of spirituality in their literature. It is neither possible nor, I think, desirable to give a singular view for how spirituality inheres within things in the body of work I analyse and the chapters in this book reference a wide range of religious beliefs, practices and traditions. However, across their work there is a sense of both the friendliness of things and the depth of thingly alterity which relates to a sense of a material transcendental – whether religious or otherwise. The various tensions and cohesions of these two modes are part of what give these texts their energy and interest.

As will be evident across this book, I am interested in the movement of things, the networks they constitute and their locations. The relation of things to and in place is a significant concern of this project. In tracing the life of things, we see their movement in and across domestic and public spaces, urban and rural environments. 'Space' and 'place' are contested terms for geographers, and definitional struggles spill over into related disciplines as the spatial turn across the humanities gathers momentum. Andrew Thacker summarizes the position: 'To a number of geographical theorists *space* indicates a sense of movement, of history, of becoming, while *place* is often thought to imply a static sense of location, of being, or of dwelling'. However, much modernist writing 'complicate[s] any sharp and easy division between a conservative sense of place and a revolutionary sense of space'.[4] Doreen Massey also urges the departure from ossified opposition between space and place, suggesting that we consider space as 'the product of interrelations; as constituted through interactions'.[5] I rely on Michel de Certeau's sense of space as *'practiced place'*, while also being mindful of Massey's warnings about the problems of maintaining sharp distinctions between place and space and the assumptions that go with them (emphasis in original).[6] I also draw on bell hooks' formulation, which privileges the environment itself as generative: 'Spaces can tell stories and unfold histories.'[7]

Modernism and religion

Although the association of modernism and secularism has been a commonplace in the majority of Anglophone modernist studies for decades, there is a growing area of modernist studies concerned with reassessing the question of modernism's relationship to religion and spirituality. Recent interest in religion in modernist studies begins with Leon Surette's groundbreaking work, *The Birth of Modernism* (1993), in which he argues that occult figures and tropes form an integral part of their poetry of Pound, Eliot and Yeats. An intriguing aspect of Surette's study is his defensive tone: he clearly sees his work as pushing boundaries of acceptable academic research. However, academic interest in spiritualism and the occult within literary studies has grown significantly, as evidenced by work from Tatiana Kontou, Timothy Materer, Helen Sword, Pamela Thurschwell, Lara Vetter and Leigh Wilson (among others), while historians like Alex Owen and Leigh Eric Schmidt have explored the cultural significance of spiritualism and the occult in rich detail.[8] More recently, John Bramble has continued this trend; *Modernism and the Occult* (2015) takes deeper cognizance of global influences that came into Western occult forms at the height of European imperialism.[9]

In *Religious Experience and the Modernist Novel* (2010), Pericles Lewis argues that spiritual concerns have generally been overlooked in studies of the modernist novel but that despite growing secularism, modernist writers continued to grapple with matters of religious experience. Taking his title from William James, Lewis reads several modernist novels alongside thinkers such as James, Weber and Freud, taking a largely psychological approach which argues for the interiority and privatization of spiritual impulses. Lewis's work resonates with mine in his analysis of transcendence meaning 'experiences that originated in the ordinary world … but that opened some sort of insight beyond the realm of the ordinary', but his privileging of interiority loses sight of the public implications of such private musings, while they also disregard the complex relationships with institutional religion explored by many writers.[10]

Turning to more thematically focused studies, in her work on angels in modernist literature, Suzanne Hobson argues that 'in their sheer variety, [angels] register the complex and variegated pattern of belief and disbelief which more accurately characterizes modernism's "religion" than the old disenchanted version'.[11] Alexandra Peat brings the trope of pilgrimage to bear on modernist interest in journeys and location in *Travel and Modernist Literature: Sacred and Ethical Journeys* (2011) while in *Modernism and Christianity* (2014), Erik Tonning reads orthodox Christianity as a source of creativity to many modernist writers.[12] The significance of religion to the aesthetics of the Harlem Renaissance is explored by scholars such as Houston A. Baker, Judylyn Ryan, Mark A Sanders, Jean E. Snyder and Elizabeth J. West.[13] This work considers the influence of both Black Christianity and the legacies of West African traditions on African American writing.

There has also been growing interest in paganism in studies of late nineteenth- and early twentieth-century literature. This work charts literary engagement with the spiritual aspects of the Greek revival and the emerging discipline of anthropology's interest in ancient religions.[14] Margot K. Louis traces a strain of Romantic emphasis on the mystery cults as 'a way to celebrate the sacredness of this life, of sexuality and the life force' that continued through the Victorian era.[15] Late nineteenth- and early twentieth-century Anglophone literature saw a myriad of heroines aligned with earth goddesses and dryads, while Modernists sought to overcome the pessimistic vision of the Decadents with a renewed emphasis on a 'celebration of life'.[16] In *Modernist Mythopoeia: The Twilight of the Gods*, Scott Freer argues for close integration of myth and spirituality and suggests that modernist engagement with myth as a form of metaphorical theology acknowledged more room for the unknown.[17]

Taken together this body of scholarship charts the wide-ranging and creative engagement of modernist writers with numerous forms of religion and spirituality.[18] However, women writers are still under-represented in this scholarship: notably, Tonning's book does not include any women writers, while Pericles Lewis limits his engagement to Virginia Woolf and Scott Freer only includes H.D. The work on the occult and spiritualism tends to have better representation, likely because women were so strongly present in these movements. The recent collection, *Modernist Women Writers and Spirituality*, goes some way towards addressing this lack. The collection addresses canonical and more marginal writers along with a range of spiritual expressions from the mainstream to the more esoteric.[19]

In her introduction to the first issue of the journal *Feminist Modernist Studies*, Cassandra Laity points to Urmila Seshagiri's comment that feminism and gender appear both 'everywhere and nowhere' in the many conference papers and articles emerging from the Modernist Studies Association and its journal *Modernism/Modernity*.[20] Although for decades scholars have 'acknowledged gender as a constitutive category of modernism', it is still largely treated as an 'add-on' in the main institutions in the field.[21] In this book's focus on spirituality and things, I risk confirming Laity's concern that feminist scholarship remains 'subsumed under modernism's broader intellectual expansions', yet I hope my focus on women writers will enable me to foreground the feminist concerns of this book and contribute to the growth of feminist modernist studies called for by Laity, Anne Fernald and others. My focus on women writers gives a particular perspective to my central concern with spirituality, things and spaces. Women's traditional association with domestic space and their experiences of it give rise to a charged relation to ordinary things both within and outwith the home. Additionally, women's position on the margins of traditional religious and academic institutions (women were often leaders of the more radical and avant-garde religious explorations of the late nineteenth and early twentieth centuries like Christian Science, theosophy and spiritualism) tends to give them an experience of lived religion that is less formal and often adversarial or heterodox. With leadership in the academy and the church closed to them, writing became a forum for women to explore spiritual ideas and experiences.

Much of the work cited above focuses on European or American texts, with Christianity and European paganism and the occult as the dominant traditions (with the exception of scholarship that considers the influence of African Indigenous religions on African American texts). Even Peat's and Bramble's works on the Eastern influences on the modernist understanding of the sacred are still largely concerned with European texts. Work remains to be done not only on bringing a fuller representation of women writers into the scholarship but also in addressing the complexity of engagements with the diversity of world religions across the global matrix of modernisms. This project aims to join scholarship initiated by Baker, Bramble, Peat, Vetter, West and others to widen the frame of reference and to bring a more diverse body of literature and spiritual expressions to the table (albeit in the limited way required by a tightly focused thematic project). Most scholarship on modernism and religion deals only passingly with material culture as such, although in *Modernist Writings and Religio-Scientific Discourse* (2010), Lara Vetter foregrounds sexuality, gender, race and the vulnerability of the body, to explore how writing concerned with ideals and otherworldly aims can be grounded in the material and political.[22] My book makes a unique contribution in bringing a close attention to materiality into exploration of modernist spiritualities. By focusing onto the material, issues of transcendence and otherworldliness often associated with religion are displaced for a view from below that takes a more earthy emphasis. This indicates a kind of spirituality more in tune with Indigenous animist traditions, the radical incarnationalism of some aspects of Christianity and contemporary theological engagement with discourses of new materialism. I will return to this point, but first I wish to consider modernist studies engagement with materiality.

Modernism and things

The new modernist studies have taken material culture to be central to the study of modernist literature.[23] Landmark works include Douglas Mao's *Solid Objects* (1999) and Bill Brown's *A Sense of Things* (2003) and *Other Things* (2015). Both scholars insist on the alterity of things, what Mao calls the object's 'otherness', that marks their resistance to interpretation and co-option into subjectivity.[24] Brown describes this alterity as a 'potentiality within any object ... that repeatedly points to the uncanniness of the ordinary, the oscillations between the animate and the inanimate'.[25] I do not find the distinction between object and thing particularly helpful as a working terminology, but I appreciate the sense of thingly mobility that Brown emphasizes, this accords with my focus on things in process.[26] According to Brown, 'The thing thus names a subject-object relation' and this relation is dynamic, an event, rather than an ongoing state.[27] In his interest in the way 'objects grasp you', Brown decentres the subject but does not do away with it entirely. In this he distinguishes his work from object-oriented philosophies that attempt to excise the subject completely.[28]

Mao addresses the charge that modernism suffers a 'cold aloofness' with a defence that brings affect into the equation: 'Yet in their approaches to the object – which they almost invariably treasured as something out of the reach of subjectivity ... modernists show how partial is the truth of this indictment, with its unwarranted assumption that love always demands the closeness of joining and holding, never the distance of respect and longing.'[29] I appreciate Mao's introduction of affect and his defence of modernism's respect for objects with a life of their own. However, I would suggest that my corpus of texts (and others beyond this study) indicate a different view of the modernist love affair with things. I argue that in this work we do indeed see many accounts of holding and joining between subjects and objects, but that this does not indicate dominance but rather a respect for the spiritual autonomy of the loved thing that draws the subject themself into a process of becoming. This focus on intersubjectivity between humans and things is supported by the work of Rochelle Rives. Her work on objects and affect in Mary Butts's writing is crucial to the understanding of intersubjectivity developed across this project. She analyses how the placement of objects enhances their capacity to provoke an opening and dispersal of subjectivity.[30] It is important to remember that things in literature are not the same as things in the world. In dealing with the language of texts written by human persons there is always a level of subjectivity: writers may take pains to represent the thing's autonomy but they can never remove themselves entirely from the text. Things may be brought to speech but they cannot tell their own stories in human writing.

Although I am influenced by Mao's and Brown's accounts of the significance of material objects in modernist writing, and their gestures towards animacy and alterity, in failing to consider the connection between alterity and spirituality they miss an important aspect of the way things function in many modernist texts. In considering the spiritual life of things in modernist writing, we see not only how these texts represent things (mimesis) but also how they participate in world building (poesis). Moreover, as in the bulk of writing on modernism and religion, Brown's and Mao's texts do not include gender parity in their author selection (unsurprisingly, Woolf features prominently in both *Other Things* and *Solid Objects*). The omission of a fuller account of the contributions of women writers by scholars such as Brown and Mao means that they miss an opportunity to engage in gender analysis alongside the study of materiality.[31]

Animism and material religion

Religious studies is no stranger to the material turn across the disciplines. In recent decades scholars began to pay closer attention to practice over doctrine, and this included a focus on the material objects and places that accompany religious activity.[32] More recently, David Morgan has argued that belief itself is enmeshed in material culture, while Manuel A. Vásquez argues for a non-reductive material approach which values particularity: 'Embodiment and embeddedness in time and place enable and constrain diverse, flexible, yet patterned subjective experiences that come to be understood as religious.'[33] In explicitly drawing together materiality and spirituality, I turn to animism as an important discourse for current work in religious studies, anthropology and ecology as well as the early twentieth-century modernist intellectual milieu. In anthropology and religious studies the term can be traced to the work of

Edward B. Tylor, who used the term to describe what he considered the basic principle of religion as containing 'belief in spirits'.[34] Martin D. Stringer argues that if we disregard the developmental trajectory (from supposed primitive to high culture) Tylor supposes, we are left with 'a way of being religious' in which 'all material objects, and primarily the human, have a spiritual dimension and so the fundamental engagement with the world is understood to be an engagement with the spiritual'.[35]

Following critique of Tylor (among other early anthropologists), anthropologists and scholars of religion are returning to animism in an attempt to engage with the worldviews of Indigenous peoples more respectfully and accurately.[36] Graham Harvey emphasizes a relational worldview as key to animist understandings of 'the world [as] full of persons, only some of whom are human'.[37] Harry Garuba describes West African animism as 'a mode of religious consciousness ... [which] spiritualizes the object world'.[38] In modernity, this 'animist unconscious' functions through the '*continual re-enchantment of the world*' in which new developments in science, technology or bureaucracy are absorbed into a magical worldview (emphasis in original).[39] Robin Kimmerer's discussion of animism and language is highly suggestive for a literary study such as this. She describes her process of learning Potawatomi, her tribes' language and the moment when she realized that many words that English would assign as nouns were verbs in Potawatomi and related languages:

> To be a hill, to be a sandy beach, to be a Saturday, all are possible verbs in a world where everything is alive. Water, and, and even a day, the language a mirror for seeing the animacy of the world, the life that pulses through all things, through pines and nuthatches and mushrooms ... This is the grammar of animacy.[40]

Kimmerer suggests that the structure of language can reveal dynamic intimacy with the living world.

The concept of spirited matter suggests the more radical purposes of this project: rethinking transcendence to locate it materially in *this* world. Early studies of comparative religion linked animism to fetishism and the figure of the fetish highlights my focus on things. Fetishism as described by early anthropologists has been justly critiqued as misrepresenting Indigenous animist worldviews, but the concept has been re-evaluated by anthropologist Peter Pels, who emphasizes the unity of material and spiritual in fetishes: 'Materiality is not transcended by any [foreign] voice ... the thing's materiality itself is supposed to speak and act; its spirit is *of* matter.'[41] Pels suggests that the fetish prompts a new (to Western modes of understanding) way of approaching religion: the 'untranscended materiality [of the fetish] provide[d] the Enlightenment with a radically novel, because atheological conception of religion'.[42] The unity of spirit and matter indicated by veneration of things and their ritual significance gives us an understanding of religion firmly anchored in material practice. An animist understanding of religion that relocates transcendence within the material has been interpreted in a range of ways: Tim Ingold's writes of 'Spirit [as] the regenerative power of … circulatory flows [of materials]' while Emma Restall Orr traces an alternative western philosophical tradition that rejects dualism and embraces animism as '*a relational ontology*' (emphasis in original).[43]

The notion of untranscended yet sacred material is antithetical to much of the Christian theological tradition (with its legacy of Platonism) that has shaped Western thinking, as well as to post-Enlightenment views that emphasize a mechanistic, disenchanted universe. However, there are streams of the tradition more hospitable to animist thinking. Caroline Walker Bynum charts a history of 'living holy matter' in late Medieval Europe.[44] A tradition of radical incarnationalism which sees divinity present in all things can be seen in the concept of haecceity (this-ness) developed by Duns Scotus and given poetic form by Gerard Manley Hopkins who celebrates how each unique being expresses itself – 'Each mortal thing … / Deals out that being indoors each one dwells; / Selves – goes its self; *myself* it speaks and spells' and also their relation to divine incarnation: 'For Christ plays in ten thousand places.'[45] Eastern Orthodoxy holds a sacramental understanding of all matter being taken into divine; sacramental awareness is not limited to the blessed elements but encompasses all the material world.[46]

Turning to the contemporary moment, some constructive theologians take a more radically materialist view of transcendence. Catherine Keller finds resources in the Christian mystical tradition as well as contemporary thinking from physics (Karen Barad) to performativity (Judith Butler) to posit new ways of thinking about the divine unfolding in the material world and the interconnections among things, persons, galaxies.[47] She formulates transcendence emerging from process thought as 'movement beyond: not beyond, to another ontology, but beyond the given, to the new'.[48] Likewise, Mayra Rivera argues for a notion of transcendence that preserves divine alterity (and the ethical implications for it as a model of human difference) while reconfiguring traditional understandings of the beyond. She offers a vision of a horizontal, relational transcendence that exists 'within creation and between creatures'.[49]

My project engages with a diversity of contemporary approaches to animist spiritualities in two ways. First, I consider how my authors engage with the discourses of their own time that indicate a lively, sacred materiality. For example, H.D.'s interest in Hermeticism, spiritualism and other occult practices in tandem with Moravian Christianity touches on an occluded tradition of Christian animism, while Mary Butts's life-writing demonstrates a strong syncretic connection between her pagan aesthetics and her Anglo-Catholic practice (influenced by Eastern Orthodox theology).[50] Second, I use new work from anthropology, philosophy and religious studies as a framework for interpreting these literary texts and considering their relevance for current thought. In its engagement with both imagination and experience, literature can make a greater contribution to genealogies of ideas than is always acknowledged. As a white, American scholar, working in the Scottish academy, I refer to Indigenous knowledge with care, acknowledging my lack of scholarly expertise and lived experience. In presenting such material here, I risk distortion by bringing it away from its original cultural context.[51] However, scholars such as Juanita Sundberg and Zoe Todd remind us that exchanges between Indigenous and colonial knowledge systems and cultural practices have been ongoing for centuries (accompanied by extreme violence towards Indigenous societies by European colonists), while the worldviews of Indigenous spiritualities resonate with the attention to the sentient cosmos evident in the turn to ontology in the Anglo-European academy.[52] Therefore, failing to acknowledge the place of Indigenous cultures in European and American history or the significance of the work of Indigenous scholars for contemporary theorizing seems to me the greater violence.[53]

Vital materialism

Religious traditions that see lively materiality as sacred or divine resonate with the turn to the material across the humanities, which not only gives greater attention to material context and culture but also has begun to develop an understanding of materiality as lively and agential. Contemporary theorists explore host of thinkers (Baruch Spinoza, Anne Conway, Alfred North Whitehead, Henri Bergson, Gilles Deleuze), as well as creative work from the arts and sciences, to uncover a genealogy of vitalist thinking. In drawing together the resources of animism, new materialism and literary modernism, the present book contributes to this project. My work participates in the project of developing a 'prehistory of the current interest in the vitality of matter and object agency'.[54] New materialists like Jane Bennett have disavowed a religious element to their projects, yet one of the problems of naming of this field of inquiry 'new materialism' is that this nomenclature occludes the many ways in which such thinking is not in fact new but replicates the relational ontologies of Indigenous knowledges in particular.[55]

In her book *Vibrant Matter* (2010), Jane Bennett defines vitality as 'the capacity of things – edibles, commodities, storms, metals – not only to impede or block the will and designs of humans but also to act as quasi agents or forces with trajectories, propensities, or tendencies of their own.'[56] For Bennett, agency is entangled with affect: 'Organic and inorganic bodies, natural and cultural objects … *all* are affective. I am here drawing on a Spinozist notion of affect, which refers broadly to the capacity of any body for activity and responsiveness.'[57] Her work connects to the relational ontology described by physicist Karen Barad. Bennett names the ethical intent of her project as a call to attend to the vital materiality of which we are a part, 'to direct sensory, linguistic, and imaginative attention to it' in the hopes that this will prompt a more horizontal, ecological orientation.[58]

Bennett notes that 'a newfound attentiveness to matter and its powers will not solve the problem of human exploitation or oppression, but it can inspire a greater sense of the extent to which all bodies are kin in the sense of inextricably enmeshed in a dense network of relations.'[59] Relations are crucial to new materialist philosophies.[60] Humanities scholars and social scientists are increasingly turning to Barad's exploration of the entanglement of matter and meaning in the field of quantum physics, which reveals the liveliness of matter at the tiniest of scales.[61] She describes a distributed and dynamic understanding of agency in which 'distinct agencies do not precede but rather emerge through, their intra-action.'[62] Barad uses 'intra' rather than 'inter' to emphasize that agency is shaped through encounter rather than exiting prior to it. This yields a dynamic view of matter: '*Matter is substance in its intra-active becoming – not a thing but a doing, a congealing of agency*' (emphasis in original).[63] Thus Barad claims a relational ontology in which phenomena are inseparable, always already entangled.[64] She is most interested in how 'matter makes itself felt' as ['it'] feels, converses, suffers, desires, yearns and remembers.'[65] Human persons are formed in dynamic relation to an emerging network of thingly agencies, which depend on generative difference rather than deadening sameness.

Catherine Keller emphasizes the turn to relations between bodies: 'Bodies sensuous, disabled, queer, vital. Not just fellow human ones, not even just fellow mammals, but bodies all the way down.'[66] The notion of a 'body' – human, animal, mineral, assemblage – allows me to maintain my focus on things. We can understand a thing as a confluence of the flow of materials that forms a body that may endure for a period of time, gathering affect, histories and actions, but one that is always already passing away. Serenella Iovino and Serpil Oppermann describe 'material phenomenon' as 'knots in a vast network of agencies' and argue that the development and movement of matter can be read as narrative: 'All matter … is a storied matter.'[67]

An ethical dilemma posed by a relational ontology is the question of the integrity of marginalized subjects whose subjectivity is yet to be recognized by an oppressive world order.[68] However, Karen Barad points out that 'it has become increasingly clear that the seemingly self-evidentiary nature of bodily boundaries … is a result of the repetition of (culturally and historically) specific bodily performance.' The 'givenness' of bodily boundaries has been contested by scholars of postcolonial, feminist, queer and disability studies.[69] Catherine Keller speaks to this concern for the dispossessed in her analysis of relational ethics. A relational ontology will see subjectivity as a process: 'I flow forth manifold … [n]ot because I have captured the other as my own self, not because I have discarded myself, but because myself, replete with others, becomes more.'[70] Keller draws on Judith Butler to develop an ethics of responsibility: 'I do not augment myself with my virtuousness when I act responsibly, but I give myself over to the broader sociality that I am.'[71] Likewise, Barad sees ethics as inherent to a relational ontology that does not erase difference but attends to the connections amid differences: 'Differentiating is not about Othering, separating, but on the contrary, about making connections and commitments … Ethics is therefore not about right responses to a radically exteriorized other, but about responsibility and accountability for the lively relationalities of becoming, of which we are a part.'[72]

Where, then is the coincidence of new materialism with theology or spirituality? While Bennett rejects the language of soul, refusing an identification of vitality with 'a spiritual supplement', we can turn to Catherine Keller's reading of quantum physics of Barad and others alongside the unknowing of negative theology: 'Once one glimpses the mindful animation of minimal creatures, the plenum of creation itself comes alive. And then how do we name that life?'[73] Keller does not suggest that we call this wildly dynamic, expansive, entangled materiality 'God', but she does indicate that nicknames for this all-in-all may be 'darkly suggested', reminding us that we relate 'as persons to – that all-in-all. And by quantum logic it would already be relating to us – personally. If after all it enfolds all, its infinite impersonality includes the personal that it embodies'.[74] The authors in this study express animist materiality in diverse ways, but they share a sense of the sacred nature of encounters between human persons and lively things.

Bennett freely confesses the elusive nature of matter's vitality: 'It is too close and too fugitive, as much wind as thing, impetus as entity, a movement always on the way to becoming otherwise, an effluence that is vital and engaged in trajectories but not necessarily intentions.' She acknowledges the difficulty of dislodging our ingrained grammars that bestow 'activity to people and passivity to things'.[75] In aiding efforts to think otherwise, we may turn to literature. This book takes up Bennett's challenge, considering whether early twentieth-century literature may go further than philosophy in dreaming of 'fabulously vital materiality'.[76] The animacy of things in modernist writing shows how modernists conceived of newness itself as alive.

Enchantment and post-secularism

Bennett's work on vital materiality is rooted in her earlier work *The Enchantment of Modern Life: Attachments, Crossings, and Ethics* (2001), in which she argues that encouraging a mood of enchantment promotes attachment to the material world which in turn fuels an ethic of generosity. While she rejects a religious understanding of enchantment, there is a latent spiritual element to her emphasis on wonder that undermines the separation of secular and sacred. Enchantment is related to wonder, which implies awe and curiosity. Both enchantment and wonder signal an acute awareness of the sensory world around us (not at all other-worldly), but enchantment also speaks to the liveliness of the world we are entangled in: 'A vibrant, quirky, and overflowing material world.'[77] Rather than a mechanistic universe or an ordered cosmos directed by a detached deity, enchantment suggests the wondrous interconnection of things. Marc Schnieder understands it as related to wonder and transformation as enchantment moves us beyond our present understanding: 'To be enchanted is thus different from being "deeply delighted" or "charmed" … since we are faced with something both real and at the same time uncanny, weird, mysterious or awesome.'[78] Enchantment sees the mystery in the world, it looks otherwise, seeing dynamic, vibrant relation. Conventional readings of modernism accept sociologist Max Weber's thesis that the modern world is disenchanted.[79] This reading has been challenged in recent scholarship: in divorcing enchantment from religion and spirituality, a substantial portion of the vibrant texture of modernism is lost. Roger Griffin argues that the search for 'hidden perennial truths in art and occultism can both be seen as *modernist* experiments in the re-enchantment of the world.'[80]

The foregoing discussion leads me towards current debate on the relations between secular and sacred. Pericles Lewis notes that in the late nineteenth and early twentieth centuries, the English-speaking world remained largely religious, while scepticism was a preserve of the educated elite.[81] Moreover, he argues that many modernists continued to engage with questions of religion and spirituality long after Arnold heard 'Faith['s] … melancholy, long, withdrawing roar'.[82] Alexandra Peat examines how many modernist writers retained an interest in spirituality and the sacred alongside their scepticism towards mainstream religious traditions.[83] Scholars interested in spirituality in modernism join a wide range of scholars across the disciplines who challenge the secularism thesis, that is, 'the idea that modern civilization implies, demands, or depends upon the rejection of belief in the sacred or the supernatural' and the claim that the secular 'is a simple break' from the religious.[84] Across the humanities we are seeing a growing interest in post-secularism, a complicating of simplistic models of secularism, and an excavation of how secular modes themselves relate to religious frameworks.[85] In religious studies, a greater emphasis on everyday life shows that a strict demarcation between secular and scared does not obtain for many people.[86]

Much post-secular scholarship is concerned with the large canvases of public domains, civil religion, global politics and so on. Post-secular feminist scholars such as Saba Mahmood and Joan Wallach Scott analyse both contemporary feminism's alliance with secularism and the way that the emergence of secular nation states is inherently gendered, with women and religion assigned to the private sphere.[87] This stream of scholarship complicates debates on secularism and religion, public and private, through the complicating third factor of sexual difference. However, this work still tends to emphasize the public sphere. My project is more closely aligned with the recent work of Rosi Braidotti, who argues that vital materialism hosts 'the residual spirituality at work in critical theory'.[88] Braidotti turns to the conjunction of affect and materialism to signify a post-secular spirituality that seeks to generate 'sustainable futures' through intimacy with the world.[89] My project contributes to the feminist post-secular project, in particular its complication of the division between public and private, which feminism has long worked to dismantle. In attending to everyday objects, domestic environments and relations, this book yields a different perspective on the post-secular that is less concerned with nation-states and more with domestic relations, less with civil religion than with heterodox spiritual practices. Attending to the liveliness of matter and entangled intersubjectivity between humans and non-humans give us a fine-grained analysis that provides a more ground-up view. Looking to the small things, spaces and practices adds richness and depth to our understanding of modern(ist) enchantment. For thinkers such as Michel de Certeau, the everyday, what has been excluded and invisible, gives us resources for making interventions in dehumanizing systems, of making 'innumerable and infinitesimal transformations'.[90] In turning to domestic spaces and everyday practices, the political does not disappear but is reconfigured.

Material spirituality in modernist women writers

Recent scholarship has contested the conventional dating of modernism as ending with the Second World War.[91] My project argues for the persistence of modernism through its choice of authors and texts. Reading H.D. (who published from the 1910s until her death in 1961, with many texts published posthumously) and Gwendolyn Brooks (who published from the 1930s to the 1990s) alongside Mary Butts, Virginia Woolf (who both died before the end of the Second World War) enables a reading of modernism which moves beyond the early 1940s. My grouping of two English writers (one a sometime expatriate), an American expatriate and an African American writer enables a trans-Atlantic exploration of the urban, domestic and rural spaces of modernism that puts pressure on representations of racial and class difference. Other authors could have been included in this project: the liveliness of things and the spiritual valences of the interconnection of humans, things and places is evident in the work of Zora Neale Hurston, Mina Loy, Katherine Mansfield, Dorothy Richardson and Sylvia Townsend Warner, to name a few. I have limited this study to four authors to allow for sufficient space to be given to each. This book takes a case study approach rather than a more comprehensive history. My hope is that this work will inaugurate further discussion of spiritual materiality in modernist women's writing.

The volume's first chapter considers how H.D.'s engagement with crafting material things formed a spiritual response to the time of crisis in which she wrote her mature poetry and prose. A range of objects, materials and their circulation and transformation enable an exploration into some of the key concerns of H.D.'s writing in the 1940s: war trauma, the search for consolation and her reflection on the process and practice of creativity. H.D.'s literary work of this period resonates with ideas in process theology and anthropology in its emphasis on process as a mode of continual becoming and the movement of materials. After analysis of the gift in H.D.'s writing from the early 1940s, the chapter examines materials and process through the role of needlework in H.D.'s life and work. Tapestry provided a way for her to link her spiritualist interests of the war years with her post-war writing. With the crafting of Christmas decorations, the giving of gifts, the stitching of embroideries and the movements of pattern through textiles, we see clearly that it is the process of making that is most important to H.D.

The second chapter analyses how objects speak of affective and spiritual realities in Mary Butts's work. Her animistic understanding resonates with romantic modernism, pagan pantheism and incarnational theology as she finds the divine within the things around her. I explore the spiritual resonances of things first through an analysis of the Grail in *Armed with Madness* (1928), which features a modernist version of the Grail quest, before turning to her life writing. Reading Butts's journals alongside her autobiography, *The Crystal Cabinet* (1937), enables an exploration of the significance of things, spirituality, landscape and home for Butts in both her remembered Dorset and her later home in Cornwall. Not only does Butts's home at the time of writing intrude on the text but so, too, does her late conversion to Anglo-Catholicism. This chapter explores the myriad forms of syncretism in the text as Butts seeks to unify her recent commitment to Christianity with the paganism that had always enchanted her.

In the third chapter I bring together discussions of materiality and consciousness in an exploration of material mysticism in Virginia Woolf's writing. This material mysticism is demonstrated in the sacred charge of everyday objects, mystical consciousness emerging out of mundane locations and the redeployment of key tropes of the mystical tradition. In the tradition of negative theology, darkness and silence are frequently used to describe the divine as transcendent, unknowable and absent. Yet in Woolf's novels darkness and silence are located in the mundane, the material and presence. The chapter uses the work of feminist theologians on the materiality of the mystical tradition to consider the possibilities for reading material mysticism in Woolf. In Woolf's work we see how the boundaries between person and thing, inside and outside are rendered porous. The chapter traces material mysticism in the formation and disruption of domestic spaces.

Chapter Four focuses on the African American Gwendolyn Brooks's novel, *Maud Martha* (1953), asking how analysis of her writing brings issues of class and race to the fore in consideration of the formation of domestic space and the role of things in its maintenance and destruction. Critics have focused on the representation of the struggle for subjectivity (particularly for the Black female subject) in Brooks's work, yet a neglected aspect of her work is the significance of objects in both enabling the coming to subjectivity and their status as markers of the problems for subjectivity and expression caused by racism and sexism. The chapter takes up questions of the relation between inside and outside posed by earlier chapters and considers how the permeability between inside and outside registers in crowded urban space. In *Maud Martha*, the fraught relationship between women and domesticity exposed by Woolf is rendered more complex in its relation to Black female subjectivity. Bell hooks's exploration of home as enlivened space for Black creativity and agency enables my reading of lively objects in Brooks's work. This chapter looks to the way objects in her texts testify to an occluded spirituality of the everyday.

The final chapter turns from domestic space to the urban environment. All the authors in this volume share an interest in urban space. The chapter considers how things move from domestic to public space, provoke wanderings, act as sacred markers and generate the urban environment which moves subjects even as subjects move through it. In Mary Butts's Paris stories objects provide a focus for the troubled journeys of young innocents in Paris in which past and present, sacred and profane, ordinary and uncanny are layered. We then move to London and chart the way things and urban places organize affect in Woolf's essay 'Street Haunting'. Finally, the chapter turns to an analysis of bleaker, more painful engagements with public space. The war-torn streets of London are viewed starkly in H.D.'s *Within the Walls* (2014), while Brooks's poem 'In the Mecca' (1968) explores a complex relationship between public and private space while confronting poverty and violence. Voices, bodies and things are brought together, leaving us to question the slippage between life and death and the animism of things.

1

Threads and silver paper: Spirituality of gift and process in H.D.'s war writing

In 1933, H.D. began an analysis with Freud. In 1944, reflecting on the analysis, she wrote that at her first session he had said 'you are the only person who has ever come into this room and looked at the things in the room before looking at me'. Indeed, Freud's study and the things in it form a significant part of the analysis. H.D.'s written rejoinder to Freud is that 'you are contained in the things you love'.[1] Freud suggests an opposition between himself and his things which H.D. denies.[2] Here the boundary between subject and object is troubled as the antiquities shape and contain subjectivity. H.D. might be forgiven her social lapse if we consider Freud's study; it is a room full of shelves and cabinets of books and antiquities, objects from ancient cultures (largely Roman but also Greek and Egyptian). His collection of antiquities moves the study beyond the typical cluttered Victorian interior into the realm of the museum. Yet Freud's study is clearly not a museum as he would frequently handle various objects, move them around or offer them to H.D. for comment. Many of them were lined up along his desk, forming a screen between the desk and the analysand's couch, itself covered with richly detailed rugs and cushions.[3] Antiquities are a certain kind of object, ancient, beautiful, expensive, markers of cultural capital and cultural memory, the opposite of the ephemeral and ordinary.[4]

This chapter will consider Freud's antiquities alongside other objects in H.D.'s work with a humbler provenance: domestic gifts, Christmas decorations and embroidery. These things enable an exploration into some of the key concerns of H.D.'s writing in the 1940s: namely, war trauma and the subsequent search for consolation which she found in relationships, spirituality and creative practice. Both during and after the war, H.D. sought strategies for continuing to create in the face of conflict and loss. Material destruction and scarcity brought an intensified appreciation for objects and materials. H.D.'s literary work of this period resonates with ideas in process theology and anthropology in its emphasis on process as a mode of continual becoming and the movement of materials. Materials have their own peculiar life as they participate in continuous motion, moving in and through various gatherings that become things.[5] This understanding of the flow of materials indicates the deep connectivity of the living world, which resonates with H.D.'s emphasis on the connection of all things, a worldview derived from Hermeticism.[6]

H.D. was the pseudonym for the American writer, Hilda Doolittle. She first travelled to Europe in 1911, subsequently settling in London. She began publishing poetry as part of the Imagist movement, publishing her first poems in *Poetry* in 1913 and her first volume *Sea Garden* in 1916. Shortly after the First World War, she began a relationship with Bryher – the writer, heiress and arts patron – that would last the rest of her life. They lived primarily at Bryher's home Kenwin in Switzerland, although they also travelled extensively, until they returned to London at the outbreak of the Second World War. H.D. stayed in London through the entirety of the Second World War despite the efforts of many friends to persuade her to return to the United States. The prolonged stress and malnutrition led to a breakdown in her health in 1946. H.D. spent the next fifteen years moving between residential hotels and sanatoria in Lausanne and Lugano, while continuing to write prolifically until her death in 1961.

For H.D., writing forged a connection between the material world and divine mystery. Like many modernists, she was interested in the transformative potential of art. However, she saw art as a way of developing and expressing spiritual understanding rather than as a secular replacement for religion. H.D. drew upon a number of different religious and esoteric traditions, engaging with spiritual concerns in her writing without subordinating it to the dictates of doctrine. Her spiritual interests ranged from Moravian Christianity to astrology, from spiritualism to the cult of St Teresa. In H.D.'s writing, these varied modes of spiritual practice, expression and beliefs are consistently taken up in relation to questions of creativity and materiality; encounters with the divine are enmeshed in the material world.

Gardenias and Gods

H.D.'s memoir 'Writing on the Walls' was serialized in *Life and Letters Today* in 1945 and 1946 (and later published in *Tribute to Freud* in 1956). She did not have access to her notes from the analysis (they remained in Villa Kenwin in Switzerland when H.D. returned to London at the start of the war) and the memoir is a series of impressions rather than a straight record. She had gone to Vienna in 1933 in hopes that Freud would help her overcome the writer's block she felt was caused by unresolved traumas from the First World War. However, she soon came to feel she could not discuss her war-horror with him, conscious as she was of the escalating crisis in Europe and the threat to Jews. However, she could and did explore the spiritual experiences she had in the Scilly Islands in 1919 and her tour of Greece with Bryher in 1920. Throughout the memoir H.D. draws connections between spirituality – whether the peculiar visions she saw on the wall in Corfu as she attempted to follow the path to Delphi or her memories of a Moravian Christian childhood – creativity and psychic health.

In considering the significance of Freud's antiquities in H.D.'s memoir, critics have tended to focus on their role in H.D.'s engagement with, and challenge to, Freudian theories around transference, female creativity, sexuality and religion.[7] The most sustained attention has come from Adalaide Morris in considering the antiquities in terms of exchange.[8] Morris's theorization of gift economy has wider implications for H.D.'s work in this period, so it is worth outlining here. H.D. sent gardenias to Freud in celebration of the arrival of his antiquities which were shipped to London after he fled Vienna in 1938. H.D. noted the flowers were 'to greet the return of the Gods' and Freud subsequently shared a joke with her, describing the note that accompanied the flowers and adding 'other people read: Goods'.[9] Adalaide Morris reads this exchange as part of a larger gift economy based in generosity. The gardenias themselves mark an earlier exchange in which Freud and H.D. swapped stories of visiting Rome (he had remarked 'the gardenias, in Rome, even I could afford gardenias').[10]

Morris draws upon the work of anthropologist Marcel Mauss to articulate two ways in which the exchange between H.D. and Freud is marked as part of a gift economy rather than an economy of scarcity: temporal lag and a third partner.[11] H.D. had long wished to give Freud gardenias; she attempted to give them on a number of birthdays and failed. When she finally does so, it is several years after the initial exchange of memories. The gift marks intimacy; H.D. knows Freud's memories of gardenias and his ongoing desire for them. The passage of time also allows H.D. to demonstrate that she recognizes the significance of his gift of reminiscence. Furthermore, telling the tale of the gardenias at the beginning of H.D.'s memoir, titled *Tribute to Freud*, suggests that the text is the larger gift, one that proceeds over a decade after the analysis (which was itself Freud's larger gift to H.D.) and after Freud's death. Morris notes that this demonstrates how Freud's gift was transformative; it takes H.D. time to absorb the gifts of the analysis and put them into circulation again.[12]

Morris goes on to argue that a third partner is essential in a gift economy. Giving-in-return involves two people and a static structure; however, giving-in-turn opens outward: 'Before a return donation the gift must leave the boundary of the ego and circle out into mystery'.[13] 'The spirit of things' or the 'god in the goods' increases as the gift is passed on only after the intervention of a third party. This dynamism puts the gift into process.[14]

Like most of the critical engagements with the gift in the American and European academy in recent decades, Morris is in dialogue with anthropologist Marcel Mauss's seminal text *The Gift* (published in 1925 as *Essai sure le don*). Mauss's work draws on ethnographic data from a number of diverse societies, focusing on non-Western, non-capitalist, Indigenous groups. Although he attempted to avoid the primitivism of colleagues in suggesting similarities between Indigenous economic modes and so-called modern modes of exchange, Mauss himself is subject to a similar critique of distancing 'the West and the Rest' in affirming a temporal distinction (i.e. that Indigenous, non-capitalist societies are archaic).[15] Graham Harvey points out that Mauss misunderstands Maori worldview in interpreting *hau* (the excess abundance that yields from gift giving) as a spiritual or mystical force rather than a social one. Harvey argues that *hau* is social because Maori see trees, rocks and land as persons, and therefore they are including in the circulation of gift giving and gifting excess (rather than profiting from it).[16] This point is underlined by T. P. Tawhai's description of the purpose of religion as 'to seek to enter the domain of the superbeing and do violence with impunity'. Thus the personhood of rocks, trees, plants and animals is acknowledged and the violence inherent in using other persons for one's own end (i.e. eating, building a house etc.) is made possible through 'seek[ing] permission and offer[ing] placation'.[17] I argue that we do not have to read the gift in terms of opposition between the spiritual and the social. If we understand spirituality as an aspect of the material world, than the sacred nature of gift exchange does not isolate it in an otherworldly category but retains it as part of everyday spirituality. In H.D.'s gift of gardenias, the antiquities form the third party: they are persons to be included in gift exchange, while the gardenias represent the *hau*, the excess that yields from the gift of analysis. The things themselves are part of the dynamic, sacred nature of the gift economy, not merely items to be exchanged.

The French theorist Hélène Cixous explores the concept of a feminine libidinal economy that escapes the constricted logic of giving-in-return in an early essay 'Sorties'.[18] Cixous argues that 'there is no 'free' gift. [–] But all the difference lies in the why and how of the gift, in the values that the gesture of giving affirms.' Cixous's understanding of the feminine economy is that such giving is positive, it does not circle around or attempt to cancel out lack but instead 'gives *for*'.[19] The dynamism we see in Morris's understanding of a sacred gift economy (drawn from Mauss) is crucial to Cixous's theorizing. She emphasizes movement when she theorises 'a cosmos where eros never stops traveling.'[20] Difference is both within and without as boundaries are porous. Sal Renshaw argues that Cixous, like Derrida, argues that the gift as such is impossible – but that this very impossibility prompts us to consider how giving might happen in spite of this impossibility. For Cixous, the masculine economy is one that privileges closure, the gift always affirming the subjectivity of the giver at the expense of the other and foreclosing difference by the expectation of return. The feminine economy is based in plenitude and celebration of difference such that the other's subjectivity is not marginalized by the assertion of the giver's agency.[21] For Cixous such gifting necessarily involves the sacred as it must be experienced 'like grace falling from the sky' in order to circumvent the giver/receiver binary that prompts exchanges tending towards closure.[22] This chapter explores themes of difference, love and circulation, through the relations between humans and object. In looking at H.D.'s work, we see how such graceful giving may be approached through the consideration of materials and things.

H.D.'s gardenias are addressed to the antiquities, labelled 'Gods'; this introduces a third partner moving the exchange into the realm of the sacred and 'directs gratitude beyond the personal, temporal, and quantifiable'.[23] Gardenias are in some ways the opposite of the antiquities. They are ephemeral rather than ancient and do not bear the same weight of religious and cultural symbolism. Yet they are also valuable and rare – if on a rather different scale – and are associated with Rome, the source of many of Freud's treasures. The spirit of the gift and the process of giving-in turn draws together disparate objects, revealing both their commonalities and their differences. Gardenias and antiquities, the things in the room that are simultaneously goods and Gods, mobilize a gift economy and, perhaps more radically, trouble the boundary between subject and object. This type of giving in turn is common in H.D.'s writing of the period and, as Morris argues, is symptomatic of an ethos that pervades her life and work. Although her exchange with Freud has garnered critical attention, the ubiquity and importance of gift-giving across her work invite further analysis as it surfaces in a number of different locations across both her creative writing and personal correspondence.

H.D. and wartime gift exchange

The presence and maintenance of intimate communities is an important theme in H.D.'s writing from the 1940s.[24] Rebecca Colesworthy discusses these networks in terms of 'queer kinship' in which homoeroticism has the potential to disrupt heteronormative modes of social structure.[25] What is particularly relevant to my work is the dynamic relationship between objects and persons within these social networks. H.D.'s letters frequently reference gifts exchanged within her circle of friends and this becomes even more prominent during the war. Certainly rationing and scarcity led to the increased market value of material goods, but there is also an excess value of affection mobilized by such gift-giving. The circulation of letters and materials extended H.D.'s circle of friends from those nearby who shared stresses and privations of wartime Britain to those across the Atlantic who were eager for first-hand accounts from the UK and in turn sent parcels with food and other supplies. Beyond the significant material support indicated in such gifts, there was a sense of solidarity and extended community marked by these exchanges. The objects themselves circulate. H.D. describes receiving parcels from American friends and in turn making up parcels from their contents to share with other friends in England. Edith Sitwell wrote a gushy letter in response to one such wartime gesture, thanking H.D. profusely for both her letter and the tea that accompanied it.[26] The giving-in-turn of domestic goods such as tea, honey, flowers or fruit nurtures these circles of friendship, as do the letters that record generosity and gratitude.

Similar exchanges are found in H.D. and Bryher's correspondence, but they reveal greater intimacy over a longer stretch of time. H.D. frequently returned to significant shared experiences in her letters and autobiographical fiction. For example, in March 1938, she wrote tenderly in response to a gift from Bryher: 'A most lovely thing, one of those great wood boxes has just come and masses and masses of daffodils that come before the swallow dares … The room is filled with you and 1919, and all you did and ever do for me … They are especially lovely and have that fragrance, like ether almost, forgetfulness and healing.'[27] H.D. alludes to Shakespeare's *The Winter's Tale* in describing the flowers 'that come before the swallow dares', a quote that may have been a coded passage between herself and Bryher (the two often used a private shorthand in their letters).[28] H.D.'s daughter's name, Perdita, comes from the same play and the reference may also indicate H.D. and Bryher's shared maternal role.[29] Reparation and healing are central to Shakespeare's narrative and may have influenced H.D.'s choice of name, given the importance of these themes across her life and work. In H.D.'s work, human relationships are bound up in the objects exchanged between individuals. The material properties of such objects are not incidental to the relationships. These objects do more than signify, they embody the relationship in their particularity.

Poetry and the gift

In 1950, H.D. had a small group of poems printed as a chapbook titled *What Do I Love?*; this slim volume was given as a Christmas gift to a number of her friends.[30] The chapbook contained three war poems ('May 1943', 'RAF' and 'Christmas 1944') that H.D. had written between 1941 and 1944 but did not feel fit with the sequences of lyrics in the volumes of *Trilogy*.[31] This volume highlights poetry as gift, both materially in terms of the printed poems given in tribute and more abstractly in the immaterial language of the poems themselves.[32] Gifting also informs the content of 'Christmas 1944', yielding another exploration of the role of things in wartime.

The poem begins in celestial company as the angels are given a choice between rising out of the realm of aerial combat or descending to share in the human experience.[33] The speaker considers whether to transcend the arena of strife and loss but then concludes that a more important consideration is to ask 'what do I love?'[34] The poem's speaker considers what beloved object should be taken from 'all, all your loveliest treasures' if only one thing is allowed to be carried away 'as gift, / redeemed from dust and ash' (here we see a reference to the anxiety over the loss of home and possessions threatened by the war).[35] A number of objects, a clock, a lump of amber, a painted swallow, even a cat, are chosen; all are precious for their emotional associations as well as their beloved physical details. Yet this list of objects is immediately made more complicated as the speaker indicates that all of them have already been lost, broken or given away. The cat is a memory or a dream and the objects are only held in the speaker's memory. She defiantly claims to hold onto all of them, despite the injunction to choose one, but also worries '*is it too much?*'[36]

The speaker likens herself and her comrades to lost children and identifies with the Christ Child who was made homeless, losing the security of the shelter of the Inn for the more precarious shelter of the manger. The speaker offers up her beloved objects to Christ, thus the things become gifts once again. In 'Christmas 1944' we see how objects that are lost, broken or given away are also cherished; 'redeemed from dust and ash', they carry memories of a time of peace. Heaven touches earth, first in the angels who gather the 'loveliest treasures' and invite the speaker's choice, then in the Incarnation, portrayed as God's solidarity with all those who have been cast out and made lost.[37] The speaker draws close to divine life in communing with the angels and in offering up her treasures to another lost child. In 'Christmas 1944', H.D. offers the divine objects that are broken or lost, yet still beloved. There is a sense here in which even things which are lost are not gone; memory proves a consolation in a time of great loss. In giving the poems themselves as a Christmas gift several years after the war's end, H.D. invokes the memories of wartime, prompting her readers to also consider what they love.

Craft and children's creativity

H.D. invokes the spiritual dynamism of things more explicitly in her autobiographical novel *The Gift* when she muses on her childhood memories of Christmas. The text oscillates between H.D.'s childhood in Pennsylvania and her experiences in London during the Second World War, drawing on the Moravian traditions of her childhood as well as the history of the Church in the eighteenth century in Bohemia and the American colonies.[38] Through the text the child Hilda searches for the meaning of 'the gift', one that includes both artistic talent and spiritual wisdom. The gift that is spiritual and creative draws these abstractions into connection with the gifts that are material objects.

H.D.'s descriptions of the Moravian Christmas are heavily detailed, focusing primarily on her family's domestic traditions. The family's preparations are many and varied, involving complex decorations. H.D. begins her narration obliquely, approaching the festival by connecting a Saint Bernard dog that appears in dreams with the Egyptian Ammon-Ra and the Roman Aries or 'gold-fleece Ram': this is typical of her habit of layering mythologies and memories. She then shifts to a more domestic scene, connecting sheep made of cotton wool to this larger mythology: 'Our Ram however, had not gold-fleece, his fleece came from Mamalie's [H.D.'s grandmother] medicine-cupboard. It was pulled off in tufts from a roll of cotton for making bandages … or for borrowing to make a quilt for the new bed for the doll-house.'[39]

What follows is a fairly elaborate explanation of this seasonal domestic craft, known to all within the Moravian community but mysterious to outsiders: 'You may wonder what mysterious occult ceremony requires cotton-wool from Mamalie's medicine-cupboard, a knot of wire and the gardening-shears which did not belong on [her grandfather's] desk, match-sticks, a lump of clay. You yourself may wonder at the mystery in this house, the hush in this room.'[40] Domestic objects are out of place and ordinary materials transformed. With the clay, matchsticks and cotton-wool H.D.'s grandfather makes sheep, which go on the Moravian putz, a nativity scene set under the Christmas tree on living moss.

The children also participate in the Christmas crafting and H.D. takes their work as an opportunity to draw together the context of making, the objects of creation and the activity of creativity itself. The narrator plays up the element of suspense by introducing an unknown 'thing', but we soon find out that this mysterious 'thing' is not an object but an activity:

> The 'thing' could not begin if there were not an old end or several almost burnt-out stumps of last year's beeswax candles … It was not only the smell of the moss, it was not only the smell of the spiced ginger-dough that was waiting under a cloth in the biggest yellow bowl on the pantry-shelf, and yet it was all these; it was all these and the forms of the Christmas-cakes … The 'thing' was that we were creating. We were 'making' a field under the tree.[41]

Here, as in Bryher's gift of flowers, fragrance is significant. The 'thing' is a process that includes both fragrances and forms; it requires ordinary objects to come into being, things seen and unseen.

The intimacy of process and object, the suggestion that a process too, might be a thing, is suggestive of the gift economy as the things and activities not only circulate among the family members but also transform the home into a spiritual space. H.D.'s emphasis on the coming together of materials and sensory experience leads me to the anthropologist Tim Ingold's work on making. He argues that our distinctions between form and matter, nature and culture, object and materials, maker and made force false dichotomies that distort our understanding of the world. He argues instead for a focus on the flow of materials. He resists considering objects as static things and instead suggests that they consist of 'substances-in-becoming' that carry on in a process of continual modulation. This has implications for our understanding of human action: 'Making, then, is a process of correspondence: not the imposition of preconceived form on raw material substance, but the drawing out or bringing forth of potentials immanent in a world of becoming. In the phenomenal world, every material is such a becoming, one path or trajectory through a maze of trajectories.'[42] What I find so fascinating here, and this has particular relevance to H.D., is how Ingold employs the language of Hermeticism in his argument. As well as using the term 'correspondences' which in Hermetic terms indicates the concept that everything is connected to everything else and that what happens in the heavens is echoed on the earth, he makes explicit reference to the alchemical worldview. He argues that alchemists knew materials by what they did, most specifically 'when mixed with other materials, treated in particular ways, or placed in particular situations'.[43]

Ingold makes an argument about the way scientific understanding has changed over time, and how a reinvigoration of older modes of thinking may release us from unhelpful, anthropocentric models. Yet alchemy and the Hermetic worldview that underpinned it was a mode of spirituality as well as scientific inquiry and H.D. draws upon Hermetic understanding as is evident from the centrality of alchemy to *Tribute to the Angels* (1945), the second volume of her war trilogy.[44] The language of the sacred emerges in Ingold's text in compelling ways; in claiming that 'materials are ineffable' he is arguing for a mode of engagement that involves careful attention to the phenomenal life of materials, but that also implicitly invites openness to the kind of mystery that H.D. alludes to in the passages above. Ingold addresses animism, arguing that it is a worldview less about attributing life to inert objects but than about a way of being 'alive *to*' the world: a world that consists of things understood as 'particular gathering[s] or interweaving[s] of the threads of life' which 'draw us in, along the very paths of [their] formation'.[45] Thus I would argue that Ingold's work is helpful for understanding a spirituality of materials. Not only can the world be seen as a 'flow of materials' but this flowing, living matter is generative, entangling us in and through its movements. Such generativity and attention to materials in flux can be seen in H.D.'s writing on the Christmas preparations of her childhood home.

In her reading of Cixous, Sal Renshaw suggests that 'God [is] that ultimate signifier of unknowable gifting'.[46] In her evocation of the Moravian Christmas, H.D. emphasizes the mystery inherent in this domestic activity as the source of the creativity that is itself a gift. She then moves to consider the objects of the children's creativity. She describes the creation of Christmas cakes and decorations as a spiritual activity that instantiates the Incarnation:

> God had made a Child and we children in return now made God; we created Him as He had created us, we created Him as children will, out of odds and ends; like magpies, we built him a nest of stray bits of silver-thread, shredded blue or rose or yellow coloured paper; we knew our power. We knew that God could not resist the fragrance of a burning beeswax candle![47]

H.D. suggests that the domestic creativity of children recasts divine creativity. God is seduced into being. Offered beauty, God is unable to resist. H.D.'s imagery anticipates the liberation theologian Dorothee Soelle's claim that human creativity engenders divine increase: 'The more a person develops her creativity … the more God is God.'[48] God is understood to be changeable and subject to growth. The children's activity resonates with Walter Benjamin's evocative description of the children's tendency to make discoveries in the interstices of culture: 'They are irresistibly drawn by the detritus generated by building, gardening, housework, tailoring, or carpentry. … In using these things they … bring together, in the artefact produced in play, materials of widely differing kinds in a new, intuitive relationship.'[49] In setting up a parallel between the childlike and divine creativity, H.D. suggests that God also creates out of scraps and odds and ends.

The theologian Ann Pedersen argues, 'To engage in that which is beautiful is to become part of the imagination of God.'[50] H.D. frequently emphasizes a close association between divinity and beauty throughout her work; this is particularly pronounced in her writing from the Second World War where she explores the vexed question of the value of art in wartime.[51] The Second World War saw widespread damage and destruction to civilian arenas such as churches, galleries, palaces and businesses, as well as more personal losses in private homes, and thus a frequent concern of H.D.'s is the loss of beautiful objects and buildings. Yet she also grapples with the pragmatism of wartime that would suggest such concerns were frivolous against the massive loss of life and the practical needs of mobilization, that is, should paper be used for books or for weaponry?[52] The fragility and mutability of objects are underscored throughout H.D.'s wartime writing. In her epic poem, *Trilogy*, she mourns the destruction of books and rejects the suggestion that manuscripts are best used for cartridge cases.[53]

The writing style of *The Gift* reflects this activity of making out of scraps as H.D. patches together narrative fragments of different times and different places. The ritualized language surrounding this emphasis on the material suggests that writing itself is another activity that sacralizes the mundane. H.D.'s densely layered imagery and incantatory, repetitive language evoke this scene of creation for the reader, placing us in the position of God – also seduced by the beeswax candle. The children's creation of God out of beeswax and tissue paper is reflected in the writer's creation of a nest for divine (and readerly) becoming through the use of metaphorical scraps and narrative fragments. The scraps with which children make a world suggest the provisional nature of their creative activity; the 'thing' H.D. describes is dependent on the smell of gingerbread and the biggest yellow bowl. Thus the larger context of war, which dominates the narrative of *The Gift*, is indicated even in the childhood scenes as the objects are mutable, subject to change and precariously aligned. In the closing chapter of *The Gift*, H.D. draws a more explicit connection between her meditations on Christmas and the context of conflict within which she wrote:

> I could not visualise civilisation other than a Christmas-tree that had caught fire.
>
> There had been a little Christmas-tree here on the table, where the lamp now was. That was the first tree we had had since the 'real' war and the fragile glass-balls, I had boasted, had withstood the shock and reverberation of steel and bursting shell … unpicking shredded green tissue-paper from a tinsel star, I said, 'look at this, it's as bright as ever and this glass-apple isn't broken.[54]

Here we have another configuration of the relationship between scraps and wholeness. The shredded tissue paper harkens back to the children's nest for God and the glass apple is another instance of incarnation, sheltered by tissue paper. The apple remains unbroken and for H.D. this is both solace and hope: a witness to ongoing life.

H.D.'s model of creativity out of odds and ends picks up the imagery of chaos as the ground of creation in Genesis 1. In *The Face of the Deep*, Catherine Keller develops a theology of *creatio ex profundis*, in opposition to the classical *creatio ex nihilo*. Hers is a biblical model of creativity, finding commonality between the God of Genesis 1who broods over the formless deep and the God of Genesis 2 who creates humanity out of dust. Keller draws on Whiteheadian process theology to argue for beginning as not a singular point of origin but a 'beginning-in-process, an unoriginated and endless process of becoming'.[55] This understanding of creation as unfolding from the chaotic, formless deep undermines the traditional distinction between divine and human creativity in which God creates from nothing, humanity creates from something. In this alternative, non-hierarchical view, creation is part of the gift economy, giving-in-turn involves creating God out of the scraps of the world – a radically relational and material view of divine, human and thingly becoming. H.D.'s writing on the becoming of crafted objects demonstrates the intimate connection between materials in process and the gift that does not take.

H.D.'s embroidery

H.D.'s emphasis on materials on the move in the process of creation also finds expression in her post-war prose, where tapestry forms a central part of her novel, *The Sword Went Out to Sea*. Here we will attend to the flow of materials in the movements of thread through the historical practices and literary engagements of needlework, the warp of symbolism and dream and the repetition of practice as hand and thread join to craft beauty, psychic health and memory. During the war, H.D. turned to domestic craft as a source of relief from the incessant anxiety entailed by living in London.[56] In a letter to her American friend Viola Baxter Jordan, she described her practice of embroidery:

> I started a number of large [pieces] in London while we sat around waiting for the last trump. … three huge original Cluny designs meant for mantle-piece; they are copied from [the] original Cluny Museum in Paris. Bryher always said 'but what will you DO with them?' I have just loved them and the designs of huge grape leaves, pomegranates and small animals, just kept me alive.[57]

Embroidery played a crucial role for H.D. personally during and after the Second World War and it frequently appears in her writing of period. Tapestry provided a way for her to link her spiritualist interests of the war years with her post-war writing. The creative practice of forming patterns in thread aligns with both deciphering messages from the séance table and the patterning of literary creation. Bringing these tropes together gave H.D. a means to explore possibilities for both personal and social healing following the trauma of the war years and to express her hopes for a world without war. Moreover, H.D. used tapestry as a metaphor that allowed her to explore her affiliation to nineteenth-century poets, particularly William Morris, while also enabling the development of her modernist style to a more extreme dynamic of rupture and connection. Using a metaphor drawn from women's work gave H.D. space to approach the work of her male contemporaries while also exploring the concerns of feminist modernism.[58]

My primary text for the remainder of this chapter is the post-war novel, *The Sword Went Out to Sea*, composed from 1946 to 1947 and revised between 1948 and 1950. Despite H.D.'s high esteem for the novel (she referred to it as 'the crown of all my effort'), it reminded unpublished until 2007 when the University Press of Florida released a critical edition edited by Cynthia Hogue and Julie Vandivere.[59] William Morris, the designer, socialist activist and writer, is a significant influence and spectral presence in both this and H.D.'s subsequent novel, *White Rose and the Red* (written between 1947 and 1948 and published in 2009). The novel's title is drawn from his early poem 'The Sailing of the Sword', from his first book, *The Defence of Guenevere* (1858) and the poem's theme of war, separation and unrequited love resonates with the narratives of conflict, love and loss recounted in H.D.'s novel. Morris is particularly significant for my project as he also was concerned with the significance of process and materials in the development of the practicalities and ethos of the Arts and Crafts Movement.

In 1957 H.D. recorded a dream of Morris and calls him her 'guardian, the godfather I never had'.[60] She goes on to consider how she did 'have him' indirectly through textual introductions, first by a school teacher who gave her a volume on furniture and later by Ezra Pound who passed on his poetry, and also by design influence; her father had built a bench and some bookcases from Morris designs (the connection between designer and poet, physical material and abstract language is emphasized here). In her late memoir of Pound, H.D. again recalls the importance of Morris to the literary development of both herself and Pound.[61] It is this 'godfather', the creatively enabling Morris of *Sword* that I am interested in here. I will situate H.D.'s embroidery in the context of women's amateur textile craft and Morris's work in textiles and literature before considering her use of tapestry as a creative practice and metaphor in *Sword*.

Subversive stitchery

H.D.'s emphasis on leaves, fruit and small animals in her embroidery is reminiscent of both the verdure tapestries that developed in the late Middle Ages and many of William Morris's medieval-inspired designs.[62] H.D. describes a project as 'real Morris period tapestry', but it is more likely that she means the medieval patterns that so enchanted Morris rather than an actual Morris design.[63] What is clear is that H.D. saw her work as sharing the spirit of Morris's. Her repeated use of the word stitching in other letters suggests that her work is embroidery rather than weaving, although, as we will see, in her written engagement with textile arts she tends to elide the distinctions between woven and stitched tapestry (although the term tapestry usually signifies large woven pictorial textiles, the term is also widely used in relation to smaller, needlework projects, usually worked in woollen thread). The significance for her is that both are fabrics made with thread. Embroidery patterns were sometimes taken from woven tapestry, while tapestry and embroidery also drew on common sources found in paintings or prints.[64]

After the war, H.D. continued to stitch. While recovering in Switzerland she asked Bryher to send her tapestry work to her and then wrote again in thanks for the wool, while in 1947 she wrote to Bryher expressing the pleasure she finds in her current pattern and reiterating again the value she had found in stitching during the war.[65] These were lengthy projects: she once wrote to Bryher asking for more wool (naming specific small skeins) and then a week or so later writes again to say she has enough to keep her going for six months.[66] At the time of beginning these projects H.D. was more ambivalent about their value. She wrote to Viola Jordan about her embroidery in 1942 in a far more deprecatory style: 'It sounds inane but there is nothing like it for keeping one's mind off things.'[67] The formation of material in one's hands distracts the mind from contemplating the material destruction all around. The ability of needlework to enable the practitioner to 'keep one's mind off things', inducing a meditative state and having a positive effect on mental health has been widely commented on.[68] I will return to this point but for now I wish to point out that after the war, as we see in her letter to Jordan, H.D. was prepared to defend her choice of activity despite her earlier concerns about its seeming inanity or Bryher's bemusement. The later letter shows H.D.'s resistance to assigning a use or exchange-value to these stitched projects. Instead she configures them as part of a network of spiritual, creative and relational value.

In *The Subversive Stitch*, Rozsika Parker argues that embroidery has been both an instrument of female subjugation and also an opportunity for creative work and autonomy. As with so much of women's work, it was something that could be done while also doing something else, that is, housework and caring for children. It allowed women to support themselves and their children – barely – but this labour was exploited, especially in the eighteenth and nineteenth centuries, through the rise of piecework, the growing distance between seamstresses and commissioners and the increasing tendency to equate skill with speed. Whether in factories or at home, women worked long hours in poor conditions for extremely low pay and suffered physically because of their trade, particularly through damaged eyesight.[69]

Despite industrialization, much embroidery was still undertaken as a domestic craft and a marker of leisure. Its place in the home is also ambivalent, described by nineteenth-century writers as a means of inculcating submissive femininity, stunting intellectual development and depriving professional embroiders of a living but also an opportunity for independence, creativity and consolation.[70] Parker cites an example from Colette about the potential of needlework to disturb: 'I shall speak the truth: I don't much like my daughter sewing … Bel-Gazou is silent when she sews, silent for hours on end, with her mouth firmly closed … She is silent, and she – why not write down the word that frightens me – she is thinking.'[71] H.D.'s anxieties around the 'inanity' of stitching reflects a pejorative view of needlework that still flourishes.[72] However, both historic and contemporary practices of needlework are currently gaining significant critical attention.[73]

The status of the amateur embroiderer has long been a vexed issue. Historians of craft and design have tended to be scornful of amateurs and the use of transfers or copied designs.[74] Hierarchies of art versus craft, professional versus amateur, innovation versus copying and embroidery as creative expression versus therapeutic exercise continue to denigrate and exclude much of women's amateur practice.[75] Current interdisciplinary work on needlework and other forms of domestic craft suggest that the boundaries between these terms can be porous.[76] Parker notes that William Morris's famous dictum 'have nothing in your house that you do not know to be useful or believe to be beautiful' echoed the strategies of nineteenth-century women's magazines for advertising embroidery patterns as 'uniting use and beauty'.[77] May Morris appears to have shared the privileging of design innovation, writing in a 1892 publication *Plain Handicrafts*, 'The old medieval embroiderers certainly made their own designs, and whoever invents and plans the work he is going to carry out himself, will realize what freedom of thought, of fancy, and of execution such an arrangement allows of'.[78] However, this didn't prevent Morris's companies from issuing many embroidery patterns as transfers or preprinted kits. These were highly successful and elided the boundary between design innovation and amateur stitching practices.[79] Commenting on women's magazines in the 1930s, Fiona Hackney argues that they reveal communities of women makers and emphasize 'agency, expression, style quality, and economy'.[80]

British needlework practice changed during the Second World War due in part to rationing and changing patterns of work. The 1940 editorial of the magazine *Embroidery* urged readers to take up patchwork as a less expensive needlework option although embroidery was often used to embellish otherwise plain clothing or to hide the many seams in patchwork garments.[81] As well as fabric, thread was in short supply and was obtained by unravelling old-knitted garments or using string and other plain materials. Despite the scarcity of materials, embroidery kits were issued to soldiers in hospital and soldiers on leave were encouraged to attend needlework classes at local art schools. A more direct contribution to the war effort is described by Constance Howard, a teacher at the Kingston School of Art during the 1940s: 'We embroidered large maps for the Air Force … working on a very tough, waterproof fabric that gave us sore hands from the effort of pushing the needles through the close weave. We worked wooded areas in French knots, placed solidly together … These maps were, apparently, more accurate than photographs in depicting relief because of the raised stitches'.[82] Given the scarcity of materials for embroidery during the war, H.D.'s projects are indeed a luxury rather than part of the 'make-do-and-mend' ethos of the time.

H.D. acknowledges this in her correspondence, particularly valuing the colour and quality of her wool.[83]

Spectres of Morris

H.D.'s practice of embroidery makes its way into her post-war literary writing, appearing most explicitly in the autobiographical novel *Sword*. The narrator refers to embroidery in relation to literary influence and genealogy: 'I had heard personal reminiscences and anecdotes about Swinburne, Browning, Rossetti and William Morris. William Morris designed medieval tapestry. I had worked on a panel of fruit-trees – it seemed useless work – for three years. Now it seems the only thing that matters.'[84] Both meanings of the word 'matter' inhere in H.D.'s language: the tapestry as materiality and the tapestry as significant. Here H.D. again figures a shift between disregarding embroidery and claiming it as a worthwhile endeavour. In *Sword* this shift is marked by the association of stitching with spiritualism and Pre-Raphaelitism. H.D. aligns her embroidery with the professional work of William Morris rather than with traditional domestic femininity, although, as I have discussed, these two approaches to embroidery are not as distinct as they may first appear. Not only is there slippage between the professional and the amateur in Morris & Co.'s production of embroidery patterns and kits but Jane and May Morris were involved in William Morris's early experiments in dying, weaving and embroidery at home (May Morris eventually took over the embroidery side of Morris & Co.). H.D. is more interested in William Morris's textiles in relation to his writing and association with the Pre-Raphaelite brotherhood and does not engage significantly with the Morris and Co. as a producer of craft objects and patterns.

William Morris is a spectral presence in both *Sword* and its sister novel, *White Rose and the Red* and my project contributes to a recent critical trend re-evaluating the relationship between nineteenth-century poetry and modernism. Elizabeth K. Helsinger makes a compelling argument for the significance of Pre-Raphaelite poetics to modernist developments. She demonstrates how the emphasis on the concrete that Rossetti brought into English verse via his translations of Dante is formative for Pound and other modernist poets.[85] Talia Schaffer and Kathy Alexis Psomiades draw a genealogy that emphasizes women's aestheticist writing, tracing influence from Christina Rossetti through Swinburne to H.D. while Vincent Sherry argues that decadence (the inheritor of the aestheticism begun by the Pre-Raphaelites) has been occluded from the history of modernism but continually interpenetrates modernist aesthetics and practice.[86] My focus here is on H.D.'s engagement with Morris as mediator between spiritualism and creativity, in terms of both textile craft and writing.[87] Although Morris's connection with the Pre-Raphaelites waned in his later life, H.D. engages with him as part of the Pre-Raphaelite Brotherhood, as is evident in *White Rose and the Red* where he appears alongside representations of Elizabeth Siddall, Dante Gabriel Rossetti and others.[88]

Wendy Parkins notes that Morris's sense of history is both material and spectral:

> In 'Gossip About an Old Place on the Upper Thames', Morris described the faded Elizabethan tapestry … as making 'a very pleasant background for the living people who haunt the room.' Morris's conceit, in which the living rather than the dead haunt a space, emphasizes the palpable sense of the past that historical artefacts like the tapestry evoke, seemingly more alive than the living.[89]

This notion of life as ghostly is echoed by H.D. in *Tribute to Freud*, 'We are all haunted houses.'[90] If, as Parkins suggests, Morris's understanding of the past's intrusion on the present is more 'historical and material' than spectral, then the historical Morris provides substance for H.D.'s activity of bringing together material and spiritual while she also crafts her fictional Morris as an individual who is interested in both the past as source for literary romances and the manifestations of the past through ghostly return. The fictional Morris dabbles in spiritualism, but this appears to be an invention by H.D. There is evidence that Jane Morris believed in ghostly appearances. She attended séances with Dante Gabriel Rossetti in the late 1860s. Biographers suggest that Rossetti's scepticism gave way to an uneasy interest after the death of Elizabeth Siddall. There is no evidence that William Morris was ever anything but sceptical about spiritualism, although he did have an interest in Theosophy through his friendship with Annie Besant.[91] However, H.D. is not overly concerned with biographical verity; she is more interested in interpreting Morris as a figure who would enable her search to unite creative and spiritual practices.

In *Sword*, H.D. uses the pseudonym Delia Alton for both author and protagonist. The first section, 'Wintersleep' concerns Delia's spiritualist experiments during the war, when she received messages from fallen RAF pilots. It describes her breakdown at the end of the war and subsequent recovery. The second part of the novel, 'Summerdream', contains a fantastical, disorienting time-slip sequence as Delia moves through a series of historical vignettes, drawn from her own past and different historical epochs: classical, medieval and Elizabethan, in which the struggle for peace and reconciliation in times of social change and crisis are repeated. The text is also a palimpsest of forms: modernist strategies including rupture and multiple centres of consciousness (as we see in Woolf's novels); romance in its emphasis on quest narratives; science fiction in its use of time travel and life-writing in its autobiographical sequences and recounting of dreams.

In *Sword*, Morris's presence is mediated through his belongings and his writings. This presence allows H.D. to connect spiritualism and embroidery with her own writing. H.D. briefly practiced as a medium during the 1940s and the table she used for the séances she held in her own home was a small tripod table that had originally belonged to William Morris.[92] The Morris table appears in a similar role in *Sword*. The table is significant because Morris owned and used it not because he designed it. We hear little about the table's design except for its tripod form. This is an important symbol to H.D. as it stands for the Delphic oracle and was a shape that appeared in her visions of 1920.[93] In the novel, H.D. connects her spiritual experiences of 1920 and the 1940s. When the medium Ben Manisi makes reference to her previous visionary experiences and the name Hal Brith, which Delia later connects with William Morris and Hallblithe, the hero of his prose romance, *The Glittering Plain*, she is drawn to him and begins to undertake séances with him, his mother and Gareth (Bryher). Morris is enmeshed in Delia's spiritualism through both artefact and literature. In a letter to Bryher from 1947, H.D. thanks her for arranging to procure the table at auction and indicates that the novel itself is a gift of the table.[94]

Later in the text H.D. uses the pattern of another table to connect the Morris table with the image of thread. After Delia's breakdown, she recovers in Lausanne and then Lugano, where she finds a table in her room that reminds her of the Morris table as both are tripod in form. After a long meditation on the table's pattern of four superimposed squares which form a sixteen-pointed star and its similarity to patterns found in cultures across the globe, Delia imagines the pattern as a tapestry:

[The pattern] is dexterously woven on the upper or right side of the tapestry, but it is woven from threads, worked on the underside, so long ago in London.

It is the legitimate reward of my devotion to the 'work,' the intense, broken sessions when I concentrated so feverishly on the messages from the RAF … I found the thread and followed it through the labyrinth. … Although I didn't know it at the time, and although I was working blind on the wrong side of the tapestry, I had begun to weave that very thread into this symbolic, decorative motive. Now, I stand on the outer or right side of the tapestry and look at the polished surface of the table. (113–14)

Here the 'work' of séances and the 'work' of embroidery merge into the woven tapestry whose pattern is only revealed when the weaver moves to the right side of the tapestry. In her analysis of Morris's printed patterns, Caroline Arscott points out that the patterns are dense, with a great deal of overlap, and therefore depth, and little negative space. She argues that these designs emphasis growth and change: 'The viewer's conviction that *this* is above *that* always remains provisional. Firstly, we understand that positionality in living matter is subject to change. Secondly, the complexity of the twisting forms is such that the following of a single line can throw up doubts.'[95] Morris's tapestries and embroidery patterns do not contain as much density and overlap as his printed patterns, and yet they do move in this direction. In the medieval tapestries that inspired Morris there is little negative space as the background itself is full of life: flowers, fruit, small animals. The curving lines of Morris's designs align with H.D.'s emphasis on curving lines connecting disparate times and places in *Sword* and allowing for alternative perspectives on history. H.D. draws together geometric and organic designs, abstraction and realism; the meeting point between them is evident in Morris's stylized flowers and leaves.

The pairing of Morris's table with the table in Lugano enables the connection of embroidery and spiritualism that is important to H.D.'s text. In the letter thanking Bryher for the Morris table 'and all [it] brought,' H.D. writes, 'I owe everything to you and to the miracle of all that marvellous real Morris period tapestry – I am sure it helped me get into the rhythm and vibration and kept me sane.'[96] The tapestry here is related to the rhythms of both spiritualism and writing. The subtitle of *Sword* is 'Synthesis of a Dream' and this dream is both spiritualist vision and literary text. For H.D., the synthesis is enabled by patterns made of thread.

By the time she wrote *White Rose and the Red*, H.D. was steeped in Morris's prose, having eagerly read and reread many of his romances. However, she notes in a letter to Richard Aldington that it was 'just as well' she had not read much Morris while initially drafting *Sword*.[97] In the novel H.D. is more concerned with Morris as a creative and spiritual muse than as historic figure and author and Delia searches for correspondences between herself and Morris via spiritual as well as literary means. We see this firstly in the figure of Hal Brit (Hallblithe) from Ben Manisi's séances and secondly in the word 'wings', which maps a complex network of associations: the Viking ship with wings from Manisi's visions that is associated with the RAF pilots Delia meets in her séances; Delia's spiritualist and other companions through the war years; and the Morris poem 'Golden Wings'.[98] I have argued that Morris's most significant presence in *Sword* is found in the tripod table and textiles; however, H.D. is concerned with connecting both of these with writing and the traces of the literary Morris in the novel are also important. In a pattern as complex as any of Morris's intricate prints, H.D. layers the creation of tapestry with the quest romance form reminiscent of Morris, combining a literary project with a spiritual quest. In *The Glittering Plain* Hallblithe rejects the deathless stasis of the Plain for a return to the everyday world with its fullness of life, including mortality.[99] This theme is repeated via the ghosts of the fallen RAF pilots who do not share tales of a glorious afterlife but insist on communicating political messages to deter another war. Cynthia Hogue and Julie Vandivere argue that H.D. presents a revision of *The Glittering Plain* in presenting a woman, 'not [as] the quest's object' but an active agent seeking 'self-reclamation' while retaining Morris's rejection of static immortality.[100]

Morris's early poem 'Golden Wings' is also a significant intertext for H.D.'s novel. Hogue and Vandivere emphasize the poem's setting of a feminine stronghold, the castle of Ladies' Gard, and the struggle between pacifism and the need for military action.[101] The drama of the poem concerns the tension between love and war and ensuing loss – of both loved ones and beloved community. The final historical vignette of *Sword* takes place in Normandy around the invasion of Britain in 1066; many of its characters' names are drawn from Morris's poem and the poem's themes of passion and violence are repeatedly invoked. H.D. folds the Battle of Britain (1940) and the D-Day invasion of Normandy (1944) into her medieval frame, suggesting the contemporary resonance of her narrative.[102] In H.D.'s mythic tale, the Duke of Normandy is fated to unite the sacred sites of Britain/Avalon with Brittany-Normandy/Lyonnesse. Rose Beauvais, the Delia figure, is a wise woman, a witch who interprets signs and portents supporting Normandy's aims but also warns her young protégé, Blanchfleur, of the costs of political-marital alliances. Rose urges Blanchfleur to consider 'that a woman may have, may one day have a complete life of her own' (250). Her own marriage had given a justification for aggressive action which resulted in a secure landed position but also the death of her husband. As a wealthy widow Rose has a certain level of autonomy and the erotic tension between her and Normandy is evident even through the narration of the innocent Blanchfleur.

Rose's passion and prescience are reminiscent of Jehane de Castel beau of Morris's poem. Jehane marks the contrast between plenitude and yearning in Morris's poem: the ladies wear roses but Jehane's are withered through her sorrow and loneliness. Her defiant disrobing – 'And she took off her scarlet shoon, / And bared her feet; still more and more / Her sweet face redden'd' – and subsequent search beyond the safety of the castle walls for her lover indicate a twining of female desire and agency.[103] However, Morris denies Jehane fulfilment, she ends the poem 'slain' 'where the water meets the land'.[104] In *Sword*, Rose Beauvais quotes 'Golden Wings' directly, repeating '*Ladies Gard must meet the war*' – echoing the poem's end but with a fierce intent to prevent Morris's vision of death and destruction.[105] Here H.D. reveals the tension between her repudiation of war and the need to defend a beloved community.

The poem's rich sensory detail also resonates with H.D.'s prose. The cost of violence is measured by disruption to seasonal progression and fruitfulness; the beginning of the poem describes a 'happy poplar land' in which 'red apples shone' while at the poem's close 'the apples now grow green and sour / … / Before they ripen there they fall'.[106] We can imagine here both the rich colours of tapestry thread and see the connection with the gardens in H.D. earlier war poem *Tribute to the Angels* (1945). In this text, H.D. has a vision of a 'half-burnt-out apple-tree / blossoming', indicating that regeneration is possible in the midst of destruction.[107] The landscapes in *Sword* are bleaker, more in line with Morris's vision of the desolation that follows war. And yet there are also hints of hope to be found in the patterns of tapestry and table and the details of Delia's surroundings. The first half of the novel, 'Wintersleep', closes with two chapters in which Delia begins to explore the connections and patterns that emerge upon reflection on her spiritualist experiences. She provides numerous details of the Lugano *pensione*, a setting which links the two parts of the novel. Delia notes the decoration of 'an arabesque of fruit, leaves and flowers' and the presence of camellias and bowls of lilacs (107–8). The scent of lilac reminds Delia of her Pennsylvania childhood and this, along with other flowers, gives 'traces of direction' that help her understand the intricate pattern: 'The sun-pattern on the table, with its inner circles of smaller petals, becomes by the alchemy of memory, an actual flower' (118). The lilacs link the embroidery patterns of 'fruit, flowers and small animals' and the geometric pattern of overlapping squares of the table they rest on. The urgency of Delia's spiritual quest then is marked not only by both the foregrounded dramas of love and war but also by the background details of colour, texture and pattern. The quest itself is the prevention of war and H.D. finds the expression of this message in the synthesis of writing, stitching and spiritualism.

Typing and typestry

H.D. wrote prolifically throughout the war, as she wrote to Viola Jordan in 1942, 'I go on working a little every day, typing and do typestry [*sic*] stitching inbetween.'[108] Here she makes a telling typo, connecting typing and stitching, writing and tapestry. Morris commented, 'If a chap can't compose an epic poem while he's weaving tapestry, he had better shut up' and it is tempting to imagine H.D. ruminating over her epic *Trilogy* while she stitched her flowers and leaves.[109] Textiles as metaphors for writing have a long history and the relationship between the pen and the needle could be a vexed one for the women writer. Sandra Gilbert and Susan Gubar have written of the pen/needle parallel as suggestive of anxieties of authorship for women (a mode of silencing women writers was to urge them to take up not the pen but the needle).[110] However, Kathryn R. King argues that there are also examples of the needle serving as a useful metaphor for women's creativity that is happily allied with the pen, as in the eighteenth-century novel by Jane Barker, *A Patchwork Screen for the Ladies* (1723), in which 'writing for print publication emerges as an extension of traditional forms of women's work'.[111] This is a similar relation to the metaphors of quilting we see in contemporary feminist writing.[112] In feminist discourse, the metaphors of such domestic activity (needlework notoriously slips between labour and leisure) are reclaimed as enabling for intellectual activity. In *A Room of One's Own*, when Woolf's fictional author seeks out the unknown women to record their stories, the metaphor is one of sewing: 'Mary Carmichael will have out her scissors and fit them close to every hollow and angle.'[113] Woolf employs the image of cutting, leaving aside the stitching that will be required in order for a woman's garment, or story, to actually be useful. She stays with the moment of deconstruction, emphasizing that the project of writing a woman's life is still in process.

Likewise, H.D. does not appear to sense antagonism between the needle (or shuttle) and the pen (or typewriter): 'In describing her life, H.D. would often use the metaphor of a tapestry, a weaving of different places, histories, colors and moments.'[114] For H.D. the tapestry metaphor enabled creativity and connection in both life and art and could bring the two together. She uses the images of threads and weaving frequently in her prose, as in 'Advent', written in 1933, where she writes: 'It is obviously Penelope's web that I am weaving' in reference to her repeated attempts to write the novel of the First World War and her subsequent spiritual experiences in Greece.[115] Susan Stanford Friedman argues that Penelope weaving, un-weaving and re-weaving is an apt metaphor for H.D. as she continually reworked texts and had many recurring plots and characters across her highly autobiographical prose oeuvre.[116] However, only in her work from the 1940s does the metaphor of tapestry come to prominence as a structuring device.[117] In *Sword* she emphasizes the pattern of a finished piece of work. However, her emphasis on process is maintained through the overlapping and repeating plotlines of the vignettes that make up the latter part of the novel. In H.D.'s later writing 'form is process,' her style expresses a 'mode of being in the world [that] was always interrogative and exploratory.'[118]

When H.D. writes about sharing reminiscences with Freud in *Tribute to Freud*, she conceives this in terms of textiles, using phrasing that will be repeated in *Sword*: 'The years went forward, then backward. The shuttle of the years ran a thread that wove my pattern into the Professor's.'[119] In *Sword*, tapestry threads bind together disparate times and places and embody creativity and history:

> I worked the wrong side of the tapestry; the threads reached from Philadelphia to Tauris, from London to Paris, from London to Athens and to Karnak, from London … to Lausanne … The years between wars, the years before wars, the years after were no longer profitless and barren … when I stepped forward, to look at last, on the finished picture, I saw not … a disproportionate space of private desolation … but a circle of Greek maidens, all blessed by the gift of Love, and I myself, among them. (104–5)

The pattern reveals isolation giving way to connection and desolation to love. However, it is notable that this passage appears in the middle of the text, and the repetition of violence in the historical sequences supports a move ambivalent reading. As I noted earlier, H.D. tends to move between stitchery and woven tapestry without clearly marking the distinctions between them. The practice of working a woven tapestry from the back, so that the pattern only emerges on completion becomes a more apt metaphor for H.D. than the embroidery where the embroiderer works on the front of a pattern.

I would argue that H.D.'s practice of stitching informs the weaving we see in *Sword* because she refers to both as 'tapestry' and focuses on thread's ability to produce a patterned fabric. Her earlier references to tapestry in the text suggest that her own experience of embroidery is foregrounded when she introduces her connection to Morris but when she wishes to engage with a more complex layering of history and geography she needs to revise the textile metaphor. The slippage between H.D.'s lived practices, her life-writing and her fiction is frequent, as textiles appear in all three modes, yet it is important to remember that the textiles referenced in her texts are fabricated in language rather than thread and are flexible in different ways. The connections between these myriad forms of creative practice are important, as are the differences. As mentioned earlier, at various points H.D. refers to stitching, writing and spiritualist séances as 'work'. The sense of actively following or manipulating a thread allows her to link the three activities. The connections between spiritualism as tapestry and tapestry as writing allow her to relinquish her spiritualist practice (which she had come to see as dangerous to her mental health) and yet hold onto its insights.

Craft as memory work

In his study of the relationship between craft and industry, Glenn Adamson analyses the tendency of craft to be represented as always already in decline and, therefore, in need of revival.[120] William Morris is a key figure in this discourse and Adamson highlights the incongruity of Morris's claims about an absence of handcraft while outsourcing much of the production for Morris, Marshall, Faulkner & Co. to skilled workers in other companies.[121] The rhetoric of Morris and Ruskin contributed to the invention of craft 'as an absence … as a memory that haunts the present.'[122] Adamson attributes the enduring cultural power of this understanding of craft to its ability to act as a screen for the traumas of modernity. However, he goes on to argue that craft is a dynamic activity and as well as screening trauma, it may also function therapeutically. He goes on to present various examples of craft as therapeutic memory work from the embroidery and appliqué of suffragettes (including embroidery by those who suffered imprisonment and force feeding) to the contemporary art work of Aya Haidar.[123] Haidar embroidered photographs of war-torn Beirut where stitches 'conceptually … act as "colored bandages," gestures that simultaneously denote the site of a wound and heal it.'[124] In these examples of craft as memory work the element of public display makes the work politically activist as well as personally therapeutic.

This understanding of craft as memory work illuminates the significance of H.D.'s alignment of tapestry with both spiritualism (with its disruption of past and present, death and life) and the temporal shifts in her novel. As the threads bind together disparate times and places into a coherent, if complex, pattern, Delia Alton finds her own traumatic past contained and redirected to more creative ends.[125] Although H.D.'s embroideries do not form a public intervention, she does see the pattern formed within the written text as significant beyond her own recuperation. Despite her failure to publish to the work, she still regarded it as a message that would reach at least a few individuals. She writes to Norman Holmes Pearson in May of 1951 that what is important is that the book 'goes on living and vibrating and reaches a few people.'[126] The ability of thread to bind together while simultaneously creating patterns provides H.D. with a means to explore a complex and dynamic experience of time, history and particularity.

The patterns contain things, figures, abstract lines and negative space, allowing for a continued invitation to the dead to remain present, for life and death to meet, for material stuff and ineffable mystery to mingle.

Stitching modernism: Things in process

In *Sword*, H.D. crafts a text which layers historical epochs, diverse geographies and multiple literary intertexts. The novel can be read as a transitional work that reprises many of the concerns of *Trilogy* while its questing, questioning heroines anticipate the Helen of her late epic *Helen in Egypt* (1961). In *Sword*, H.D. figures a broad historical canvass, crafting a transnational vision of diverse cultures and geographies.[127] Just as she turns her sights to the past, focusing on her debt to the Pre-Raphaelites, she simultaneously creates one of her most formally innovative and challenging texts that is startlingly prescient in its environmental concerns. The novel is largely read as concerned with the Second World War, as I have done here. However, the threat of a third world war and nuclear apocalypse, which runs through the novel, reminds us of its composition at the beginning of the Cold War. This, again, marks H.D.'s shuttle moving backwards and forwards, as she presses the Victorian literary heritage into service of her modernist spectral and material poetics.

Using traditional women's work as a structuring device and creative metaphor is both humbler than the mythopoetic vision of *Trilogy* and more ambitious in its audacious claim to hold space–time together with thread. H.D.'s strategy is radical in its choice to elevate stitching and claim it as an everyday activity but one that is challenging and complex. The subversion suggested by Rozsika Parker's richly allusive title applies to both H.D.'s stitchery and her modernism. In their expression of women's creative agency, they align with Lily Briscoe's defiance of the dictate that 'women can't paint, can't write'.[128] The metaphor of stitching or weaving a tapestry emphasizes connection. However, in employing a patterning device that draws the fragments together without concealing their edges, H.D. expresses a modernist poetics of diversity. She holds together oppositional modes: connection *and* rupture, mourning *and* healing practice, material *and* spirit, stitching *and* writing. To return briefly to theology, Catherine Keller suggests a view of the divine as that which makes difference possible.[129] Her view of the interconnectivity of all things – persons, planets, quarks – is founded on relationality in and across difference. Thus we can read H.D.'s urgent search for, and crafting of, connection as hospitable to difference.

H.D.'s writing from the 1940s emphasizes a concern with the objects – both ordinary and extraordinary – that make up daily life. These texts reveal a celebration of things and anxiety about their fragility and destruction in war. In this chapter I've considered several different kinds of things: flowers, antiquities, home-made Christmas decorations, embroideries. H.D.'s texts emphasize how these disparate things are all in process. Even Freud's antiquities are not static. They move from Vienna to London and mobilize the gift economy, intervening in H.D. and Freud's relationship. Turning to the Christmas decorations and her needlework we see more clearly that it is the process of making and the vibrancy of materials that is most important to H.D. Mariana Ortega expresses this dynamism in her reading of the gift as an event rather than an object. She claims that the gift in giving 'makes us who we are' and 'opens up a world to us.'[130] Such dynamism is crucial to the generative openness of the feminine gift economy explored by Cixous. Cixous's theoretical writing partakes of both the genres of manifesto and utopia (making a world), and we see similar commitment to hope in the midst of violence and loss in H.D.'s writing. The unfolding of divinity in the world, through children's creativity, the circulation of gifts or the traces of literary genealogy suggests that materials themselves instantiate relationships and draw the world into being.

2

'The pebbles were each one alive': Animism and Anglo-Catholicism in Mary Butts's writing

The first memory Mary Butts recorded in her autobiography, *The Crystal Cabinet* (1937), involved falling purposefully into a puddle of yellow mud in order to discover if it tasted as good as it looked. She was disappointed. Another memory swiftly follows, this of a small box covered with shells and crimson velvet that she discovered in a shop in France. Her mother refused to buy it, purchasing a doll instead. Butts insisted that the box was beautiful and rejected the doll, eventually burying it in the garden.[1] These two memories mark enduring concerns of the text: the child's interaction with the natural world and the significance of small objects, beautiful to the child if not to others. Butts's childhood world was replete with objects that spoke of affective and spiritual realities. Her animistic understanding resonates with both romantic modernism and incarnational theology as she found the divine hidden and revealed within the things around her. Her relationship with things, her activities of crafting, collecting and caring for them form an essential aspect of her spiritual and creative development.

In *The Crystal Cabinet*, the child's creative engagement with materials and things becomes a way into considering questions surrounding imagination, divine life and the spiritual meaning of the object world. In Butts's work, things mobilize creativity, traverse interior and exterior space and stage the interaction between the numinous and the mundane. Butts may come across her treasures in ordinary life but they are often ornate, exquisite or in some way unusual, yet their quotidian setting is crucial for the development of a material spirituality anchored in the domestic and daily landscape. The spirituality of things in Butts's fiction and life writing can be traced to a number of influences including Romantic pantheism, incarnational theology and early studies of comparative religion. In this chapter, I consider the role of the Grail, as both object and idea, in her fiction and life-writing and then move to an analysis of the life of things and relation of these things to landscape and domesticity in her late memoir.

Mary Butts was a modernist writer who seems to be most noted by her contemporaries for her flaming red hair and her exuberant participation in the hedonistic expatriate circles in post-war France. After spending most of the 20s in France she returned to England in 1930 where she would remain until her death in 1937. She moved to Cornwall in the early 1930s and settled at Sennen Cove, on the north coast not far from St Ives. She once expressed a prediction that she would be remembered as an English writer and her work has most recently been seen as part of a turn towards the local following earlier decades' emphasis on empire and cosmopolitanism.[2] Certainly her most famous work celebrates the landscape of her native Dorset, however, it is important to remember that she also ranged from Paris to ancient Egypt to Cornwall in her fiction. She was a committed writer and published several novels, both highly experimental analyses of the post-war condition of England and historical fiction. In addition she published many short stories, essays and reviews, and her final book, the memoir, *The Crystal Cabinet*, which focuses on her childhood home of Salterns in Dorset.

In the early 1920s she visited the notorious Aleister Crowley in Sicily in search of spiritual meaning following the shattering experiences of the First World War. But Crowley's milieu did not suit her, and after numerous occult experiments she concluded that spiritual realities were best discovered through art rather than astral journeys, commenting in her journal in 1921: 'I'd sooner be the writer I am capable of becoming than an illuminated adept, magician, magic master of this temple or another.'[3] Throughout the interwar period her journals and letters emphasize the significance of the arts for revealing spiritual realities 'obliquely … like the knight's move'.[4] Her search for spiritual realities and her interest in the myriad ways humanity has pursued such questions continued to be an abiding passion, and shortly after settling in Cornwall she converted to Anglo-Catholicism.[5]

A concern across Butts's oeuvre is the haunting presence of the First World War. The shattering of a generation, the immensity of loss and the scale of psychic damage appear in text after text. In *The Crystal Cabinet*, Butts makes explicit a recurring trope: the bones of the land, the stones, trees and prehistoric formations provide an anchor against the dissolution brought about by war trauma. The land is restorative not merely through consolatory bucolic reveries but through its very strangeness. The sense that the stones have a life of their own and a significance that transcends human comprehension gives Butts numinous glimpses that sustain in the midst of despair. Butts has been criticized as ungenerously elitist in her conservationist stance.[6] Rather than promoting greater access and environmental education as part of a holistic concern for both environmental and human flourishing as many early conservationists did, Butts stressed an exclusive ethos in which particular wild, sacred places remained the preserve of those with a historic connection to the area.[7] This is evident in her pamphlet *Warning to Hikers* (1932) as well as *The Crystal Cabinet*. This affinity was largely a matter of birthright rather than class (Butts frequently criticized the snobbishness of her mother and others of her generation), based on rather grandiose constructions of lineage. In her later fiction, such as *Death of Felicity Taverner* (1932), her environmental concern takes on an increasingly xenophobic edge. The widespread concern for the preservation of natural beauty was only beginning to gather momentum in Butts' lifetime, alongside suburban development and loss of green space. In the 1920s and 1930s, while land use in Britain was changing at an unprecedented rate and suburban growth threatened green space, access to the countryside often trumped ecological concerns.[8] In this light, Butts's concern for environmental degradation and her view of natural spaces as valuable in themselves can be seen as prescient, although the exclusions she upholds are extremely problematic. Sam Wiseman points to notions of 'static dwelling' evident in *Warning to Hikers* but also notes Butts's ambivalence she demonstrates 'a sensitivity to the epistemological potential of movement, defamiliarisation and outsider perspectives'.[9]

From her most esoteric period Butts remained grounded in the physical world. Despite astral travel and other occult exercises she was sceptical of the ultimate benefits of such experiments: 'The danger of "magic" & its enquiry is that it may diminish, "despiritualise" the "material" world … art, love, scholarship, dancing, tobacco … Nothing will take away from me the sense of the terrific and absolute importance of phenomena.'[10] Butts had no desire to evaporate into an astral plane, her aim was to realize sacred realities within materiality. We can see in *The Crystal Cabinet* the emphasis on locating an understanding of the spiritual and magical within the material world. She writes of a rare visionary moment at her boarding school in St Andrews (a place she generally found alienating):

> Quiet in the playing fields – I had made myself a little rosary, of nutmegs and tiny macrocarpa cones, carved beads from the east and pierced tonquin beans the Salterns drawing-room used to smell of, and one or two ivory knobs … out on the grass … there was a tree … a birch I think, with something gold

as oranges glimmering in its branches, only more golden … A magic thing to remind me that all the inside things were true.[11]

The significance of things to spiritual and emotional health is repeatedly marked in her autobiography, and we also see it in her journals. When she was taken to London after collapsing of malnutrition and drug abuse in Paris in 1930, she writes, 'Remember: Home again. All the things of beauty I've known since I could first see & love "as though they were persons"' (emphasis in original).[12] Despite the fact that Salterns, the family home, has been sold, the familiar objects from her childhood home give her solace when at her lowest ebb.

'An odd cup of some greenish stone': The Grail in *Armed with Madness*

Butts' s biographer and the editor of her journals, Nathalie Blondel, argues that her engagement with landscape is primarily classical as she sees the land around her as suffused with the spirit of Greek deities. Blondel rightly emphasizes Butts's education and its impact on her writing.[13] However, as well as Greek gods and myths, Butts was fascinated by the Grail. It is a continual presence in her fiction, her journals and her memoir, suggesting that later European mythology also had a hold on her imagination. For Butts the Grail was both a thing and an idea, closely aligned with sacred landscape. Following the medievalist Jessie Weston, Butts felt the Grail formed the meeting point between paganism and Christianity.[14] Like many writers of her era she was significantly influenced by the work of classicists Jane Harrison and James Frazer.[15] In later life this work helped her reconcile her newly discovered commitment to Christianity with the European paganism that had always fascinated and delighted her. I begin my exploration of the Grail in Butts's work with her novel, *Armed with Madness* (1928), which features a modernist version of the Grail quest. I then turn to the more abstract representations of the Grail in her later life writing, where it enables syncretism between paganism and Anglo-Catholicism.

Armed with Madness participated in the modernist dialogue with the classical pagan revival begun in Romanticism. Margot K. Louis notes that the Romantics dismissed the mythology of Homer in order to champion the 'Mystery cults of the chthonian deities Persephone, Dionysos, and Adonis'. A strain of this Romantic emphasis on the mysteries as 'a way to celebrate the sacredness of this life, of sexuality and the life force' continued through the Victorian era.[16] Late nineteenth- and early twentieth-century Anglophone literature saw many heroines aligned with earth goddesses and dryads from Hardy's Tess to L. M. Montgomery's Anne Shirley. Modernists like Mary Butts sought to overcome the pessimistic vision of the Decadents with a renewed emphasis on a 'celebration of life'.[17] This modernist urgency was heightened by the trauma of the First World War. Butts's heroine, Scylla Taverner, described as a 'witch and a bitch', is an assertive Persephone who seeks her own lovers, has an intense identification with the Dorset landscape and articulates the 'disease' the characters sense within and around them.

Armed with Madness focuses on a band of young people damaged by the war (two are veterans), sojourning in a house in Dorset which is surrounded by a mysteriously silent wood. The uncanny setting resists easy identification and becomes even more charged when one of the characters discovers a cup of 'greenish stone' in an old well.[18] This peculiar find sparks a series of strange adventures, love affairs, violence and reconciliation. Identifications slip and slide as different characters take on characteristics of questing knights, sometimes failing, sometimes achieving sacred vision, or the wounded Fisher King. Like Percival, they struggle to articulate the right questions and the answers are illusive and fraught with uncertainty. Butts's analysis of the modern condition is similar to T. S. Eliot's and she noted that her novel could have been called 'The Wasteland' as she and Eliot were working on a parallel, although he was 'on the negative side'.[19] Unlike Eliot, she 'deploy[s] mythology not merely as an expression of mourning and loss, but as a source of regeneration.'[20]

The grail quest in *Armed with Madness* is decidedly pagan rather than Christian. This is no tale of medieval chivalry and quest for Christian purity. The gods invoked are Persephone, Zeus and the unnamed spirits of wood and tree. There is no hint of Eucharistic devotion despite the intervention of the vicar after the questors have scattered. Here Butts's humour shows itself; the vicar is both a nod to stereotypes of rural England – according to the American Carston he 'looked and spoke right' – and a peculiar oracle (137). He unravels the riddle of the cup for Picus and Carston: 'It seems to me you are having something like a ritual. A find, illumination, doubt, and division, collective and then dispersed. A land enchanted and disenchanted with the rapidity of a cinema. Adventures. *Danger and awe and love*' (140). Although he commends a day of ecclesiastic devotions to Carston, he indicates that the 'splendour of midsummer filtered through old glass on cold stone' is as spiritually sustaining as the church service (138).

Retellings of Arthurian legends had gained in popularity since Tennyson's *Idylls of the King* (1859–85).[21] Yet in her memoir Butts dismissed the romances of Arthur, Lancelot and Guinevere, asserting that the Grail was the only thing that mattered.[22] Butts's Grail narrative was inspired by Weston's argument that the medieval tales contained a Christian gloss over older, pagan tales in which the grail was a relic of woman-centred religions presided over by Eastern and female goddesses.[23] Mimi Winick explores Weston's work as 'scholarly enchantment' dedicated to the late nineteenth- and early twentieth-century investment in a comparative method that sought to reveal a historical, psychological or spiritual coherent whole as a source for meaning in the world. Weston's concern with the occult and explication of a 'world saturated with meaning' would have been extremely appealing to Butts.[24]

Like the medieval Grail stories, *Armed with Madness* assumes congruence between the health of the land, human well-being and the presence of the sacred cup.[25] The Grail story's inconclusiveness was important to Butts and this provokes the plot of her novel.[26] The identity of the cup of greenish stone with strange markings is ambiguous and never ultimately resolved. It attracts many names, functions and descriptors: 'Sanc Grail', 'the question mark to the question we can none of us answer', 'stone of exile', 'stone of joy', 'a piece of worn jade', an Indian poison cup, loot, a Keltic chalice, an ashtray (37, 25, 137, 141). The thing is strange and compelling. Although seeking renewal, the characters have no easy task and Scylla reminds them that 'I never heard of the Sanc-Grail doing anyone any good' (20).

Some of the questions raised in the novel are answered, for instance, we discover that Picus – the novel's trickster – put the cup in the well in the first place and later hid it in Carston's luggage. Yet for all these manipulations, the cup retains a sense of uncanny autonomy. It is never entirely clear whether the characters manipulate the cup or the cup moves them to act. The cup's resistance to signification creates webs of meaning, mystery and affect. After Carston returns it to the well at the end of the novel, we are left wondering when it will reappear. Just as its provenance remains mysterious, so its ritual significance as a possible Grail continues, even after Picus's jokes are revealed. At the end of the novel, Felix returns to Dorset from Paris, with a new character, the Russian refugee Boris. This stranger parallels the cup as another chancy find who may well start another cycle of adventures. Yet Boris's coming is harmonized with the landscape and the domestic scene. No longer portrayed as menacing or aloof, the house is open to the elements and smells of honey and the sea. The cup's discovery, circulation and eventual removal from display [but not from the vicinity] have ameliorated the disease so evident in the novel's opening.

Rochelle Rives argues that an affective relationship with things (specifically, possessions) and their appropriate placement in space enable empathy and 'soluable sense of self', a kind of intersubjectivity (my term).[27] Rives reads an implicit critique of imperialism in Butts's concern with things that have been loosed from all affective bonds through disruption, theft and endless circulation. Categorized as loot, these things, and those persons coming into contact with them, are unable to form empathic bonds that provoke an opening of subjectivity. Additionally, Butts criticizes the stasis of displayed objects: they are unable to interact and generate living space. The cup is eventually identified as part of Picus's father's collection of antiques, but in displaying objects without using or communing with them, Mr Tracy quenches the life in things. Thus for Butts, the tension between the movement of objects and the boundaries around this movement is crucial. Things must be able to move in order to foster affective bonds but the "discrete integrity" of things remains; boundaries are porous but not entirely erased.[28]

The 'soluble sense of self' in Butts's prose is formed in relation to things and an empathic openness to the external world.[29] We see this in Scylla's relationship with the wood around the house: 'She played an old game, that she was lying out on the wood's roof: translating the stick and leaf that upheld her into herself: into sea: into sky. Sky back again into wood, flesh and sea' (67–8). The relational ontology that draws together cup, human persons and environment is formed through mana. Mana was an important term for Butts. It's likely that she drew on her reading of Jane Harrison when she defined mana as the 'wild, enchanting incalculable force in nature … the non-moral, beautiful, subtle energy in man and in everything else, on which the virtue of everything depends'.[30] In *Themis* (1912), her book on the origins of early Greek mystery religions, Harrison describes mana as a 'vague force in man and in almost everything … constantly trembling on the verge of personality'.[31] For Harrison, mana forms a '*continuum*', indicating 'a world of unseen power lying behind the visible universe' (emphasis in original). Yet this does not mean a kind of otherworld but a power that can communicate 'from stone to stone', indicating a 'fluid substantiveness'.[32] Harrison's ideas were crucial to Butts's as she developed her understanding of the connected nature of things. Across her work she 'comes increasingly to align her narrative voice' with mana as 'a sense of flow between individual and group, among person, animal, plant'.[33]

The word 'mana' entered English in the mid-nineteenth century, via studies of Maori culture in Aotearoa/New Zealand (and similar concepts in Polynesian religions found in Hawaii and Samoa) by early European anthropologists.[34] The term may have come into more popular usage via William James's final text *Some Problems of Philosophy* (1911), where he defines mana as 'mysterious energy' as well as Jane Harrison's discussion of it in *Themis*.[35] For Butts, the circulation of this energy depends on a dynamic of connection and differentiation. Peter J. Mataira outlines the relational worldview of Maori in which relationships take place in the transitional place between connected opposites (light/dark, life/death, etc.). This interconnection then allows the power of the gods to be given to human persons.[36] Mataira argues that colonialists misunderstood mana, suggesting it to be a positive force while *tapu* was a negative one, but in Maori terms, *tapu* is the sacred state and mana 'the endowment *process* through which spiritual power was given by the indwelling spirit that presided over it' (my emphasis).[37] While I do not suggest that Butts possessed any great knowledge of Maori culture, I would like to draw attention to the importance of process and circulation in her use of mana.[38]

Throughout the novel Butts explores the possibilities for the connection of things, persons and the natural and built environments. The cup emerges from an old well (signifying the connections of elements like stone, earth and water with human agency) and the house and the wood create a mysterious silence together: 'The silence let though by the jays, the hay-cutter, and the breeze, was a complicated production of stone rooms, the natural silence of empty grass, and the equivocal, personal silence of the wood' (3). This silence dwells beneath the everyday noises of birds, farm equipment and wind. The 'complicated production' emerges from the synthesis of different spaces and the variety of *genii loci*. Here Butts moves past Harrison's formulations into a more positive claim for the personal liveliness of mana and the material, personal connections it forges. While emphasizing that the cup forms 'the question mark to the question we can none of us answer', Butts *does* provide an answer, if an ambiguous one: 'Wonder was the answer, and familiar objects out of their categories' (140). The movement of things and disruption of categories leads to wonder and this allows the characters to open to each other and the spiritual energies that surround them.

Pagan-Christian syncretism: The Grail in Cornwall

When Butts moved to Cornwall in the early 1930s, she found a wild and strange landscape, a place where she felt both at home and a stranger. She retained the animistic view of the land evident in her earlier fiction. In Butts's life-writing of this period, we see the Grail becoming more diffuse. A divine energy coalescing in and emerging from the landscape, it became a name for a sacred ecology rather than a discrete object. For Butts the Grail is both present and to come: on the 11 December 1932, she wrote: 'I think that the Grail might be seen here this winter. It is time, anyhow,' and a month later, 'I believe the Grail is stirring at Sancreed.'[39] In the 1930s, leading up to her conversion, the Grail becomes more evidently the locus of a mystical Christian Mass, yet her journals show how it continues to hold her imagination as emblematic of a pantheistic nature-focused paganism. We see here, and elsewhere in her writing of this period, how she approaches a variety of thinkers to elaborate the idea of Christianity as fulfilment of earlier religions. In this she participates in the Victorian ideals of development and progression that later scholarship has found so problematic. But at the same time, across her writing there are also traces of an undermining of hierarchy and notions of progress (she follows Jane Harrison's privileging of ancient rites and her emphasis on their modern relevance). In her pagan-Christian syncretism the paganism holds its own.

She frequently draws connections between Christianity and paganism in her journals and other writings in the 1930s. She was enchanted by the old churches and crosses of Cornwall as well as its dramatic landscape. In August 1933 she wrote of a visit to St Ives and Zennor: 'Remember ... At Zennor, peace in the church & magic by the great stone.'[40] This syncretism is also rife throughout *The Crystal Cabinet* where she writes about 'Our Lady, who was the same as Artemis, whom I asked God if He minded me saying my prayers to, and He didn't.'[41] In a review of a gardening book she commented, 'In gardens there is all that we have of a nature religion left to us.'[42] In an essay on Cornwall she evoked the ancient deities more directly when she lamented the villagers' failure to propitiate the gods. In her list, the classical deities merge with an image for Mary that emphasizes her relation to Aphrodite.[43]

Butts's journals show how paganism joined with Anglo-Catholicism in her spiritual, imaginative and intellectual approach to religion. The worldview in which the divine is manifestly present in materiality is not confined to paganism but also takes its place in a sacramental view of the landscape. Butts used her journals as reading notebooks and in August 1936 she muses on the nineteenth-century unorthodox Eastern Orthodox theologian Vladimir Soloviev. Her understanding of the uniqueness of Eastern Orthodoxy was its emphasis on humanity's deification, understanding that religion would not be complete until every soul experienced a theophany.[44] Soloviev used the name of divine wisdom, Sophia, to refer to this dispersed incarnation.[45] Eastern Orthodoxy holds that not only humanity, but all of matter will be deified, or taken into God.[46] The contemporary theologian John Chryssavgis articulates a sacramental sense in which the material world holds creation, incarnation and redemption simultaneously: 'For it is in the sacraments that the world not only looks back in historical time to the moment of creation and to the event of the incarnation, but also simultaneously looks forward in sacramental time to and even anticipates the redemption and restoration of all things – of all humanity and of all matter – in Christ on the last day.'[47] This is a mystical paradox in which all matter is divine, both already and not yet.

Turning to Western Christianity, there is a strand of sacramentalism, or radical incarnationalism, which celebrates the glory of God revealed in all things.[48] This Franciscan spirituality is perhaps most widely recognized in the poetry of Gerard Manley Hopkins and has been most recently explored in the context of ecotheology. A growing number of theologians insist on the intimate connection of the divine with the material.[49] As the Brazilian theologian Ivone Gebara writes, 'We no longer speak of God as existing before creation, but, in a way, as concomitant with it. We no longer think of God first and creation later.'[50] In this view then, things are animated by their connection to the divine energy that flows through, in and between all matter.

Many theologians writing in the traditions of radical incarnational or sacramental theology take pains to distinguish their position from pantheism.[51] Catherine Keller argues that pan*en*theism is a more appropriate formulation because it indicates that God is in all things (and all things in God; Keller emphasizes this enfolding and unfolding process) rather than asserting that all things *are* God. Keller is concerned that the *pan* in pantheism denotes a problematic unity that collapses difference. Interdependence and relation depend on separation as well as connection.[52] Theologians like Keller (and others less radical) are concerned with retaining a sense of transcendence, in which the totality of the divine is not limited by the material. Gebara writes of this difference in terms of possibility,

> It signifies openness to the possibility of all that is different, unpredictable, and
> unutterable. It means we should not build a closed discourse, a discourse in

which the unknown the as-yet-unthought, or even the non-existent has no
chance of being included … I like to say, then, that to speak of pan-en-theism
is to consider the potentialities of the universe, the potentialities of life, and the
potentialities of human life as always open-ended.[53]

While I am sympathetic to the concern for retaining difference, I also want to
point out distinguishing themselves from the polytheism and pantheism of
surrounding pagan traditions has been a concern of monotheistic religions
since their emergence in antiquity. Even the most progressive of contemporary
Christian theologians may not escape this anxiety. To return to the question of
difference, Grace Jantzen argues that a collapse into a sovereign oneness is not an
inevitability in pantheism but that divine transcendence can be reimagined as a
'horizon of becoming' within the world that embraces complexity and change.[54]
Mary-Jane Rubenstein elaborates on Jantzen to outline a definition of 'God-world
[as] … not a monist totality but rather an irreducible mutliplicity.' She draws on
the thinking of Jane Bennett and Karen Barad to remind us that 'our multiple-
universe [is] an untotalizable and shape-shifting product of narrative-theoretical-
material assemblages that are neither reducible to, not constitutive of, "oneness".'[55]

Mary Butts was a creative writer, not a systematic theologian, although she did
read widely and brought her considerable intellectual powers to bear on spiritual
concerns that interested her, and her work shows a mixture of pantheism,
panentheism and even more anti-material traditions like Neoplatonism.[56] In her
journal, Butts elaborates on Soloviev, describing his work on theosis as a legacy
from Greece and the mystery religions.[57] She ties this to the early church fathers
and links them to Joseph of Arimathea (according to legend, he brought the cup
from the first Eucharist to Britain), the Grail and the healing of the Waste Land.
Here we see how the Grail is coming to stand for the syncretism of Christian
and pagan religious systems. The 'Mass said at Corbenic' becomes the source for
the theophany to all souls.[58] After her conversion, Butts brought her more pagan
ideas in-line with her Christainity, but the persistence of the pantheistic remains
in her understanding of a living landscape, as is evident in her late memoir,
The Crystal Cabinet. The rest of this chapter concerns the liveliness of things in
this text.

The Crystal Cabinet

In 1934 Butts first mentioned her memoir in her journals. Her new book would
explore 'My childhood – how God, art & magic were learned. Praise of my father,

praise of Salterns – both dead.'[59] The three categories of divinity, artistry and magic are not distinct but are subtly interconnected in shifting ways throughout the memoir: the divine suffuses art and the mode of apprehending the one and crafting the other is magic. Butts's home of Salterns and the surrounding landscape is the place that shelters and provokes her growing understanding while her father was the first to foster her love of words and of place.

The manuscript of the memoir was finished in 1936 and after various difficulties with publishers (Heinemann found it too hot to handle, rejecting it for fear of libel), a heavily edited version of the autobiography was published by Methuen in 1937, a few months after Butts's sudden death from a perforated ulcer.[60] The full text was published in 1988 by Carcanet in Britain and Beacon Press in Boston. As indicated by her journal entry, the text is elegiac in many ways, mourning the loss of both father and childhood home. A major emphasis of the book is the celebration of Salterns, the Dorset house where Mary Butts grew up, and its surrounding estate and landscape. After her father's death in 1905 and her mother's subsequent remarriage in 1907 the house was altered. Eventually most of its contents, estate, and finally the house itself were sold; Butts felt this loss sharply.[61]

The text is a Künstlerroman yet this is also a spiritual autobiography as Butts makes clear in her journal. Scholars have commented on the text as containing a mystical vision of the sacred within the natural world, yet Butts's conversion to Anglo-Catholicism prior to writing the text has not been fully considered.[62] The narrator's Christian perspective is evident although the protagonist does not always share it. We can see the influence of Butts's high Anglicanism when she describes learning 'the superb Liturgy which is the matchless inheritance of the English child'.[63] She disparages much of the Low Church religious practice of her childhood, emphasizing the importance of sacrament and ritual, and claiming that her father inclined towards her (later) understanding of piety without much real evidence for this (54).[64]

The memoir takes its title from a poem by William Blake and perhaps the most precious objects within Salterns were the Blake paintings collected by Mary Butts's great-grandfather. As Nathalie Blondel notes, 'Gradually she absorbed "the kind of seeing that there was in William Blake," which would have a far-reaching effect on her writing, portraying as it does the surface of things whilst also intoning their resonance, their place in a pattern underlying and transcending the merely phenomenal world.'[65] The Blake paintings lead Mary Butts towards an appreciation of a visionary style which she will transmute into her writing.[66] Heather Walton notes the formal correlation between the

Romantics' concern with the inner life and creative self-expression and the interest of Protestant writers in the inner life as spiritual quest. She describes how many of the images and idioms of the Romantics were easily adopted by devotional writers including 'the transformed heart, the renewed mind, the indwelling spirit and the self-shaking of sublime encounters'.[67] Clearly Butts is no orthodox devotee, nor does *The Crystal Cabinet* follow the formulae of traditional spiritual autobiography; however, it does present its own adoption and adaptation of Romantic selfhood.

Salterns and Tebel Vos

Butts only began to write directly about her childhood after she settled in Sennen Cove in Cornwall.[68] Her small cottage near the Cornish cliffs was hardly a grand estate, yet she called the house Tebel Vos: house of magic. Her journals make it clear how the Cornish landscape, the proximity to the sea and the house itself nourished her. Cornwall features in her short fiction and essays of the period and her writing of the landscape is compelling and evocative. Just as *The Crystal Cabinet* demonstrates a strong correlation between Salterns and the surrounding Dorset landscape, so in Butts's Cornish home the house and the landscape are intimately connected. The landscape inhabits the house: 'The wind is strong, roughening the sea … Polished the fine furniture & did small things to beautify the place, with the wind rushing through the house for accompaniment.'[69]

For Butts, gardening and homemaking could partake of sacred, ritualized labour.[70] She describes an afternoon's gardening in which flowers, earth and sun are sacramental elements, as restorative to the soul as receiving communion: 'a nature sacrament'.[71] Earlier in the journals she writes of Tebel Vos as a place she has responsibility for nurturing and which in turn blesses her with moments of numinous vision.[72] As well as rhapsodic descriptions of the house, garden and landscape, Butts makes practical notes in her journal: '*household hint:* Polish your glass as well as your brass – but it's a magical discovery really'.[73] Butts took great delight in making her home in Tebel Vos. Her journals are rife with references to things added to the house: gifts from friends, her own new acquisitions, family heirlooms sent from her mother in London: 'THE MOVE here, & the beautiful things that came from London. (The view from the window which would stop any quarrel.) The marvellous "finds" unpacking, books & curious treasures &

beautiful things.'[74] Butts values beautifully crafted and rare objects but insists on a domestic setting rather than a museum, the things are there to be lived with and loved. For Butts, the landscape and the domestic scene are mutually implicated. The view from the window is jumbled up with the 'beautiful things' and the householder becomes archaeologist, unearthing treasure in the midst of unpacking. The things, old and new, join with the garden and the wild landscape beyond to create a harmonious whole.

Anim-fetishism: Lively things in *The Crystal Cabinet*

If *The Crystal Cabinet* is the story of Butts's relationship with Salterns and its environs, then it is evoked by the very small as well as the grandeur of the house itself. Salterns is made up of things as well as walls, roof and windows. Some of the earliest memories that Butts chooses to record are to do with her own possessions and growing love for particular small objects. Daniel Miller argues that 'objects create subjects much more than the other way around'.[75] Butts frequently returns to the idea that these precious things are alive, albeit in a way that is unknown and other to us: 'Grown-up people say that children like to pretend that the things they love are alive. This is nonsense – they *are* alive, and animism a natural possession of childhood. Alive, not with a copy of their own life, but with the life, the mana, proper to the thing itself' (81).

In using terms such as 'animism' and 'mana', Butts invokes early studies of comparative religion. In this book's introduction I traced the history of animism as a term in Western discourse to Edward B. Tylor's problematic formulations of the development of culture. However, the term continues to be useful for anthropologists and others interested in exploring an inspirited material world. In drawing together animism and mana, Butts yokes life with sacred power. Not only are the objects other (their life is not like human life but distinctly their own), but their alterity is sacred. In focusing on things in the context of animism, I suggest that the fetish can provide a useful interpretive framework. In developing his theory of commodity fetishism, Marx drew on the anthropological theories of the fetish as an object endowed with life and worshipped by a primitive tribe.[76] Isobel Armstrong notes that both Marx and Freud (who used the term to denote sexualities focused around phallic lack and substitution) participated in the racism of their time by not considering the significance of the fetish in its Indigenous environment. In combining anthropological ideas and the grotesque, Marx 'burlesqu[ed] the fetish' and 'instantiated – or perhaps perpetuated – a hostile subject-object world in which each stands over and against the other'.[77] Conversely, Armstrong suggests that things can function as a third term that provides a way out of the hostile subject–object binary. We can see this enabling mode if we return to anthropology's engagement with the fetish.

Tylor considered fetishism to be an elaboration upon animism, whereby 'spirits [were] embodied in, or attached to, or conveying influence through, certain material objects'.[78] However, Peter Pels argues that Tylor fundamentally misunderstands the nature of fetishism because this formulation suggests a transcendent spirit that is other to materiality itself. Pels argues that the fetish foregrounds 'untranscended materiality' because it speaks for itself: 'Fetishism says things can be seen to communicate their own messages. The fetish's materiality is not transcended by any voice foreign to it. To the fetishist, the thing's materiality itself is supposed to speak and act; its spirit is *of* matter'.[79] The term 'fetish' emerged out of Portuguese traders' interactions with West African communities. The pidgin word describes not so much African Indigenous religions, as the Portuguese misinterpretation of them. The word 'fetisso' may refer to a failed translation of an African word and may be related to the Portuguese word *feitiço*, (meaning "magical practice" or "witchcraft").[80] As the term began to circulate it became both an 'other thing' to commodity capitalism and Dutch traders' Protestant Christianity.[81]

Michael Taussig notes that the word's emergence in a pidgin language underlines the instability inherent in language: thus the fetish is 'bound to a sense of richness and mystery in elusive word-magic, the fetish of the fetish, we might say, testimony to etymologies and histories cosmic and violent'.[82] The term magic hearkens back to the etymology of 'fetish' and reminds us of the interplay of material and spiritual. The instability of meaning is mirrored in the otherness of the fetish object itself, its refusal to submit to human modes of control: 'It maintains an aesthetic value that radically distinguishes it as a material object from the subject it confronts. In this confrontation the fetish always threatens to overpower its subject, because – unlike our everyday matters – its lack of everyday use and exchange values makes its materiality stand out, without much clue as to whether and how it can be controlled'.[83] In Butts's writing, as elsewhere in this volume, we see ordinary objects that become extraordinary by exceeding their everydayness in their emergence into radical differentiation. Resistance to control and anthropomorphism is evident in her formulation of 'the life proper to the thing itself'.[84] However, although Pels stresses issues of power and control (dependent on the opposition described by Armstrong), we may also see a relational ontology in the differentiation of the fetish's materiality. The importance of relational ontology in her approach to objects can be traced through Butts's predilection for the term 'mana' and its movement through objects, persons and landscapes, drawing them together into a relational network of difference-in-connection.

Butts goes on to relate her understanding of childhood with adult life: 'Blessed are the grown-up people who have not lost it [communion with a beloved object] – a reminder of the conditions under which we enter the Kingdom of Heaven' (82).[85] Butts's choice of language is particularly interesting here. In describing a sense that may be lost with maturity, she appears to invoke a kind of innocence aligned with animism. Yet the language of the Gospels reminds us that entering the Kingdom of Heaven may be difficult and the message of the Beatitudes is as stark as it is comforting ('Blessed are the poor in spirit … Blessed are those who mourn').[86] Butts inverts a traditional understanding that heaven can only be gained by a denial of earthly pleasures. Here, attachment to objects engenders a communion that brings its own kind of sanctification.

Stones

Early in *The Crystal Cabinet*, Butts devotes a chapter to stones. In introducing her delight in possessions, she notes that part of her growing awareness of herself as a person was discriminating between things she did or did not wish to possess (8). Her passion was for books and stones: 'I desired, from the very beginning, books, and things I had found myself, birds' eggs, but with a deeper pleasure, bright pebbles and shells. These tastes persist. Today I cannot touch a lump of crystal, coral or amber, lapis or jade, without the deepest sensual joy' (8). Again, we see the connection Butts draws between the experiences of childhood and adulthood. She affirms that her sense of sensory pleasure in small stones does not erode with time. As is common in writers' memoirs, Butts will give space in *The Crystal Cabinet* to her passion for books and the role of various authors in her creative and spiritual development. However, equally important from an early age are small stones. This is just one of many times in her writing where Butts draws together the object world with the realms of imagination and culture. Of course, books are also objects; they have the peculiar property of being both material constructions of paper, ink, glue, thread and so on, and immaterial creations of language. However, books and stones would initially seem to have little in common and Butts does draw distinctions between them. Here the distinction of stones is that she discovers them herself (the implication, which is verified later, is that books are given to her by others).

The stones that Butts discovers reveal the animism of the object world:

> As they lay on the path or in pockets on the moor, the pebbles were each one alive. Alive, in communities, in the stone-world … It was there I found it, a pebble the size of a blackbird's egg, one side sliced off to show a cluster of crystals of violet quartz. Nothing would persuade me that I had not discovered a great jewel … Nor to this day can I go to a place where the earth is made out of any substance so essentially satisfactory without returning with samples … deriving from them still communion and delight. (8–9)

Butts notes the extraordinary quality of the stones she discovers and yet they are hardly diamonds, merely the beautiful bits and pieces of the natural world to be found in a day's walk along beach or moor. Perhaps the magic of these pebbles resides in this mixture of ordinary and extraordinary.

She goes on to consider how the intimacy with her collection of pebbles leads her into the understanding of the peculiar life of stones:

> In their chink and shine and colour and lick … [I] began to learn the meaning of stone. The life, the potency that lives in the kind of earth-stuff that is hard and coloured and cold. Yet is alive and full of secrets, with a sap and a pulse and a being all to itself. So that now, living in a country [Cornwall] with all its bones showing, whose fabric and whole essence is stone; standing stones on the moors, cairn and castle and 'coty-house' … neither stone nor flesh are without contact one with the other, in extension of the contact made so many years before on the nursery floor. (12)

We see here how Butts is drawn to the esoteric. Ordinary stones are the guardians of secrecy and thus possess an aura of compelling mystery. Butts presents herself as the initiate on the threshold; not entirely privy to the secret life of stones and yet growing in awareness of its meaning. She aligns her early experiences with stones with her adult life again: first, emphasizing that the communion she experiences with stones forms a continuity between childhood and adulthood, second, referencing her sense of emplacement while writing *The Crystal Cabinet*. We are reminded that the 'now' of writing is not the time of her Dorset childhood but her later life in Cornwall. The two places of home overlap. She suggests that her early contact with stones assists her becoming at home in Cornwall, a stony country.

Stump

The next object that I want to discuss here is a strange one. It is more of a backdrop or stage setting than anything else, yet it is seen to be singular in itself and also earns its own chapter in Butts's memoir. I am referring to an object Butts discovered in a hedge that her mother christened 'The Stump'. This is an old chunk of an oak tree, 'worn, smooth and unrotted, in to the model of a small mountain. Perfect and complete, with *everything*, cover and cliffs, pools and an open valley, all rising to a central peak' (80). Butts is enchanted by the *Stump* and when it is delivered to her nursery it becomes central to her developing imagination and creative powers. She is private about the intensity of her engagement with The Stump, considering it 'a mystery to be guarded' and part of the animism that pervades her childhood: 'The Stump to me was a live thing. Alive with personality, the character proper to a large, worn, wise lump of old oak' (80, 82). The Stump may be the broken body of a tree (trees are spirit-filled in *The Crystal Cabinet*, again sounding the note of residual Romanticism), but here it has a second life, a second self both like and not-like an oak tree. The Stump becomes the site of world creation and – as Butts gets older – the site for more complex dramatic enactments of myth and adventures:

> One's business with the Stump was really to make worlds, and those endless games were images of the whole of everything one could think about, and express in terms of a mountain which was an island, and a magic island, which lived in the Greek sea … The sensual delight in grouping, shaping and arranging, the utmost expression of sight and touch, the long joys of finding things to go on it out of the garden, I feel to this day. (84)

Here we see Butts's engagement with Greek mythology and how in her mind it is enfolded within Salterns and Dorset. The child's creation of tableaux using an old stump and cast-off materials and objects gestures towards a spiritual depth to her home and surrounding landscape that partakes of a vibrant pantheism.

The stones we considered earlier find their way into the world-life of The Stump as they 'came out of their drawer now and found their proper setting' (84). Butts used a variety of materials in her creations: stones and other bits from the garden, plasticine ladders, small dolls. Butts avoids what we might conventionally expect, a life of dolls as mirroring the life of their owner, arguing 'while stone and shell and even bead and button took on vitality and character, not human but their own, the dolls remained nameless and quite dead. *They were symbols, properties, part of the landscape*' (85). Here again Butts suggests peculiar crossovers between nature and culture. the inert dolls are both symbols and landscape, while the stones come from the land yet have a life of their own, as do beads and buttons which are manufactured objects. Butts's creative bricolage of scraps from nursery, house and garden accords with Walter Benjamin's assertion that children focus on the discarded remains of culture, as discussed in Chapter 1.[87] In Butts's description of her creation of tableaux, material from house, garden and field mingle in a ritualized creative activity that partakes of mystery and magic and the spirit of stone and tree.

Things and a soluble self

It is easy enough to critique Butts's description of Salterns as a paean to private wealth, mystified by tropes of lineage and naturalized by references to birthright. However, Rochelle Rives's more nuanced reading of objects in Butts's fiction also applies to her life-writing. Rives's analysis of the placement of objects and resulting affect yields a phenomenological engagement with object life rather than a direct critique of consumer capitalism. Butts's relation with stones in *The Crystal Cabinet* reprises this empathic economy in which the stones move in and out of a dynamic collection that has a life of its own. The affinity of small pebbles with the standing stones of Cornwall hint at a concern with sacred ritual that joins with Rives's ethical argument to suggest that porous boundaries open the self to the world of spirit as well as materials. The emergence of the divine in between these moving-yet-boundaried 'quasi-objects, quasi-subjects' indicates that spirituality may be a matter of surfaces, placement and interaction as well as the depth of individual subjectivity.[88]

Butts's writing on stones and stumps could be seen as a romantic longing for union with the natural world.[89] The loss of Salterns becomes emblematic of the loss of childhood innocence and the wider loss of peace, stability and psychic health following the First World War. However, there are two elements in the text that undermine such a reading. The first is that the pulse and life of the stones refuse to be entirely subsumed into a narrative of longing and loss; their strange inner life and interactions between themselves and other objects continue as a performance of peculiar presence. Second, as I have discussed earlier, a feature of *The Crystal Cabinet* is the narrator's continued commentary on the integration of her early life with her life at the time of writing. Butts's relationship with stones is not lost along with childhood innocence but forms a crucial part of her mature understanding of the world. Her sense of affinity with

Dorset is placed in dialogue with her sense of belonging in Cornwall, one that is more complex and partial. In Cornwall she is both at home and not at home; and this uncanny relationship with the landscape of her later life calls into question the supposed seamless integration of self with childhood home. The subject of the text may be Salterns, its grandeur and loss, but the ghostly presence is that of Tebel Vos, her beloved, small Cornish bungalow.[90]

3

Darkness and dirt: Virginia Woolf's material mysticism

Recent treatments of the role of religion in Virginia Woolf's novels have posited a tension between religiosity and secularism, but this chapter explores the conjunction of spirituality and materiality in Woolf's work.[1] I argue for an unorthodox view of spirituality in which the mystical and the material are deeply interrelated. This material mysticism is demonstrated in the liveliness of everyday objects, the way in which 'moments of being' emerge out of mundane locations and the redeployment of key tropes of the mystical tradition of negative theology. In negative theology, or apophatic mysticism, darkness and silence are frequently used to describe the divine as transcendent, unknowable and absent. Yet in Woolf's novels darkness and silence are located in the mundane, the material and presence. Following from Chapter Two's exploration of the liveliness of things and their relation to domestic and natural environments, this chapter analyses the uncanny nature of objects and assemblages in Woolf, in particular relation to domestic space. The life of domestic objects and the house itself provides a locus for reading material mysticism in Woolf's work.

I am engaged with the relationship between Woolf's writing and Christian mysticism, and, more specifically, the discourses of apophatic mysticism. There are, of course, other spiritual traditions relevant to Woolf, including the Eastern mysticisms that were circulating in Europe in the late nineteenth and early twentieth centuries and various occult traditions and practices. Some of these, such as Theosophy, were inspired by Eastern traditions, others drew from hermetic sources and Jewish Kabbalah.[2] Christian mysticism itself draws from many traditions including Judaism and Greek paganism but a precise delineation of these relationships is beyond the scope of this chapter.[3]

Mystical Woolf: Critical positions

Mystical Woolf is a contested term. Criticism on mysticism in Woolf's oeuvre ranges from Jane Marcus's claim that Woolf's mysticism was influenced by the teachings of her Quaker aunt, to Val Gough's delineation of the irony and ambivalence surrounding mysticism and religiosity in Woolf's texts, through Julie Kane's exposition of mysticism in Woolf as part of a journey of developing self-confidence to Pericles Lewis's consideration of Woolf and enchantment.[4] Other critics have dismissed or critiqued any notion of a mystical Woolf, but she won't quite go away.[5] More recently, Donna Lazenby has argued that Woolf's work presents a mystical philosophy in her affirmation of the power of language to represent transcending vision while also engaging with the 'fracturing' and 'dissolution' that troubles such representations; a dialectic of cataphasis and apophasis.[6]

In her engagement with ancient and medieval sources, Lazenby departs from critical habit. Analysis of mysticism in modernist texts tends to concern itself with the discourses of mysticism found in the late nineteenth and early twentieth centuries, following the work of William James, among others. Early anthropologists and philosophers of religion searched for social origins and sought commonalities across time periods and differing traditions. Both of these intellectual projects have since come under critique as scholars have become suspicion of models of progress and false universalizing that elides cultural differences. I do think it is important to consider writers in relation to the thinking of their times and that intellectual history should not be divorced from literary criticism, nevertheless I agree with Lazenby that there is value in considering Woolf in relation to earlier philosophical and theological traditions. The turn of contemporary discourses of both critical theory and theology to medieval mystical texts as well as recent work in medieval studies on the liveliness of objects suggests that such texts may also be fruitful for current readings of Woolf.[7]

I find much value in Lazenby's scholarship and her perceptive reading of Woolf, but I want to point out a problematic area, namely, the issue of the material and the ordinary. Lazenby insists that Woolf's mysticism is continually imbricated in the material, everyday world. Yet her text pays very little attention to this material everydayness and is much more concerned with abstraction. I think this stems from a similar problem in her source material. In its debt to Neoplatonism and its idealism, negative theology has a strong tendency towards transcendence and a flight from the material and the body. Bringing the work of feminist theologians to bear on the discussion of apophatic theology takes us in a different direction in relation to what I call a material mysticism in Woolf.

Apophasis, feminism and materiality

Negative theology argues that God is completely other to anything that could be said or known about God. Apophasis is the process of 'unsaying' everything that has been said about God. It is the *via negativa*, the way of ignorance, of unknowing. Language collapses, leaving only silence. Some theologians contrast apophasis (the negation of images) with cataphasis (the affirmation and proliferation of images). Others claim that cataphasis itself is subsumed within apophasis. Denys Turner argues that for classical negative theology, which stems from the writings of the sixth-century Syriac monk, Pseudo-Dionysius, what is required is to say all things of God, negates all of these things and then go on to negate the distinction between them. Apophasis is then the destabilization of language that is accomplished by this final negation.[8] Although Turner urges readers to remember Dionysius's claim that the cataphatic and apophatic are inextricably linked, his focus on apophasis and his sense of apophasis as the ultimate mystical expression undermine the significance of cataphasis.

Beverly Lanzetta advances a more radical reading of apophatic mysticism. She posits a liberating openness in which 'nothing' is figured as the dynamic ground of being. She reads the medieval mystic Meister Eckhart as pointing to a nothingness beyond God (rather than a God-beyond-God) which goes beyond the usual discourse of negative theology towards an even greater negation: 'Mystical experience breaks open to the liberation of consciousness, and to the negation not only of all *conceptual* claims, but to the *intradivine* negation in which *God* unbecomes.'[9] Such mysticism may not be as divorced from atheism as one might expect.

What is problematic in these understandings of apophasis, especially from a feminist perspective, is the potential, if not the actual, denial of materiality and embodiment. A number of theologians explore a third way which affirms a dynamic of cataphasis and apophasis in which the two modes are linked but one does not supersede the other (this is Lazenby's understanding of both ancient mystical theology and Woolf's mystical writing). Amy Hollywood discerns the interplay of cataphatic and apophatic languages in the writings of medieval mystics. She emphasizes the significance of imaginative visions to apophatic mysticism, claiming that visual images can be used apophatically as the mystics inscribe images in their texts and then work to destabilize these images by suggesting their inadequacy. In the medieval text, the *Rothschild Canticles*, veil imagery connotes the divine as a hidden presence; the presence of the veil indicates that absence is never absolute while simultaneously suggesting that presence is never fully revealed.[10]

In the work of Turner, Lanzetta and Hollywood we can begin to discern the resonances between apophatic mysticism and deconstruction. Scholars have considered the relationship between Derridean deconstruction and negative theology; both are practices focused on the instability and undoing of language.[11] However, as Catherine Keller points out, such post-structuralist theological discussion has tended to ignore materiality and the entanglements and relations that emerge from it. Keller's work performs an important intervention when she yokes apophatic mysticism with feminist theology. She aligns the fifteenth-century Nicholas of Cusa's 'cloud of impossibility' with the 'dual dynamic of obstruction, a redoubled density of impossibility' that faces feminist theologians in the task of critiquing andromorphic norms within religious traditions as both non-religious feminists and patriarchal religious gatekeepers query how a woman could be 'a feminist *and* a Jew/a Christian/a theologian'. Keller notes that the feminist strategy of 'unsaying and saying anew' may be aligned with apophatic discourse.[12]

Keller resists the tendencies in negative theology to distance itself from materiality. In *Cloud of the Impossible* (2015), she explores negative theology and planetary entanglement, taking the discourses of apophatic mysticism into the complexities of a radical relatedness that considers the entanglements of quarks as well as persons, considering ecology on a vast as well as minute scale. She argues that the 'knowing ignorance' of Nicholas of Cusa 'does not close in on itself in defeat or exhaustion. It finds in the limits, ruptures, and fogbanks of consciousness new relations to – anything that matters. And what is con-sciousness, anyway, but first of all, a knowing-with?'[13] She explores a sense that our relations, our non-separability, our entanglements are always shrouded in mystery. This correlates with the mystical subjectivity Lazenby finds in Woolf: 'We are … porous subjects embedded within a reality that comes to us … life ceaselessly arrives to contest the settled frame.'[14] It is in this ecological, material mode of an apophasis of relation that I situate my reading of Woolf.

Material mysticism in Woolf

Unity is a central concern of much criticism focused on Woolf's mysticism. Certainly a sense of merging with the surrounding, world also called 'the oceanic', is a significant concept for scholarship on mysticism, particularly for those who focus on trans-religious phenomenology (following James).[15] While I don't dispute the many moments of unity expressed in Woolf's fiction and life-writing, my reading takes a different direction. Mainstream critical discourse has been suspicious of unities, but this does not necessarily require a dismissal of mysticism. Contemporary readings of the medieval mystical tradition suggest that multiplicity and diversity are also sites of mystical experience and open out from readings of mystical texts. Likewise, in Woolf we see a dynamic mysticism that resonates with the traditional tropes of negative theology (the destabilizing of language, the ineffability of ultimate reality, the significance of silence) while also bringing forward modes that foreground materiality, the interplay between subject and object, materiality and consciousness. We see the emphasis on multiplicity in Woolf's development of the 'choral protagonist' in her later fiction, as well as in her description of moments of being.[16] Woolf's emphasis on the 'we' that makes up 'the parts of the work of art … the words … the music' cuts against the unity of 'the thing itself', suggesting that 'the whole' is actually a multiplicity.[17] Even the 'pattern' behind daily life, may be anything but a monochrome. Patterns involve repetition, but as Derrida reminds us, repetition entails both similarity and difference, just as patterns contain a diversity of shapes, lines and negative space.

Lorraine Sim argues that Woolf resists an elevated understanding of epiphanies as out of the ordinary: 'For Woolf, the quotidian is not devalued in moments of being, nor is the cotton wool of everyday life separate from, or separable from, the numinous "pattern" she finds behind it.'[18] 'Behind' is a difficult word, as it suggests that the world of daily life may be transcended, yet I would argue for Sim's insistence on non-separability: behind may be a word carefully chosen to indicate the same (horizontal) plane and a refusal of a more other-worldly beyond of traditional understandings of transcendence. Mayra Rivera, a postcolonial theologian, constructs an alternative understanding of transcendence that can help us here. She argues, 'God is irreducibly Other, always *beyond* our grasp. But not beyond our touch.' She offers a vision of a relational transcendence that exists 'within creation and between creatures' leading to the argument, Our images of the divine Other shape our constructions of human otherness.'[19] Rivera's intervention in the discourses of transcendence suggests that the unknown otherness of the divine need not entail a flight from the material world but may indicate a sense of mystery within the ordinary. This gives us a strategy for reading Woolf's mysticism alongside discussion of the sociopolitical investments and implications of her texts.

As we saw in Chapter 2 regarding Mary Butts, the placement and displacement of things contribute to the formation of environments and subjectivity. The contrast of surfaces and interiorities appears in Woolf's work repeatedly as things shift from intimacy with persons to a marked alterity and resistance to interpretation. According to Rachel Bowlby, things have an uncanny nature in Woolf as they signify the juxtaposition of past and present and create different modes of domestic space, yet through their linguistic placement, they also highlight narrative's vexed relation to representations of time, space and interpersonal connection.[20] *To the Lighthouse* is an important text for readings of mysticism in Woolf; I will explore how we may trace a material mysticism in the interplay of things and human persons in the Ramsays' house and in the emphasis on the liveliness of material world in the 'Time Passes' section of the novel.

Discussions of mystical Woolf often consider Mrs Ramsay's solitary visionary experience in *To the Lighthouse*.[21] Left alone, she is able to shed the social expectations that define her much of the time and enter into an experience of interiority that presents a different mode of selfhood than we have seen in her interactions with her guests, children and husband: 'To be silent; to be alone … one shrunk … to being oneself, a wedge-shaped core of darkness … Beneath it is all dark, it is all spreading, it is unfathomably deep.'[22] In contrast her discussion of the pattern of daily life in 'A Sketch of the Past', here Woolf uses 'beneath' to indicate the positioning of changing modes of consciousness. This reintroduces a vertical plane, but the emphasis is downwards, towards the earth, rather than upwards, towards the heavens. The reduction of self to inarticulate 'unfathomable' darkness bears resemblance to mystical tropes of the dark night of the soul, the unbecoming of negative theology. Darkness is frequently associated with absence and negation, of self, of world, of divine plenitude. However, Lazenby places her discussion of Mrs Ramsay's darkness in her chapter on cataphasis, because she sees it as allied with a *visionary* experience that relies on unity and form.[23]

The substance of Mrs Ramsay's vision is a sense of unity with the things around her 'if one was alone, one leant to things, inanimate things; trees, streams, flowers; felt they expressed one; felt they became one; felt they knew one, in a sense were one' (54). Mrs Ramsay names elements of the natural world but she then moves to that element, at once both simple and complex, natural and manufactured: the stroke of light from the lighthouse.[24] Lazenby argues that Woolf's 'modernist self-exploration … shares insights with pre-modern exercises in self-contemplation'.[25] She compares Woolf's depiction of Mrs Ramsay's leaning into things to the Greek philosopher Plotinus's understanding of 'union with objects of world'.[26] Thus self-transcendence is a horizontal move that involves 'oneself becoming Other'.[27] It is in self-negation that the self is able to open out towards the object world, participating in the kind of intersubjectivity that I explored in the last chapter. Woolf writes about the decentring of human consciousness onto the object world in her memoir, 'A Sketch of the Past', again focusing on the natural world: 'The lemon-coloured leaves on the elm tree; the apples in the orchard; the murmur and rustle of the leaves makes me pause here, and think how many other than human forces are always at work on us. While I write this the light glows; an apple becomes a vivid green; I respond all through me; but how?'[28] Here she is remembering her family's summer home at St Ives, the inspiration for the Ramsay's home in *To the Lighthouse*. But I want to take up this sense of 'participative *kinship* with objects in the world' and 'oneself becoming Other' to pursue the implications for a material mysticism.[29]

Knitting

Mrs Ramsay's meditation on the 'stroke of light' is arguably the most obviously mystical moment in *To the Lighthouse*, but Woolf interweaves the material with the ineffable throughout this episode. Mrs Ramsay's knitting is mentioned frequently throughout the novel, especially in the first section. It is easy enough to give an entirely social reading of Mrs Ramsay's knitting: it is part of her ethic of care, it is a way of extending her domestic role to encompass the village and lighthouse (the stocking is a gift for the lighthouse keeper's son), it is associated with the other textiles in the novel (Mrs Ramsay's shawl, the clothes left in the house after the Ramsays' departure), it allows (or requires) her to remain active while sitting or conversing. But I think Woolf's frequent mention of knitting in the midst of a description of abstract reverie invites a different reading. The knitting is referenced seven times in two pages, continually providing a material anchor to Woolf's exploration of self-transcendence. The dance of hands, needles and wool in and among Mrs Ramsay's reverie provides a material quality to her contemplation; the knitting enables and influences the material direction of Mrs Ramsay's mystical moment. Woolf repeatedly underlines the connection between knitting and vision. This moment is visionary in that *looking* is the vehicle for Mrs Ramsay's changed consciousness, a point underlined by the personification of the light that looks back at Mrs Ramsay: 'She looked up over her knitting and met the third stroke and it seemed to her like her own eyes meeting her own eyes, searching as she alone could search into her mind and her heart' (53). Yet we are reminded that this is also an embodied, haptic experience. The body that looks is the body that knits. Touch and movement are as important as sight and repose.

After describing Mrs Ramsay's sense of being as a 'wedge-shaped core of darkness', Woolf notes 'she continued to knit' (53). All through this time of contemplation, Mrs Ramsay is linked to the daily and quotidian through her knitting. Yet the knitting does not interrupt her contemplation, unlike the demands of her husband, her knitting does not drain her and cause her to close up like flower at night (34). Rather, it allows her to open herself to darkness and light alike. The repetitive movements of the needle and its ongoing reminder of materiality leads to Mrs Ramsay's understanding of 'lean[ing] to thing': 'Often she found herself sitting and looking, sitting and looking, with her work in her hands until she became the thing she looked at – that light for example' (53). The knitting in her hands supports the looking and the leaning. Undergirding vision is the comfort of touch, of fibres against skin.

Later on the page the knitting is bracketed, but placed in between Mrs Ramsay's experience and the wedge of darkness: 'Not as oneself did one find rest ever, in her experience (she accomplished here something dexterous with her needles), but as a wedge of darkness' (53). We may wonder what this dexterous something is, perhaps the turning of the heel. We don't have ordinary knitting here but something more complex; Mrs Ramsay's skill is emphasized but also the active work of the needles. In this episode knitting oscillates between being an activity and a thing. Hovering between 'oneself' and 'wedge of darkness', it is not entirely clear if the knitting inhibits Mrs Ramsay's rest or is part of what enables her sense of self to alter, to 'lean into things' and become a 'wedge of darkness'. I would like to suggest that the knitting, bracketed as it is, forms the boundary between Mrs Ramsay's daily, domestic, social identity and her dispersed self, the darkness that is unfathomably deep yet has a limitless horizon. As a boundary, the knitting both connects and divides. It is passageway as much as boundary, giving a haptic, textured, material vehicle for this transformation of consciousness.

After accomplishing something dexterous, Mrs Ramsay has her visionary moment. As she contemplates the 'long steady stroke, the last of the three' of the lighthouse, 'There rose, and she looked and looked with her needles suspended, there curled up off the floor of the mind, rose from the lake of one's being, a mist, a bride to meet her lover' (53, 54). Here her needles cease to move, time is suspended as a bridal mist arises from her being. Here, as with the wedge of darkness, Woolf most explicitly draws on mystical language, which frequently employs bridal imagery for the contemplative soul. Although the needles pause, we are reminded of the knitting's continued presence and as it ceases to move, it shifts from action to thing. The movement of hands and needles may pause – action is suspended – but the knitting is not laid down, physical contact between knitting and hands is maintained and we may wonder if the intensity of the mutual gaze between Mrs Ramsay and the lighthouse would be diminished without the wool in her hands.

Mrs Ramsay's knitting does not entirely vanish from the novel with her death. Towards the novel's end, when Lily is about to finish her painting, she considers ordinary objects – 'that's a chair, that's a table' – and how their simplicity is simultaneously 'a miracle … an ecstasy' (164). This is also the moment when she is haunted by Mrs Ramsay. Seeing her on the steps Lily's sense of desire and loss also 'became part of ordinary experience' and into this ordinariness she sees Mrs Ramsay, 'sat there quite simply, in the chair, flicked her needles to and fro, knitted her reddish-brown stocking, cast her shadow on the step' (165). Mrs Ramsay's knitting is so much a part of her that it returns as an aspect of her ghostly appearance. Like Clarissa Dalloway, Mrs Ramsay's creative energies usually take a social shape, drawing together disparate people to form a coherent dinner party, bolstering her husband's fragile ego, matchmaking. Yet with the knitting we have a thing that connects Mrs Ramsay's social endeavours (we never see her knitting for herself) and her inner life. Mrs Ramsay's knitting is integral to Lily's final vision.[30] It is not light but shadow, darkness, that moves Lily to find the expression she has been searching for throughout the novel. The shadow Mrs Ramsay casts from beyond the grave contains her knitting. We are left to wonder what ever happened to the stockings Mrs Ramsay knit for the lighthouse keeper's son. Have they outlived her? What was their life once off her needles? She was near to finishing so we imagine the stockings had made their way as intended, but perhaps they have ended their life shredded by moths and home to mice (the small creatures that will make their own home in the house in the 'Time Passes' section). In *To the Lighthouse* Woolf reminds us of the ongoingness of things. They are not immortal; they change, decay and evolve, but they also extend beyond the experience of individuals. They too partake of unfathomable depths of darkness in the mysterious space beyond human capacity for thought and feeling.

The ubiquitous reddish-brown stocking on Mrs Ramsay's needles relates to another significant textile object in the text: Mrs Ramsay's green shawl. In contrast to the earthy colour of the knitting, the shawl is green with the vibrancy of life. It aligns with the leaves of trees that are so frequently compared to Mrs Ramsay (34). The cashmere shawl, a luxury item, contrasts with hand-knit stocking that will likely be knit from more common and hardwearing wool.[31] Like the knitting, the shawl also has a social function, facilitating her relationships with her husband and children.

After dinner, at which Mrs Ramsay presides in her green shawl, she goes up to the children's nursery where Cam and James are quarrelling over a boar's skull; Cam is frightened but James refuses to have it moved. Here Woolf gives us the text's most unusual object. The skull is mounted on the wall, becoming a decorative, if macabre, object, rather than the corpse of an animal. In this brief scene Woolf suggests that the transition between animate and inanimate things is uncertain and odd. The light in the room causes the skull's horns to multiply. Cam declares she can see them 'all over the room' and she calls the skull 'a horrid thing, branching at her all over the room'. Here the dead animal gains a ghostly life, appearing in shadows, moving and multiplying. Cam doesn't blame the light for casting shadows but locates agency with the originary object.

Mrs Ramsay covers the skull with the green shawl and this shroud now becomes the agent for yet another transformation, as Mrs Ramsay lulls Cam calling the shawl-covered skull 'a bird's nest; … like a beautiful mountain such as she had seen abroad … with valleys, and flowers and bells ringing and birds singing and little goats and antelopes' (93). Mrs Ramsay's description joins with the soft green cashmere folds to create a new object: firstly described as a bird's nest, then as an entire ecosystem, a mountain with valleys, flowers, sounds and (living) animals. This imagined landscape reminds us of Mary Butts's Stump that contained a whole world. By calling the shawl-covered skull a thing beloved of fairies and similar to faraway landscapes, Mrs Ramsay assists in the object becoming distant from the children. Its frightening intrusion – 'branching at her' – is removed, made other-worldly, fantastic. Mrs Ramsay and Cam join together in a ritualized repetition 'a mountain, a bird's nest, a garden … little antelopes', calling this new thing into being with words while the green shawl supports their imaginary world with its tangible, visible characteristics of greenness, softness and size (it is large enough to wrap around the skull many times) (93). Then, in an adroit manoeuvre, Mrs Ramsay persuades James that despite being covered, the skull is still there. The shawl here is redescribed as a covering or shroud rather than an agent of transformation. This strange thing, the shawl-shrouded skull of the once living but now dead animal that is both there and not there, reminds us of the veiling that indicates the presence/absence of the divine. The shawl–skull provokes our questions about the relationship between human persons, things and animals. It suggests that things that once participated in animal life may still have an afterlife as an uncanny, lively object.[32]

House as uncanny other thing

In *To the Lighthouse*, we see clearly how assemblages of objects contribute to that larger thing that is the home.[33] In the first chapter I analysed how we can see objects as a flow of materials. Arjun Appadurai argues that objecthood is inherently fragile because 'materials are ever volatile', and he stresses that the movement inherent in the social life of things means that 'all things are congealed moments in a longer social trajectory'.[34] The gatherings of things that are themselves ever evolving is reiterated across Woolf's text. The Ramsays' summer house on Skye is a pervasive presence in the novel. Early in the text we see how things are heaped up, in order to suggest the whole that is the house itself: 'bats, flannels, straw hats, ink-pots, paint-pots, beetles, and the skulls of small birds … long frilled strips of seaweed pinned to the wall … towels too, gritty with sand from bathing' (11). We see how the Ramsays' house is markedly different from that other house, the lighthouse. As we have discussed, the lighthouse is an absent presence. Rather than holding straw hats and ink-pots, it holds intangible light. It is the object of the children's thwarted desire and provocation to Mrs Ramsay's visionary mystical moment. Yet Mrs Ramsay's knitting, a gift for the lighthouse keeper's son, reminds us that the lighthouse is also a material dwelling. Thus the lighthouse is made material as a habitation as well as an ideal.

Anthropologists like Daniel Miller celebrate the mutually constitutive relationship between selves, things and homes, while Gaston Bachelard's work has become synonymous for the way selfhood is rooted in the remembered (or imagined) home.[35] Yet feminist critics have laboured long to deconstruct idealized notions of self and home (while still acknowledging their formative power), exploring the many ways in which the domestic sphere has been a place of labour (physical, emotional and administrative) and entrapment for women.[36] In directly confronting this legacy of entrapment in the patriarchal home, Woolf is scathing in her critique, claiming that women must kill the angel in the house in order to exercise personal and creative freedom.[37] Yet houses were important to Woolf. They are prominent in her fiction and life writing, from the Victorian

patriarchal houses of *Night and Day* and *The Years* to the aristocratic grandeur
of Knole celebrated in *Orlando*, from the inviolate room that shelters the woman
writer to the homes of her childhood explored in 'A Sketch of the Past' and '22
Hyde Park Gate'.[38] Victoria Rosner argues that domestic spaces are important
for Woolf as a site demanding creative transformation: 'For Woolf, the kitchen
table represents not what the modernist artist must discard but what she must
transform into the basis of her work'.[39] Thomas Foster indicates the centrality of
the vexed relationship between women and domesticity in modernist women's
writing: 'I take the phrase homelessness at home from Emily Dickinson, to name
one of the defining goals of modernist women's writing. This phrase offers a
verbal formulation of the desire to resituate possibilities for "defamiliarization
and social critique" in relation to domestic settings and the feminine personae
located there'.[40] In Woolf, as in other modernist writers, we may look for a
disorienting approach to domestic space that renders the home uncanny and
precarious. The defamiliarization of objects that resist interpretation and
co-option yet invite intimacy is realized in the home as thing.

In his study of the 'poetics of the house', Gaston Bachelard explores how 'not
only our memories, but the things we have forgotten are "housed." Our soul
is an abode. And by remembering "houses" and "rooms," we learn to "abide"
within ourselves. Now everything becomes clear, the house images move in
both directions: they are in us as much as we are in them'.[41] Thus we see how
fictional houses are so conducive to explorations of personal consciousness,
as houses are 'in us' as well as the reverse. The feminist critic must approach
Bachelard's celebration of the house that 'shelters daydreaming' cautiously.[42]
Bachelard's alignment of the house with maternity poses a particular problem
for women who might resist a requirement to provide such maternal care.[43]
While I do not wish to underplay the importance of the domestic care offered
by women, I would suggest that many women are caught between domestic
obligation and a desire to relate differently to the dwellings they inhabit. The
house as an image for the self has a long history, but what I want to consider
here is the house as thing, and how it might come to be an *other* thing with a life
of its own. Bill Brown defines the 'other thing' as an intersection of matter and
movement that indicates a vitality, an excess of being, that moves beyond the
control (and knowledge) of the (human) subject. He suggests that this attention
to the resistance of objects ('the object-event') highlights 'the uncanniness of
the ordinary'.[44] His emphasis on movement related to vitality resonates with
the flow of materials and the placement of things discussed in earlier chapters.
Brown refuses a spiritual reading of this excess of being that hovers mysteriously

around and within the entirety of the object world, but I would suggest that this alterity enables a mystical reading. We can see an extension of the material mysticism of Mrs Ramsay's habit of 'leaning to things' to the thing itself in the uncanny liveliness of the house, allowing us to ponder how the house may also have a spiritual life.

For many of Woolf's fictional houses, their liveliness is signified by the extent to which they are open to the outside. Plants, animals, soil and weather disturb the domestic interior and indicate a mode of domestic being that is beyond human dominance. The Ramsays' summer house in *To the Lighthouse* is an uncanny, mysterious thing. It is changeable, subject to growth and entropy. The house begins to decay even while the Ramsays are still resident. This is largely due to crossings between interior and exterior; the wilderness invades the house, aided by the children:

> If they could be taught to wipe their feet and not bring the beach in with them – that would be something. Crabs, she had to allow, if Andrew really wishes to dissect them, or if Jasper believed that one could make soup from seaweed, one could not prevent it; or Rose's objects – shells, reeds, stones ... things got shabbier and got shabbier summer after summer. The mat was fading; the wallpaper was flapping. (25)

This description of the shabby house foreshadows the greater decay to come. In 'Time Passes', the human inhabitants of the house are replaced by wind and the process of change accelerates: 'Those stray airs ... blustered in, brushed bare boards, nibbled and fanned, met nothing in bedroom or drawing-room that wholly resisted them but only hangings that flapped, wood that creaked, the bare legs of tables, saucepans and china already furred, tarnished, cracked' (104, 105–6). In this section the house and garden take centre stage, human activity, achievements and losses are relegated to brief comments in brackets. The human inhabitants leave material traces in their impressions on objects. The ghostliness of human persons contrasts with the liveliness of the objects left behind, as the objects reveal the presence of an absence: 'What people had shed and left – a pair of shoes, a shooting cap, some faded skirts and coats in wardrobes – those alone kept the human shape and in the emptiness indicated how once they were filled and animated' (106). Like the animal skull, the people have now become absent presences, intimated by the shape of empty clothing and the looking glass without a face.

The house assumes an even more uncanny character as things take on a greater weight and heft than formerly: 'Once in the middle of the night with a roar, with a rupture, as after centuries of quiescence, a rock rends itself from the mountain and hurtles crashing into the valley, one fold of the shawl loosened and sung to and fro' (106). The green cashmere shawl had bonded to the skull so firmly that to come away is a roaring rupture, a movement that spells catastrophe for the miniature world created for Cam. The shawl, a product of animal growth and human skill, takes on the qualities of stone and wilderness, opposite to its common associations with warmth, softness and lightness. In 'Time Passes', Woolf emphasizes cyclical time through reference to the seasons but links this with linear, historical time as objects shift and change:

> When darkness fell, the stroke of the Lighthouse … came now in the softer light of spring … But in the very lull of this loving caress … the rock was rent asunder; another fold of the shawl loosened; there it hung, and swayed. Through the short summer nights and the long summer days, when the empty rooms seemed to murmur with the echoes of the fields and the hum of flies, the long streamer waved gently, swayed aimlessly … there came later in the summer ominous sounds like the measured blows of hammers dulled on felt, which, with their repeated shocks still further loosened the shawl and cracked the tea-cups. (108–9)

The light from the lighthouse appears to have maintained intersubjectivity with Mrs Ramsay, even after her death. Like her, it leans into the things. It is witness to the loosening shawl. Here we have a discomforting juxtaposition of gentle eroticism, 'softer light … loving caress' (the stroke of light reminiscent of the stroke of a hand), and violence, 'the rock was rent'. This first violent rupture, which is likened to the rockfall that starts an avalanche, a natural image, foreshadows the more ominous violent shocks (made by people) to come as the guns of war invade the stillness in the house. The process of decay that Mrs Ramsay observes earlier in the novel becomes more profound as human habitation gives way to other animals and plants:

> The house was deserted … the trifling airs, nibbling, the clammy breaths, fumbling, seemed to have triumphed. The sauce-pan had rusted and the mat decayed. Toads had nosed their way in. Idly, aimlessly, the swaying shawl swung to and fro. A thistle thrust itself between the tiles in the larder … rats carried off this and that to gnaw behind the wainscots … Poppies sowed themselves among the dahlias; the lawn waved with long grass; giant artichokes towered among roses … the gentle tapping of a weed at the window had become, on winters' nights, a drumming from sturdy trees and thorned briars which made the whole room green in summer. (112–13)

This passage contains a wealth of detail; it is similar to Woolf's earlier description of assemblages of objects in the house. The shawl that we saw covering the skull and creating a new thing (first a nest, then a mountainous landscape) in the imagination of Mrs Ramsay and Cam has lost the sense of purpose with which it first covered the skull. As it continues to unwind, it sways aimlessly. But its sense of movement echoes the other moments in the house, the 'trifling airs', the nosing of toads, gnawing of rats, drumming of trees on the window. These sentences contradict the first statement; 'The house was deserted.' Although the house no longer plays a role in human drama, it takes on a different kind of life. The garden comes into the house with the thistle growing in the larder and the wilderness transforms the garden as wildflowers grow among the cultivated flowers and the lawn turns into a meadow. The room is green in summer, displaying growth as well as the tarnish and flapping wallpaper of decay. Green, the colour of the cashmere shawl, now signifies the whole house, which lives a verdant life apart from the human life it once contained.[45]

The hollow

In his reverie on the spaces in the house, Bachelard contemplates the small. He emphasizes the pleasure and satisfaction to be found in retreating to a small space and curling up. He has chapters on nests, shells and corners, here conflating natural and domestic images. Bachelard compares the nest to a simple house.[46] Although the Ramsays' house is not a cottage, it is aligned with the nest in its processes of change; firstly, as Mrs Ramsay makes a nest of the green shawl and the skull to soothe her frightened daughter, and second, as the swallows nest in the drawing room, a room often associated with the mistress of the house.

Despite the problems with Bachelard's correlation of the house with maternity, his emphasis on the significance of small spaces for solitude and imaginative growth resonates with Woolf's claim that a woman needs a room of her own to write. Bachelard writes about the cultivation of silence in small spaces: 'Every corner in a house, every angle in a room, every inch of secluded space in which we like to hide, or withdraw into ourselves, is a symbol of solitude for the imagination … When we recall the hours we have spent in our corners, we remember above all silence, the silence of our thoughts.'[47] This cherished memory of solitude is echoed by bell hooks's description of her constant desire for a study that is a small room, uncluttered by the books that represent the clamour of others' thoughts:

I loved tiny rooms, spaces where I could close myself in. The shacks I loved were
full of small rooms. Growing up I had always found some small tight space to
shut myself away. I could hide from the pain and the torment. I could feel the
sweetest most private peace … I never want to think or work in the same room
with someone else. I need to be alone with language.[48]

Mrs Ramsay's children feel a similar passion for small spaces. The rhythm
of domestic life in the Ramsay's household involves regular intervals of
dispersion: 'Disappearing … directly the meal was over, the eight sons and
daughters of Mr and Mrs Ramsay sought their bedrooms, their fastnesses in a
house where there was no other privacy' (10–11).

As we saw earlier, solitude is at a premium in the Ramsay's house; Mrs
Ramsay's visionary moment comes in a rare moment of solitude. Lily does not
have the room of her own that Woolf claimed a woman needed for creative
production. Lily requires daylight so she paints on the lawn, subject to all
manner of interruptions. Yet for all the lack of shelter for her creative work
to grow, she succeeds in attaining her vision. Lily disparages her work by
asserting it will be hung in the attics, or destroyed, but she also holds to her
vision as the thing that matters and thus claims a kind of ongoingness for
her work. From the perspective of the painting itself, taking up residence
in the sheltering eaves of the attic, in the company of mice, boxes and the
memory of the unnamed Swiss maid crying for her dying father, might not be
so bad. It might not be an undervaluing of artistic merit but a participation
in another kind of community of things. Moving out of the sphere of human
consumption and desire may not indicate the death of the painting but a new
kind of life.

Although Bachelard's meditations on the house are largely positive and do not
explore the unhomeliness of home, he does at times emphasize the mysterious
nature of the house.[49] Here he describes a connection between small, enclosed
spaces and alterity: 'Nest, chrysalis and garment only constitute one moment
of a dwelling place. The more concentrated the repose, the more hermetic the
chrysalis, the more the being that emerges from it is a being from elsewhere.'[50]
This sense of being from elsewhere invites otherness into the corners of the
house – as we saw with the shawl-covered skull – and aligns with Rivera's
contention that transcendence does not entail a flight from materiality, but a
sense that divine being is always beyond our grasp, while remaining intimate.
The dynamism between intimacy and otherness is at play in the nooks and
crannies of Woolf's houses.

Bonnie Kime Scott notes the significance of hollows to Woolf: 'Woolf is attracted to "hollow," sheltering spaces as they occur in nature, protecting butterflies, flowers, mushrooms, birds, rabbits, houses, or vulnerable people, and providing a sense of connection. She selects the word sixty times at important junctures in her novels.'[51] We can make a connection here between Bachelard's corners and hollows, images of the natural and built environment inspiring and forming one another. Scott notes the fragility and transience of some hollows. She quotes *To the Lighthouse*, 'So soon a bird sings, a cock crows, or a faint green quickens, like a turning leaf, in the hollow of the wave' (104). This compelling image draws together wind, water and plant: 'The wave bestows motion on the leaf, like a miniature world, briefly whirled.'[52] Scott goes on to compare this to a moment in *Mrs Dalloway* when Rezia is compared to 'a bird sheltering under the thin hollow of a leaf'[53] and suggests that both bird and woman are dependent on the leaf 'but the leaf provides a scant, fragile, temporary shelter at best.'[54]

Scott's analysis of hollows is also relevant to *The Years*, where we find a more complicated and problematic interplay of the success and failure of fragile shelters for material mysticism. Sara Pargiter has been read as a mystical character of the novel, one of Woolf's outsiders who generates alternative ways of knowing.[55] In the 1907 chapter, Sara's attempt to somatize the act of thinking leads to a moment of altered and earthy consciousness as she identifies herself as a tree root: 'She became something; a root; lying sunk in the earth; veins seemed to thread the cold mass; the tree put forth branches; the branches had leaves.'[56] She is doubly sheltered: in bed, in her bedroom at the top of the house, the garret corner Bachelard finds so well suited to imagining. Sara's moment of altered consciousness is a kinaesthetic one, where the earth also functions as an enfolding, protecting presence, more of a shelter than her own room in which she is restless. Sara as tree moves, growing branches and leaves. She finally finds peace in her small space in the attic as bed and earth come together in her awareness: 'The one sheet and the one blanket fitted softly around her. At the bottom of the bed was a long stretch of cool fresh mattress ... Her body dropped suddenly; then reached ground' (122).

Later in the novel, we have a very different domestic scene, with its own 'hollow' offering a much more limited shelter: the bath in Sara's boarding house. North is visiting his cousin in her shabby flat in a working class neighbourhood. Sara has not lit the lamp, so North attempts to recite poetry as it is too dark to read but is distracted by noises off:

He heard a sound. Was it in the poem or outside of it, he wondered? Inside, he thought, and was about to go on, when she raised her hand. He stopped. He heard heavy footsteps outside the door. Was someone coming in? Her eyes were on the door.

'The Jew,' she murmured.

'The Jew?' he said. They listened. He could hear quite distinctly now. Somebody was turning on taps; somebody was having a bath in the room opposite.

'The Jew having a bath,' she said.

'The Jew having a bath?' he repeated.

'And tomorrow there'll be a line of grease round the bath,' she said.

'Damn the Jew!' he exclaimed. The thought of a line of grease from a strange man's body on the bath next door disgusted him. (306)

This exchange is followed by Sara, rather incoherently, relating her reaction to similar, earlier occasions. She became overwhelmed with rage at the intrusion on her privacy and felt forced to seek work (in order to earn enough money to move house) yet this also enrages her as she feels it would be intellectual prostitution, and she doesn't follow through on an offer of work. Maren Tova Linett critiques this scene, noting how the 'Jew in the bath' presents a threat to the imagination (in North's mind he invades the poetry itself) and to Sara's autonomy: 'Her privacy is being infringed upon and her creativity obstructed by the Jew who shares her bathroom; but if she gets a job to escape him, she falls into a similar trap, still forfeiting her solitude and mental freedom.'[57] Linett argues that in this scene, Woolf wrestles with her concerns about the status of the disinterested artist and the importance of remaining 'outside' patriarchal culture, an anxiety that was particularly acute in the 1930s, as her work took a more explicitly social and political turn.[58]

While it is unsurprising to find a remnant of grease in the bath of a worker in the tallow trade, the description of the by-product of Abrahamson's industry participates in the long history of antisemitic associations of Jews with the body.[59] Here we have a scene in which the hollow space does not shelter Sara. The bath, or rather, the traces (audible and tangible) of its inhabitant threatens the solitude of her small dwelling. In analysing Woolf's resignification of domestic and public spaces, Thomas Foster points to Georg Simmel's understanding of the city as 'a place where it is not possible to avoid encountering … "the stranger", a person who is both "near and far *at the same time*"'. He argues that these encounters destabilize 'the spatial metaphors that establish identity by establishing an inside and an outside.'[60] Woolf addresses such encounters across *The Years*, some of which enable this disruption while others enforce the separations that secure identity.[61]

Terri Mullholland advances a similar argument to Foster when she emphasizes the porosity of the boarding house. She notes that working-class neighbourhoods, such as the East End where Sara lives, are frequently marked in *The Years* as spaces where 'the sounds of the street outside merge with the life inside the room'.[62] Mullholland reads 'the Jew in the bath' section as emblematic of both Sara's rage against the patriarchy that would 'control her economic situation and her spatial agency, confining her to a single room and a shared bath' and also of the potential for boarding houses to become space for 'society of outsiders'.[63] Abramhamson's status as outsider parallel's Sara's own as an impoverished, disabled, single woman. I agree with Mullholland's exploration of Sara Pargiter as representative of the financially constrained single woman, but I would also point out Sara's cultural capital, the letter of introduction that would aid her in securing work if she wished, and the fact that she still has means to provide a roof over her head. She lives in working-class accommodation yet does not need to work for a wage herself, unlike Abrahamson and his fiancée. Moreover, the potential for coalition is undermined by the perpetuation of antisemitic discourse. Although the boarding house may be 'a way of both containing the outsider or other, and through the proximity of shared space, forcing the inhabitants into a confrontation with that other', that confrontation fails to enable a recognition of intersubjectivity when Abrahamson is forced into a representative role (for patriarchy, for capitalism) rather than acknowledged as a person.[64]

Earlier in this chapter I have shown how Woolf tended to create the house as an uncanny thing in drawing together interior and exterior, domestic space and wilderness, cultural and natural. I would argue that the bath represents a lost opportunity for Woolf to again engage in situating objects otherwise and opening subjectivity. Sara resists an encounter with her neighbour/stranger, who is both near and far off. Yet the bath may indeed offer protection and solitude to another individual, namely, Abrahamson. Woolf gives us very few details about him and how he experiences his dwelling place. All we know is that he works in the tallow trade, he is engaged to a 'pretty girl in a tailor's shop' and he is noisy when bathing.[65] He has no voice in the text and we are given no window into his consciousness. The line of grease and stray hairs in the bath contrasts with the earth which enclosed the tree root of Sara's imaginings earlier in the text. Here we are reminded of Mary Douglas's assertion that dirt is 'matter out of place'.[66] Unlike the soil of the Browne garden of Sara's girlhood that the text celebrates, the grease in the bath is socially marked dirt, reviled by Sara and North because it is out of place, that is, it is in an intimate proximity to Sara that she does not welcome.

Although the association with the bodily has long been a weapon of antisemitism, this connection has also been re-evaluated by contemporary Jewish scholars, much as feminists re-evaluate the historically negative association of women with the body. Many modernist scholars, Linett included, are primarily concerned with antisemitism as secular, cultural issue (that depends on a construction of Jews as a racial other to white Europeans), but given my interest in mysticism, I want to turn to a consideration of Jewishness that foregrounds religious ritual and sensibility. In considering Abrahamson, we are confronted by a male, Jewish body. Daniel Boyarin alludes to the antisemetic discourse that aligns Jewish men with carnality and by extension, with the feminine. However, he argues that this association is not only made by a hostile gentile culture, but that it is also 'an assertive historical product of Jewish culture'.[67] Boyarin describes a nineteenth-century East European Jewish masculinity in which the ideal man is 'gentle, timid, and studious'. He argues that this model of masculinity has roots in traditional Jewish culture, going back to the Babylonian Talmud and 'such a man is interpreted as anything but sexless within rabbinic texts; indeed, he is represented as the paramount desiring male subject and object of female desire'.[68] While Boyarin acknowledges that Jewish women suffered patriarchal oppression in both Talmudic culture and later European Jewry, he argues that the Jewish masculine ideal holds the potential for liberatory interpretations because it is 'a positive oppositional identity to "manliness" that is neither "castrated" nor emasculate, because it does not read femininity as lack'.[69]

Circumcision is a clear marker of Jewishness on the male body. Antisemitic interpretations of the circumcised penis link it with fears of castration and related effeminacy. However, Boyarin stresses the Jewish interpretation of circumcision that reads it rather as a marker of wholeness, 'a mark of resistance and a deliberate (private) setting apart of oneself from the dominant culture'.[70] The sense of spiritual belonging to a tradition provides a metaphorical shelter of which circumcision is a bodily signifier. Moreover, elsewhere Boyarin reads midrash as indicating that circumcision is a sign of preparedness for divine vision: 'The cut in the penis completes the inscription of God's name on the body. It speaks of circumcision as a transformation of the body into a holy object.'[71]

This ritual action then marks a space where the holy and the bodily come together. The relationship of the body and space is important. Mayra Rivera draws on the work of French theorist Hélène Cixous when she notes that the body is always in process and in relation to the surrounding world:

> Flesh is always becoming. Air, water, food, sunlight, and even societies of microorganisms enter our bodies to weave the delicate tissue of our flesh. Imperceptibly to the naked eye, cell by cell, day after day, the world constitutes your body and mine. And our bodies enter into the constitution of the world. They are intimately our own, singular and irreplaceable, and yet formed by and given to the world.[72]

Ecofeminists have emphasized the connection between embracing the materiality of the body and the materiality of the earth: 'When the earth is sacred to us, our bodies can also be sacred to us.'[73] Here we can see the resources for reconfiguring the bodily (and industrial) dirt in the bath as sacred matter than can participate in the experiences of dynamic holism that includes a range of experiences and social locations rather than excluding. We can imagine Abrahamson's bath as one that shelters a particular, labouring, body. Woolf doesn't tell us how Abrahamson responds to solitude, if he feels the awkwardness of thin walls and unwelcome close contact with neighbours or if, like Mrs Ramsay, he leans into things and becomes one with the intimate object, if he takes consolation in discarding the traces of his daily work, if he rejoices in joyful flesh. The gusto with which he bathes tempts me to imagine the latter. Abrahamson in the bath gives us a moment to read against the grain in Woolf's texts, to consider the subjectivity of the other that the text fails to represent and to ponder the hidden connections between subjects, objects and spaces.

4

Radiant dandelions: Gwendolyn Brooks's domestic sublime

This chapter leaves the European scene for the American city of Chicago at mid-century. Including the work of Gwendolyn Brooks brings a greater complexity to this project by inviting consideration of how the liveliness of things may contribute to spaces that are formed in tension with racial and economic oppression. Brooks's writing engages with the questions of subject–object relations, domestic space and everyday enchantment that are the central concerns of this book. Brooks was born in Topeka, Kansas, in 1917, but her family moved to Chicago shortly thereafter and she has always been known as a Chicagoan. She wrote poetry from an early age and began publishing in magazines in 1930. She became the first African American to win the Pulitzer Prize for poetry with her collection *Annie Allen* (1949); she was involved with the Black Arts Movement and published poetry across seven decades. Although she is best known for her poetry, this chapter focuses on her only novel, *Maud Martha* (1953), and asks how Brooks's writing brings issues of class and race to the fore in consideration of domestic space and the role of things in its formation, maintenance and precarity.

Brooks's early work can be located within the mid-century Chicago Renaissance, a movement described as following the Harlem Renaissance in 'represent[ing] avant-garde political, social, and artistic thinking that eventually produced a stage upon which African American writers could redefine their relationships to American society and the world'.[1] However, as it became increasingly evident that greater social equality did not emerge from the literary outpouring from 1920s Harlem, the optimism of the earlier movement gave way to a 'more jaded, bitter outlook'.[2] Although the Chicago Renaissance is seen as following the earlier movement based in New York, Harlem Renaissance writers continued to write long after Harlem's heyday in the 1920s and there is a close interplay between the late work of some Harlem writers and the early work of the Chicago writers. James Smethurst describes Brooks's *A Street in Bronzeville* (1945) as 'later modernist or neo-modernist collective portraits of Black neighborhoods', comparable to Langston Hughes's *Montage of a Dream Deferred* (1951) and Melvin Tolson's *Harlem Gallery* (1965).[3] The choral nature of Brooks's early collection becomes more pronounced in her later work *In the Mecca* (1968) as I will explore in the following chapter.

The more pessimistic tone of Brooks's work, in terms of both the state of society and the poet's ability to adequately represent it in language, chimes with other late modernist works. However, some critics find the 'bleakness' of Brooks' vision to be 'tempered by an optimism' inherited from Harlem Renaissance writers such as Langston Hughes and Countee Cullen.[4] The 'collective portraits' form allows Brooks to 'bring ... to the surface the life of a community that is separated and suppressed, yet thriving and surviving.'[5] Brooks was influenced by James Weldon Johnson and Langston Hughes, who encouraged her to keep writing and also to read other modernist poets including Pound, Eliot and Cummings.[6] Critics have noted how her poetic techniques suggest 'the elliptical, allusive, and imagistic verse of modernist poetry' and her unique vision involves a blend of social critique and modernist style.[7] Earlier criticism tended to see the Harlem Renaissance as separate from modernism, but more recently scholarship has challenged the exclusions inherent in a narrow view of modernism.[8] In a more expansive view of modernism, we can locate Brooks's work within a trend towards greater engagement with social realism, while also noting that her style is marked by irony, linguistic intricacy and the significance of the object: features she share with more traditionally defined modernist writers.[9]

Critics have tended to focus on the representation of the struggle for subjectivity (particularly for the Black female subject) in Brooks's writing.[10] However, as seen in previous chapters, an understudied aspect of her work is the significance of objects in both enabling the coming to subjectivity and as marking the thwarting of subjectivity by racism and sexism. In Brooks's work, subjects find themselves in relation to the liveliness of things. Not only do object enable (inter)subjectivity, but they contribute to the formation of space and contribute to altering textures of interiors and exteriors. I follow Hortense J Spillers in her reading of *Maud Martha* as a text in which the character's inner life has 'the capacity to draw the outer into oneself, retranslating it into an altered exterior' and this movement between inner and outer means that Maud Martha 'thrives because she wills it through diverse acts of form, woven from the stuff of everyday life'.[11] This chapter takes up questions of the relation between inside and outside posed by earlier chapters and considers how the permeability of inside and outside registers in crowded urban space. In *Maud Martha*, the fraught relationship between women and domesticity exposed by Woolf is rendered more complex in its relation to Black female subjectivity. For Brooks, home space can be both restrictive and liberating. In *Maud Martha*, the eponymous heroine struggles to create and take ownership of domestic space. The novel's characters frequently negotiate their relationships with these spaces through objects. Bell hooks's exploration of home as enlivened space for Black creativity and agency is enabled by things, and her work underlies my reading of lively objects in Brooks's work. This chapter argues that objects in Brooks's texts testify to an occluded spirituality of the everyday.

Brooks and animism

The relationship between objects and subjects, things and human persons is particularly vexed for African American subjects given the history of chattel slavery.[12] However, in this chapter I turn to an older history of West African cosmologies that privilege the material world as a place of spiritual liveliness: 'Everything that exists possesses some portion of the universal life force.'[13] Harry Garuba describes these forms of thought as 'a mode of religious consciousness' characterized by a lack of disembodied spirits and attention to 'material manifestations' of divine spirit.[14] Garuba emphasizes that animism does not reinscribe mind/body dualism but rather posits a world in which the spiritual and natural properties of material nature are 'both simultaneous and coterminous with their natural properties'.[15] These cosmologies persist in the African diaspora, taking new forms in Voodoo, Hoodoo, Santeria, Obeah and entwining with Christianity in myriad ways.[16] In this chapter, as across this book, I am more concerned with the liveliness of things and their mutual becoming with human persons, than the objectification of persons.

In considering the spiritual life of things in Brooks's work, I look to a spirituality of the everyday as indicative of an African-inflected animism.[17] Scholars of both religious studies and literature have traced the ways African cosmologies are evident in the African diaspora. James Haskins observes that in West African cosmology spirituality is imbedded in everyday life.[18] Tribes such as the Akan (located around present-day Ghana) did not see barriers between 'sacred' and 'secular' or 'holy' and 'profane'.[19] This sense of holism, in which there are no fast boundaries between the sacred and the ordinary, enables a worldview that sees the material world as saturated with spirit. *Vodun*, practiced by the

Dahomey in present-day Benin, is an underlying reality that 'is personified as deities and that animates everything in the universe'.[20] The material realm is not seen as distinct from the spiritual and even material that appears inert is enlivened in complex cosmologies. Interconnections among deities, ancestors, humans, plants and animals indicate a worldview in which 'reality was viewed as one interwoven fabric'.[21] Will Coleman notes the commonality between such cosmologies and Hermeticism which has its roots in North African Hellenism and which also preaches the interconnection of all things: 'As above, so below'.[22] Houston A. Baker, Jr argues that as Black Africans were materially displaced, their spiritual needs intensified: 'Bereft of material, geographical or political inscriptions of a state and a common mind, diasporic Africans were compelled to seek a personal, spiritual assurance of worth'.[23] Sacred environment was important to the emerging religious sensibilities of Black cultures in the Americas: 'Indigenous West African religious memories … imbued the enslaved Blacks with sensibilities honouring all of creation and space as holy'.[24]

In his reading of the spiritual poetics of twentieth-century African American women's writing, Baker suggests that Conjure plays a significant role in this literary tradition and forms an important site of women's spiritual power.[25] Conjure (along with Hoodoo and related traditions) can be placed in the realm of the everyday practices of 'vernacular religion' and defined as 'a magical tradition in which spiritual power is invoked for … healing, protection, and self defense'.[26] In the use of physical charms and rituals and awareness of myriad spiritual powers at work in the material world, Conjure is embedded in an animist worldview, participating in the '*continual re-enchantment of the world*' (emphasis in original).[27] While Brooks's work does not identify Conjure women explicitly, I would argue that her writing can be read in this tradition that sees the material world as animate. Maud Martha, with her understanding of the interconnectedness of persons, things and environments, can be seen as part of this diasporic tradition. In *Maud Martha*, the things themselves take on the role of Conjure woman.

Maud Martha

Maud Martha, Gwendolyn Brooks's only novel, was written in the 1940s and published in 1953 by Harper & Co. The text charts the growth and development of the titular Maud Martha Brown, from her childhood to her second pregnancy at the end of the Second World War. Although the narrative is in the third person,

Brooks's use of free indirect discourse situates the narrative within Maud Martha's perspective and we are privy to her thoughts, feelings and dreams. There are numerous autobiographical elements in the novel, like Brooks, Maud Martha is a dark-skinned African American woman who grew up on Chicago's south side. Steven Caldwell Wright has noted that the novel was ahead of its time: 'Maud Martha is a daring book, coming at a time before society at large was willing to discuss the prevalent issues of race, gender and socioeconomic equality.'[28] The story is told in brief episodic chapters and critics have commented on the novel's lyrical style, which connects with Brooks's preferred form of poetry.[29] As I will demonstrate, in the text, things are crucial to the formation of particular spaces and subjectivity. In the novel, Brooks critiques consumer capitalism and its racist construction in mid-century America but does not reject material culture.

The opening chapter is titled 'Description of Maud Martha.'[30] Yet unlike conventional descriptions, we are not given any sense of what our protagonist looks like, or her character, or her interpersonal relationships, instead, Brooks's initial description consists of situating Maud Martha within a company of things: 'What she liked was candy buttons, and books, and painted music (deep blue, or delicate silver) and the west sky, so altering, viewed from the steps of the back porch; and dandelions' (1). The chapter goes on to explore Maud Martha's relationship with dandelions in more detail, and I will say more about this in a moment, but here I want to emphasize how Brooks introduces Maud Martha in relation to particular objects (candy buttons, books, painted music) and an environment (the west sky). The objects range from the ephemeral to the more enduring emblems of culture. Maud Martha's relationship to the natural environment is framed by her domestic one: her particular sky is the one seen from the steps of the back porch of her home. Two themes are introduced in Maud Martha's relationship with things that will continue throughout the text: pleasure and aesthetics. We see her sensitivity to colour and her ability to make aesthetic judgements.

Pleasure as a moral, even spiritual, domain has a significant lineage in African American culture. Dwight N. Hopkins indicates that the connections between freedom and pleasure give it a moral weight in antebellum Black culture. He describes the ways in which enslaved people would navigate the time of sundown to sunup as a space for grounding their sense of self and community in theological terms. In the interstices of forced labour and systemic cruelty, individuals found ways to reconfigure their relationship to the surrounding environment in sacred terms: 'As part of their theological strategy of re-imagining and living as free creations of the divine in a comprehensive holy environment, enslaved Africans and African Americans stole and claimed the sacred domain of pleasure … Even in pleasure, Black workers knew who they were and how to nourish themselves.'[31]

Following Hopkins, we can see how excavations of a spirituality of pleasure form an important element of Black women's writing: we may think of Janie's delight in the pear tree, Nella Larsen's jazz bar, Baby Suggs's invitation to her community to love themselves.[32]

Radiance of dandelions

While stones are significant elements of the natural world for Mary Butts, plants are more important to Gwendolyn Brooks. In *Maud Martha* the saturated radiance of flowers generate a sacred space of encounter between the protagonist and the things around her. The dandelions resonate with the pear tree that grounds Janie's 'emergence into selfhood' in *Their Eyes Were Watching God*.[33] Elizabeth J. West notes how Hurston's imagery accords with the Akan belief that land is a source of communal identity and in Brooks's writing we see that relationship to place (whether positive or negative) has a strong influence on her characters.[34] Named in the opening sentence as the final thing that Maud Martha likes, a meditation on dandelions dominates the first chapter. Paradoxically, the flowers are both precious and common: 'Yellow jewels for everyday, studding the patched green dress of her back yard. She liked their demure prettiness second to their everydayness; for in that latter quality she thought she saw a picture of herself, and it was comforting to find that what was common could also be a flower' (2).

In describing outside space as a dress, Brooks draws the natural world of the garden close to the domestic and the bodily. Here the ordinary and the beautiful are equated. In considering dandelions further, Maud Martha sees the paradox of folding the ordinary and extraordinary together. This is the power of everyday aesthetics. Brooks draws affect into the scene as well. When Maud Martha doesn't see the dandelions, she begins to doubt their charm: 'It was hard to believe that a thing of only ordinary allurements – if the allurements of any flower could be said to be ordinary – was as easy to love as a thing of heart-catching beauty.'[35] Thus the flower also marks Maud Martha's desire for love. Maud Martha sees herself in the dandelion and the dandelion calls forth the Maud Martha that she wishes to be: ordinary, yet also beautiful and beloved. The resilience of dandelions and their capacity to grow and bloom in the most inhospitable of places underlines the 'persistence of a life force' that Larry Andrews reads as the heart of the novel: 'Maud's sense of her own aliveness and the aliveness of the things in the outside world is the source of both her anger and her joy, of both her heightened sensitivity and her resilience.'[36]

In an unpublished short story, 'Gladys Gladiolus', Brooks explores the human-flower encounter further. In this story, we are introduced to Little Mama, an elderly Black woman living in a predominantly Black neighbourhood in a northern city.[37] The focus of the story is Little Mama's passion for gardening, and her friendly gardening rivalry with her white neighbour, Zora Rogers. Unlike Maud Martha, Little Mama is not captivated by wild flowers but by garden flowers, those grown and tended with care. The love and attention that Little Mama lavishes on her garden are returned by her flower's glory. Alice Walker has written about the creativity of gardeners like her mother whose creative work goes unmarked by the wider world.[38] Houston A. Baker, Jr draws on Bachelard's formulation of the poetic image as the beginning of consciousness to craft a poetics in which the image (of the garden) enables a 'shimmering irradiance of subject and object' in which the world is made anew.[39] Baker stresses the ideal image rather than the physical flower, however, he later draws material, spirit and poetics together when he draws a connection between African American poetics and 'a phenomenology of conjure'.[40] In 'Gladys Gladiolus', the relationship between woman and plant draws both into intersubjective mutual becoming. The repetitive practices and rituals of care in Little Mama's gardening give space to this relationship.

In the summer of the story, Little Mama's passion is directed to her gladioli. The first blossom comes late and is met with love and cherished. The connection between Little Mama and Gladys is one of intimacy, of recognition, of love and care: 'She felt that her gladiolus was a creation, her graceful blowing work of art, her thing of beauty, a child of her old age.'[41] Here Brooks conflates tropes of creative production and reproduction. The flower is both work of art and child. The image of the child suggests that the flower is both strange ('not me') and familiar (emerging from and connected to the self). In indicating the mutual becoming of Little Mama and the gladiolus, Brooks gives the flower a name: 'She even had a name for it. But no one ever knew that. Except possibly Gladys. She would lean out of her living room window, for Gladys was just outside the window, and touch the soft freshness.'[42] The name is secret but is known by Little Mama and 'possibly' Gladys herself. That 'possibly' is important; it suggests that Gladys's self-knowledge is unknowable by Little Mama but that a kind of communication and communion between plant and person is taking place. Equally important is the physical intimacy between the two beings. However, the story has an ambivalent ending. After a night of troubled sleep and nightmares, Little Mama awakens to find Gladys gone. The story ends with Zora Rogers coming to her house, offering gingerbread and her own gladiolus in a vase. Although this suggests care and a stronger connection between the two women, marked by gift giving, the unknown (cut) gladiolus cannot replace the beloved Gladys.

It is tempting to read a version of Levinasian encounter and ethics of response in the face of the other in both Maud Martha's interaction with the dandelion and Little Mama's encounter with Gladys Gladiolus. Yet as Mayra Rivera has pointed out, some critics argue that the structure of Levinas's account rests on 'the problematic assumption that strangeness is an intrinsic characteristic of some persons'.[43] While Rivera discusses alterity in the frame of human encounters and how we might unsettle the self/other binary, I would argue that human-thing encounters can provide another way to contest the frame that assumes otherness as intrinsic. Levinas's insistence that the face is always human places a limit on his ethical claims.[44] What Brooks's botanical-human encounters give us is an alterity that holds tension between sameness and difference, identity and empathy. These encounters unsettle notions of the other as intrinsically strange and exclusion as a precondition for becoming without supressing the strangeness that sits alongside recognition.

In both *Maud Martha* and 'Gladys Gladiolus', this extends to other kinds of objects, particularly domestic ones, as I will explore through the rest of this chapter. In *Maud Martha*, the dandelions themselves are liminal flowers; growing in the yard of Maud Martha's childhood home, they are associated with the home but bring a bit of wilderness into domestic space (they are wildflowers or weeds, not cultivated garden flowers). I will return to the significance of flowers in Brooks's work in Chapter 5, for now I want to move on to consider the assemblages of things that contribute to the formation of domestic space and to extend the conversation begun earlier in this book on the liveliness of houses.

Domestic space: Precarity and sanctuary

In Chapter 3, I discussed how domestic spaces are particularly vexed for women; they can hold that crucial room of one's own but can also be restrictive, entrapping spaces. When we bring race and class into the equation we generate a more complex vision of domesticity. Black feminists have written about how domestic space could be an alienating, oppressive sphere when it involved working in service (usually for economically advantaged white women) but that Black women's own homes could be sources of pride, comfort and seclusion from a hostile public sphere. Brooks's novel gives us a sense of the complexity of the house when racial and class indices are considered as well as gender. In *Maud Martha* we see houses that are generative, homely places and those that are oppressive. The novel explores the lives of complex, in-between homes that are both loved and vibrant things and also un-homely difficult spaces, marked with injustice.

In her critical analysis of the radical possibilities of domestic space, Susan Fraiman argues that for those marginalized subjects 'who are outsiders to polite society … domestic spaces and domestic labor mean neither propriety and status nor captivity and drudgery but safety, sanity, and self-expression: survival in the most basic sense'.[45] Fraiman goes on to argue that for too long explorations of domestic space have been assumed to be inherently conservative while in fact they are more diverse. When seen from the margins, the household is a space of multiple valences:

> Vulnerable, hybrid, heterogeneous, and dynamic – all these attributes serve to debunk received, naturalized notions of home as inert and one-dimensional. All argue, instead for the domestic as a site of change and complexity. What they suggest, too, is the invented-ness of domestic life … The *doing* of domesticity involves labor that is physical and affective as well as ideological, and women generally get the brunt of it.[46] (Emphasis in original)

In *Maud Martha* we see the ongoingness of domestic labour and the struggle to create and maintain a livable space while also seeing the value of the home and the way it contains multiple affective histories.

We can read the exploration of domesticity in *Maud Martha* in relation to Zora Neale Hurston's *Their Eyes Were Watching God* (1937). Connections between the house and self, between architectural and psychological modes of interiority and the boundaries between inside and outside play across Hurston's text. Thomas Foster notes that these boundaries are 'not fixed but shifting and resisted throughout the novel'.[47] In the text, rhetorical strategies play alongside thematic ones: 'Hurston's use of free indirect discourse [is] the rhetorical analogue to the text's metaphors of inside and outside, so fundamental to the depiction of Janie's quest for consciousness, her very quest to become a speaking Black subject'.[48] Brooks also uses free indirect discourse in Maud Martha to similar effect. The reader hovers between the intimacy of sharing Maud Martha's consciousness and a slight distance effected by the use of third person and the occasional foray into the minds of others.

Foster goes on to interrogate how gender, class and race are mapped onto domesticity in Hurston's novel: 'Janie's "classing off" takes the form of grounding her femininity in a domestic space and conforming to a falsely universalized, white, middle-class model of womanhood.' Foster reads this as a critique of 'domestic ideology and individualism'.[49] The porch is a significant architectural and social space where gender struggles are waged, community is formed and social status is established.[50] While Janie is excluded from the masculine space of the store porch by her husband, this makes the telling of her story to Phoebe on the porch of the home she shared with Joe Starks all the more powerful. The porch as a liminal space between domestic interior and outdoor public space becomes Janie's most enabling space.

Bell hooks has written about the importance of domestic spaces for herself and her siblings:

> In our young minds houses belonged to women, were their special domain, not as property but as places where all that truly mattered in life took place – the warmth and comfort of shelter, the feeding of our bodies, the nurturing of our souls. There we learned dignity, integrity of being; there we learned to have faith. The folks who made this life possible, who were our primary guides and teachers, were Black women.[51]

These spaces are particularly marked as Black, feminine and maternal. Hooks explicitly removes concepts of ownership from her formulation of homespace, focusing instead on the creation of nurturing space that enables the development of Black subjectivity and creative community. This space itself takes on a political and ethical dimension with its opposition to a damagingly racist public sphere: 'This task of making homeplace was not simply a matter of Black women providing service; it was about the construction of a safe place where Black people could affirm one another and by so doing heal many of the wounds inflicted by racist domination.'[52]

In 'An Aesthetic of Blackness', hooks muses on a particular relationship with things, which enables the development of aesthetic vision in her grandmother's home: 'Her house is a place where I am learning to look at things, where I am learning how to belong in space. In rooms full of objects, crowded with things, I am learning to recognize myself.'[53] Here we see an intricate relationship between things, space and personhood. While Bachelard presents a mode of being in domestic space that implicitly draws on tradition, he does not make this explicit.

Bachelard's child seems to be in the Romantic tradition of one who instinctively knows how to be in the world and how to foster a sense of the connectedness of things. By contrast, hooks emphasizes how an aesthetic relationship with domestic space is a *learned* process.[54] Hooks foregrounds the role of wise women who hand down their understanding of objects, homes and persons.

For hooks, the assemblages of things that make up domestic space teach her how to look and this looking leads to a sense of how to be in space and how to recognize herself. Belonging comes through a relationship to things that involves aesthetics and affect. It is not only her grandmother who teaches but also the things themselves: 'Objects are not without spirit. As living things they touch us in unimaginable ways. On this path one learns that an entire room is a space to be created, a space that can reflect beauty, peace, and a harmony of being, a spiritual aesthetic. Each space is a sanctuary.'[55] For hooks, objects have an inherent liveliness and the capacity to shape space and participate in creative work. Aesthetics and animist spirituality are explicitly linked. In forming homespace as a sanctuary, the objects enable sacred encounter. Hooks's lifelong interest in aesthetics was informed by her early environment. She notes that poverty is not a bar to an appreciation of beauty and the ability to develop critical judgement: 'One [house] cultivated and celebrated an aesthetic of existence, rooted in the idea that no degree of material lack could keep one from learning how to look at the world with a critical eye, how to recognize beauty, or how to use it as a force to enhance inner well-being.'[56] However, she also acknowledges painful domestic spaces that are marked with avarice, lack and misogynistic oppression and violence.

Home in *Maud Martha*

In *To the Lighthouse*, Woolf gives us a clear impression of the Ramsays' house on Skye as a thing in itself. In *Maud Martha*, Brooks gives us homes that are less clear as singular objects (we are given fewer views of the whole) and more evocations of a particular kind of space, one shaped by the disposition of things and the movements of people through it (in this way we might read her as closer to Bachelard, although her work diverges from his in important ways). There are four significant homes in the novel: Maud Martha's childhood home; the homes of glossy magazine pictures; the kitchenette she shares with her husband and the white woman's house in which she works for one day. These homes have a range of physical, affective and functional differences within the novel. As things, or more precisely, assemblages, their liveliness is differentiated and their relationships with Maud Martha range from enabling to destructive of mutually constituted subjectivity. The spirited nature of things that are crucial to forming creative subjectivity as described by bell hooks is evident in Brooks's fiction.

The magazine home

In the chapter 'Maud Martha and New York', Maud Martha contemplates a fantasy home, inspired by the objects and interiors pictured in magazines. It is New York not Chicago that frames this luxurious daydream. Locating her fantasy in the more familiar environment might make the contrast between her current prospects and the life she covets too stark; distance is part of the aura of desirability:

> Maud Martha loved it when her magazines said 'New York' described 'good' objects there … They showed pictures of rooms with wood panelling, softly glowing, touched up by the compliment of a spot of auburn here, the low burn of a rare binding there. There were ferns in these rooms, and Chinese boxes; bits of dreamlike crystal; a taste of leather … her whole body became a hunger. (48)

Brooks gives a visceral account of consumer desire and the power of images of things to shape a sense of self: 'The desire for these objects – this lifestyle – is termed "a hunger," implying not only the desire to possess, but a desire that, if fulfilled, could sustain one completely.'[57] Yet, Tracy Floreani argues, Maud Martha's dreams of upward mobility are thwarted by the constraints imposed on a young Black couple with minimal education. As she comes to see the racist and classist ideologies of white women who represent the lifestyle she aspires to, she begins to abandon her earlier fantasies.[58] Floreani argues that Brooks unsettles mid-century representations of Black women in mass culture by 'examin[ing] the workings of a character virtually unrepresented in the popular media at the time, that of the individualized Black woman'.[59]

While I find Floreani's analysis of Brooks's critique of the imbrication of racism and consumer capitalism insightful, I think Maud Martha's relation to objects is more complex, partaking not only of falsely induced desires but also of a love that is grounded in daily ritual and ongoing relationship. While Brooks questions the value of aspiring to glossy magazine interiors, she also suggests a more positive relationship to things that shares hooks's view of the agency of objects in creating a nurturing homespace. We can see in the novel how Maud Martha undergoes a process of training her sense of aesthetics, of learning how to see things and what to value. The importance of pleasure as a spiritual and political stake for Black women comes into play here. Margo Natalie Crawford argues that women poets of the Harlem Renaissance like Mae V. Cowdery and Alice Dunbar-Nelson critiqued the equation of beauty with whiteness and asserted that poverty was no bar to the love of beautiful things.[60] Here we can see that Brooks participates in a tradition of twentieth-century African American poetry that celebrates things.

In 'Gladys Gladiolus', Brooks makes the connection between love of beautiful things within the home and the outside space of gardening more explicit:

> What made Little Mama happy? Nothings. Bits of marble and brass, her little collection of china, some unmatched pieces of crystal, some old mahogany, polished till it burned with a half-smothered glow, her crocheted doilies and antimacassars and spread … her collection of handkerchiefs. The things the years had gathered and given. These things she could look at, and look at.
>
> And flowers made her happy.[61]

Little Mama lives within a community of things from manufactured objects to flowers. The connection between manufactured things, handmade things and grown things disrupts the discourse of consumer capitalism. The sense of being 'gathered and given' across time, even as gifts of time, brings a temporal dimension to a spatial configuration that I will return to later in my discussion of *Maud Martha*. We are reminded here of bell hooks's grandmother's house and the disposition of objects with spirit that teach one how to be and how to look at things and spaces. Little Mama's house, though it is small and in no way luxurious (she is a widow, she works a little, rents out a room and 'ate very little, not quite from choice'), echoes Maud Martha's dream home of the glossy magazines, exemplified in glowing wood, precious 'bits', crystal. Little Mama's home has been 'gathered and given' by the years, and here we see a possible future for Maud Martha: a home, an assemblage of things loved and cared for. Brooks herself can be seen in relation to Little Mama and Maud Martha. Writing of the similarities she sees between her mother and Maud Martha, Brooks's daughter, Nora Brooks Blakely notes how they shared: 'A love of "foolish food" and fine things, a need for grace'.[62] Brooks shares the celebration of harmonious domestic space with her protagonist. The connection of 'fine things' and 'grace' gives us a clue to a reading that would critique the constraints of consumer desire formed by white dominance but also celebrate the relationship of persons and things in a life well lived.

Mrs Burns-Cooper's and the kitchenette

The scenes in which Maud Martha learns to question her earlier fantasies of (white, upper-class) materialist consumption occurs in the commercial establishments designed to fuel those dreams. She experiences the shock of disillusionment when a white saleswoman visiting a beauty parlour at the same time as Maud Martha makes a racist comment (139–41). Subsequently, she tries on several hats in a milliner's shop, bargains briskly with a condescending saleswoman and then 'decide[s] against the hat' (155–6). Here the rejection of capitalism and material acquisition is empowering. The non-possession of a hat gives Maud Martha a stronger sense of self and autonomy, eroding the desires fostered by the magazine images. However, the final deconstruction to these disabling relations to commodities occurs in a domestic space: in the white woman's house where Maud Martha goes to work.

With her husband out of work, Maud Martha turns to domestic work to secure additional income. It is with reference to material things and their cost that Mrs Burns-Cooper shows the hollow at the core of the fantasy of consumption and it is partially in relation to material things that Maud Martha defends herself from the white woman's microaggressions. Mrs Burns-Cooper details her accomplishments, possessions and travels with explicit mention of their cost: 'The imported lace on my lingerie. My brother's rich wife's Stradivarius. When I was in Madrid. The charm of the Nile. Cost fifty dollars. Cost one hundred dollars. Cost one thousand dollars' (161). She uses things, or, more precisely, her verbal description of things and places, as a weapon designed to humiliate Maud Martha.[63] She destroys any potential connection with Maud Martha and extends the distance between them (while also requiring Maud Martha's presence to bolster her own sense of self – this is evident in her invasion of Maud Martha's workspace and in her cowedness in front of her own mother). However, she is unaware that for Maud Martha, the comparison is reversed. Maud Martha's own 'small' kitchen is a place of freedom, autonomy and personal dignity (even if that dignity is threatened by the problems of that particular home), unlike the more opulent but inhospitable white middle-class home (160).

Maud Martha asserts herself through the details of her own material possessions, family relations and domestic ritual: 'Why, one was a human being. One wore clean nightgowns. One loved one's baby. One drank cocoa by the fire – or the gas range – come the evening, in the wintertime' (163). Critics have commented that Maud Martha does not defend herself verbally to Mrs Burns-Cooper; her defence is to herself, but I would suggest that it is also made to her home and her things themselves and this strengthens her relationship with them.[64] A gas range may not be as luxurious as an open fire but it still enables a cosy domestic ritual. The rhythmic cadence of Brooks's language – 'come the evening, in the wintertime' – emphasizes seasonal and diurnal cycles of time that merge with space in this assemblage of things, humans and activities. Maud Martha directly aligns her humanity with repeated domestic activities (laundry and cocoa-drinking).

However, for most of the novel, Maud Martha's home is not described in such positive terms. The kitchenette apartment where she lives after her marriage to Paul Phillips is a much more constraining, difficult space. The kitchenette contains two rooms; a bedroom and a kitchen, with a shared bathroom down the hall. At first Maud Martha is determined to see only the potential of the cramped space: 'It was small, but wonders could wrought here' (61–2). She plans how she will rearrange the furniture; she will remove some of it and introduce new pieces to create a cozy, graceful space. Colour is important to Maud Martha and she imagines green drapes and a green rug, only to have her dreams crushed by a hostile landlord who refuses to allow changes to the kitchenette. I initially subtitled this section 'the resistance of things', yet the resistance we see in the kitchenette chapters is not that of the objects, but that of the difficult landlord, the Phillips' poverty and the limited opportunities available to Paul that prevent upward mobility. As GerShun Avilez argues, *Maud Martha*, among other mid-century novels that focus on Black urban life, 'demonstrates how [segregationist] housing policies not only structure where Black people live, but also undermine their relationship to domestic space'.[65]

With the kitchenette, we see a space that is a contingent shelter. This is a precarious and inhospitable homespace, hampered by the unwelcome intimacy with neighbours with whom the Phillips share a bathroom and a garbage can. In the first chapter on the kitchenette, Brooks folds affect and aesthetics together. Maud Martha describes the entirety of the apartment building as becoming grey, for all the senses: 'The sobbings, the frustrations, the small hates, the large and ugly hates, the little pushing-through love, the boredom, that came to her from behind those walls ... via speech and scream and sigh – all these were gray [*sic*]' (63–4). Here we see the effects of many lives lived in close proximity; waves of emotion come through Maud Martha's walls. Instead of the growth of community described by hooks, we have a more melancholy sense of lives of struggle in which happiness is thwarted by the domestic environment and external constraints; even the little love is grey.

GerShun Avilez argues that bell hooks's notion of Black domestic space as site of resistance depends on the ability of families to 'create and sustain boundaries that maintain a distinction between interior and exterior spaces'.[66] In Brooks's evocation of the kitchenette, we see how these boundaries are continually eroded and how this then erodes Maud Martha's sense of self and her ability to be interact more positively with her environment. Yet although this chapter describes Maud Martha's trajectory towards a lack of caring connection with the things that form her domestic space, the later chapter 'at the Burns-Coopers' indicates that precarity is not the whole story. Even in her cramped and inhospitable domestic space, Maud Martha has a freedom to develop domestic rituals that sustain her spirit and her humanity.

Kathleen Stewart writes about the affect of the practices, places, things and connections of daily life as 'refrains that etch out a way of living in the face of everything'.[67] She describes her elderly mother's continued attempts to craft such refrains in the face of increasing dependency and decreasing wherewithal to absorb change. Stewart's work makes us attentive to the way creating and maintaining such domestic rituals is difficult for the most vulnerable but also helps us see we all have a need for 'synthetic experiences [that] become generative repetitions of worlding refrains'.[68] Although Stewart does not class her 'refrains' as rituals, their repetitive, deliberate nature aligns them with ritual. Ritual allows for the accumulation of affect to inhere in particular places, assemblages and practices. Ritual as repeated activity is important, along with objects, for the formation of space. Cocoa drinking in the winter shapes the kitchen space, as much as the kitchen supports the cocoa drinking. Stewart underlines the importance of these refrains or rituals in her use of the word 'worlding'. Things, spaces and activities join together to make a world. Beyond these refrains is undifferentiated chaos, a space without meaning in which the liveliness of human persons and things is deadened. Susan Fraiman connects affects and practices in her analysis of domesticity. She emphasizes the labour, both physical and emotional, in the ongoingness of housekeeping. Fraiman's work is concerned with how this emotional labour is enmeshed in precarious domestic spaces, where 'contriving a livable space is all the more urgent, fraught, and potentially gratifying'.[69] This precarity and resulting urgency to join with things to contrive a livable space is evident in all the domestic spaces explored in *Maud Martha*.

Stewart's work on affect and practice is a departure from usual definitions of ritual, yet the idea of daily practices or refrains connects with ritual studies in important ways: they provide meaning, organization, socialization and coherence of self. I argue that through reading Brooks and Stewart together, worlding refrains can be understood as ritual as a significant part of an everyday spirituality. Brooks writes about daily or seasonal practices in a way that emphasizes the connection with ritual; the cadences of her writing align it both to poetry and to liturgy. Catherine Bell describes ritual as necessary for socialization; in Brooks's work we see a socialization of human persons with things and spaces.[70] Jonathan Z. Smith emphasizes that 'ritual is *work*'[71] and we see this not only in the social work that ritual accomplishes but also in a more mundane connection to housework.

Bell uses Foucault to unearth the ways in which ritual helps to create power relations, but she argues that ritual practice is complex and can involve resistance and appropriation as well as compliance: 'A participant … naturally brings to such activities a self-constituting history that is a patchwork of compliancy, resistance, misunderstanding, and a redemptive personal appropriation of the hegemonic order.'[72] In this episode from Brooks's novel we see Maud Martha resisting white hegemony and asserting her humanity in the form of repeated domestic ritual. In *Maud Martha* an organized relationship to things is more powerful than the accumulation of things and experiences via the marketplace as Mrs Burns-Cooper claims. In the novel, ritual is not primarily religious yet Maud Martha's dynamic relationship with her own domestic space resists a hard distinction between sacred and secular. With hooks's claim that objects have spirit, we can see a domestic spirituality developing in the novel.

Maud Martha's childhood home

I turn now to Maud Martha's childhood home: the space in the text where the life histories of things are most evident. In *Maud Martha* we see a more implicit and tenuous generational transmission than that described by hooks. Maud Martha's relationship to her childhood home is presented as unique among her family. In the chapter in which the Browns' home ownership is under threat, Maud Martha, her mother and sister Helen share an awkward period of waiting in which they respond differently to the possibility of losing their home.[73] Brooks highlights the distinctness of Maud Martha's connection to the house, which is different from her mother's and sister's. As in *Their Eyes Were Watching God*, the porch is a significant place in *Maud Martha*, yet this scene is very different from Janie's 'porch talk' with Phoebe that enables her subjectivity. This scene shows how Maud Martha is formed by her domestic environment and how the family is held by this space and yet the differences are also revealed: family solidarity is fractured. Racist housing policy and finance bring contingency and threaten the homespace. Janie and Phoebe's space is guaranteed by Janie's independence and financial security. Although bell hooks frames Black domestic space as separate from possession, Hurston's and Brooks's novels show how a lack of legal possession and financial security leads to a precarity in the homespace that can be painful and alienating.[74]

This moment in *Maud Martha* is also different from the first time we see reference to the porch (this time the back one) in the opening sentence of the novel: 'The west sky, so altering, viewed from the steps of the back porch' (1). Here the steps of the porch (even closer to the outside than the rocking chairs) are aligned with the freedom, drama and change of the sunset sky. The changeable sky is contrasted with the security of the home, both are required for the fullness of the experience. In the later chapter that marks the precarity of homespace, *Maud Martha* invokes the sky again, emphasizing the connection between the particularity of house and sky: 'She felt that the little line of white, some ridged with smoked purple, and all that cream-shot saffron, would never drift across any western sky except that in back of this house' (30).

Brooks makes the similarity between father's and daughter's love for the house more explicit in the following chapter when she writes: 'Who was it who sympathised with him in his almost desperate love for this old house? Who followed him about, emotionally speaking, loving this, doting on that?' (37–8) These sentences conclude a paragraph in which Maud Martha has noted her father's preference for her sister Helen and we understand that Maud Martha's father does not deliberately teach his daughter his love for the home or even recognize that they share this passion.[75] Maud Martha goes on to detail how she loves the house as her father does and to assert that the unlovely may still be loveable. This is not a departure from aesthetics but a re-articulation of affective aesthetics otherwise. As Jacqueline Bryant notes, 'Maud's childhood home was a sanctuary, a place of refuge.'[76] We are given the understanding that Maud Martha may follow her father in her reverence for their home, but that the generational tie is frayed. The alterity in Maud Martha's home and the affect attaching to things become more evident as the description of unlovely space unfolds. The Brown's kitchen is similar to the dandelion in its commonness that can be beloved:

> The kitchen, for instance, that was not beautiful in any way! The walls and ceilings, that were cracked. The chairs, which cried when people sat in them.

The tables, that grieved audibly if anyone rested more than two fingers upon them. The huge cabinets, old and tired … And underneath the low sink-coiled unlovely pipes, that Helen said made her think of a careless woman's underwear, peeping out. (38)

This kitchen contains the opposite of the 'good things' of Maud Martha's glossy magazines. Nor do they seem to partake of the brilliant beauty of light and colour bell hooks found in her grandmother's house. Yet these things, the chairs, tables and cabinets, also have spirit, with an uncanny life of their own. They resist use-value and yet contrive to form a livable space. They create a space that is both homely and unhomely. The kitchen's closeness to the body is made explicit in the comparison of pipes to clothing. Both house and clothing cover the body, providing shelter and warmth yet also become modes of encoding social mores, in this case, gendered modesty codes. The furniture has a sense of a being of its own that resists easy appropriation, inviting an encounter with strangeness rather than comfort.

Defamiliarization and discomfort can enable wonder as Sara Ahmed notes in her discussion of Marx's dancing table: 'To re-encounter objects as strange things is hence not to lose sight of their history … Such wonder directed at the objects that we face, as well as those that are behind us, does not involve bracketing out the familiar but rather allows the familiar to dance again with life.'[77] The life that animates objects is enmeshed in the ordinary but it also appears to come from wonder itself, or rather, between the wonder of the looking subject and the perceived ordinary-but-strange object rather than inhering within the object itself (Ahmed is largely critical of models of depth and interiority). This suggests that objects may be animate or not; the life that comes to them may also depart. The interaction between humans and furniture in Maud Martha's kitchen demonstrates the accumulation of affect; it resides among the grumpy furniture as tables grieve and cabinets bicker. Ahmed notes that for Marx this life is a false life of the commodity, life that is stolen from the workers who made it and the wood that formed it. However, Ahmed suggests an alternative reading that accords with the reading of objects that I attempt in this book:

We could approach the dancing table quite differently, if we see that the life of the table is 'given' through this intimacy with other lives, rather than being a cut-off point. A table acquires a life through how it arrives, through what it comes into contact with, and the work that it allows us to do. Perhaps this life is a borrowed rather than stolen life, where the act of borrowing involves a pledge of return.[78]

Here Ahmed makes the intersubjectivity of persons and objects more explicit. The intimacy that we see in the passage from Maud Martha suggests love despite (or perhaps because of) the strangeness of things. While Ahmed critiques a Marxist interpretation that would not admit that the life of objects may exceed that of the commodity, she does not consider how the life of the thing also exceeds the subject–object relation. The object arrives, but as Bachelard notes, it is a being from elsewhere, and this elsewhere names the unquantifiable strangeness of objects that exceeds our designs, wishes and practices. What I find most striking in Ahmed's description of the table is the sense of a return on life borrowed. The return suggests the excess of the subject–object relation and, crucially, the agency of things in their ability to redirect life.

In *Maud Martha* memory is laid down in the house; in the interplay of memory, affect and object a sanctuary is made. In a passage that anticipates both Bachelard and hooks on the significance of reminiscing on houses to a sense of self, Brooks explores the series of practices and spaces that shape Maud Martha in relation to her home:

> Maud Martha … saw herself there [in the kitchen], up and down her seventeen years, eating apples after school; making sweet potato tarts; drawing, on the pathetic table, the horse that won her the sixth grade prize; getting her hair curled for her first party, at that stove; washing dishes by summer twilight, with the back door wide open … And even crying, crying in that pantry, when no one knew. The old sorrows brought there! – now dried, flattened out, breaking into interesting dust at the merest look. (38–9)

Brooks shows the home is a place that shapes and is shaped by repeated activities (rituals) that knit Maud Martha's sense of self, her personal history, with the objects of the home. Emotion is solidified and made into a thing, but a thing that is subject to decay. Emotion becomes a thing in process with material form, first tears, then dust.

The pathways Maud Martha marks around the kitchen 'up and down' the years – baking, washing dishes, doing school work, preparing for social gatherings – blend housekeeping with other domestic practices that hint towards the wider sociality of the community and seasonal rhythms. These repeated practices become containers for memory and this provides the connectivity between time and space and between things and humans: 'Habits are not simply disembodied, meaningless experiences but memories, ways in which the house can function as "an organization of space over time".'[79] Objects move, provoke and participate in actions and practices. The living presence of things are needed in shaping hospitable space. Across the novel we see a range of possible ways of interacting with things; their alterity registers in different ways. Some things resist use and interpretation in a way that opens up possibilities for intersubjective encounter. Other times the social rejection of difference (particularly racialized difference) defeats possibility.[80]

Domestic sublime

There is a strand of modernist women's writing which evokes what Heather Walton calls the 'domestic sublime'. This sublime writing 'gathers up all the commonplace matters of existence and irradiates it with energy.'[81] We can situate Brooks's everyday sacred here, as the resistance of objects to use and interpretation promotes a different way of relating to them that recognizes alterity. Matter's resistance to human control links the domestic sublime to more traditional notions of the sublime in the sense of subjects being overwhelmed by that which is external and beyond their control. In encounters with the sublime, the very notion of coherent, internalized subject, becomes unsettled.

Walton makes an important connection between the sublime and writing. The domestic sublime is not just a matter for philosophy or experience. It provokes not only mimesis (representation) but also poesis (making); it is in the form of writing that the domestic sublime is apprehended. In such writing 'the sublimation process retains the directly referential language of realist fiction … but transforms the objects referred to into strange and holy shapes … when the world is met with attention to the particularity of its forms it emits the faint scent of transcendence.'[82] Attending to forms in the world and form within text enables an understanding of how Brooks's lyrical writing is transformational. Walton's formulation is important here; in describing transcendence in terms of scent, she emphasizes its sensory nature. It is located in this world understood otherwise not in an otherworldly space. This in turn is related to Mayra Rivera's notion of relational transcendence.[83] Relational transcendence and the domestic sublime are categories that relate to the animist cosmologies explored earlier in this chapter. Inspirited objects that participate in domestic ritual speak of a worldview that is animated by sacred energy.

Walton argues that commonplace happenings that elude representation must be 'ma[de] strange'. She writes this of Elizabeth Smart, another writer whose work is thick with material references, a writer who writes in concert with 'other women who live common, blasted but glorious lives.'[84] The process of making the commonplace strange, speaks to modernist styles which would find realism too limited. In many ways *Maud Martha* is a realist text, yet in Brooks's lyrical style, the compression of incident and lack of narrative connectivity between chapters allow the commonplace to register alterity. In Brooks's description of the home under threat, lyricism comes to the fore:

> What had been wanted was this always, this always to last, the talking softly on this porch, with the snake plant in the jardinière in the southwest corner, and obstinate slip from Aunt Eppie's magnificent Michigan fern at the left side of the friendly door … Those shafts and pools of light, the tree, the graceful iron might soon be viewed possessively by different eyes. (28–9)

We see here not only an allusion to domestic repetition but also how the particularity of objects with a history evokes an alternate relationship to time. Hortense J. Spillers analyses this passage in terms of time and eternity: 'The vocabulary of natural objects so overwhelms the house of the living that the latter takes on a spirit of timelessness, enters a domain of the immutable.'[85] Spillers terminology resonates with the domestic sublime; the house glows with a radiant life that is found in the porch, plants and pools of light.

The quality of paying attention to ordinary things made strange brings wonder into the discourse of the domestic sublime. Sara Ahmed indicates that wonder is affect arising from encounter with what has been made strange.[86] Crucial for the domestic sublime, we see here an interplay between the ordinary and extraordinary. Wonder also reveals the contingency of worlding, the dynamism and changeability of objects and all that inheres to them: 'To see the world *as if* for the first time is to notice that which is there, is made, has arrived, or is extraordinary. Wonder is about learning to see the world as something that does not have to be, and as something that came to be, over time, and with work.'[87] Ahmed emphasizes how this wonder allows us to see the historicity of objects and their worldly relations. The emphasis on memory in Brooks's evocation of Maud Martha's relation to her childhood home presents a fragment of this historicity.

Ahmed distances her discussion of wonder from traditional conceptions of the sublime. She asserts that the association of wonder with the sublime neglects the material dimension of wonder that she wishes to recover:

> The philosophical literature on wonder has not focused on wonder as a corporeal experience, largely because it has been associated with the sublime and the sacred, as an effect that we might imagine leaves the materiality of the body behind. But for me the expansion of wonder is bodily. The body opens as

the world opens up before it; the body unfolds into the unfolding of a world that becomes approached as another body. This opening is not without its risks … But wonder is a passion that motivates the desire to keep looking; it keeps alive the possibility of freshness, and vitality of a living that can live as if for the first time.[88]

I want to contest this separation of wonder, the sacred sublime and materiality. For Ahmed wonder is an emotion which, like others, arises as an effect of interactions between bodies and is felt in the body. I find Ahmed's discussion of the 'unfolding of a world' through the particularity of attention to the ordinary/extraordinary extremely helpful. Her connection between vitality, wonder and materiality underlines the threads I have followed in this chapter, but I would not exclude the sacred sublime from this triumvirate. Bennett's work on enchantment is helpful here, as Bennett also locates enchantment in material encounters: 'The world comes alive as a collection of singularities. Enchantment includes, then, a condition of exhilaration or acute sensory activity. To be simultaneously transfixed in wonder and transported by sense, to be both caught up and carried away – enchantment is marked by this odd combination of somatic effects.'[89] Bennett's choice of language here – the experience of being 'caught up' – is reminiscent of the sublime. I would argue that a sense of the lively, spirited material worlds relocates wonder and the sublime in the here and now and presents a call unfold in the world as Ahmed describes.

This discussion of wonder and the sublime brings us back to Mrs Ramsay, and my discussion in Chapter 3 of the way in which she 'leant to things' at the moment of ineffable vision. This horizontal move in which the spirited body and the spirited object open towards each other speaks of the beyondness of things: transcendence configured otherwise. Like Mrs Ramsay, Maud Martha leans to things as she is caught up in the wonder of the ordinary world. Maud Martha's greater awareness of the precarity of wonder gives her relation to the lively world a particular intensity.

Kitchenette redux: Aesthetics and justice

I would like to close this chapter with a brief consideration of the importance of boundaries and the complex relationship between private and public space in Brooks's work. Earlier in this chapter, I analysed an enabling relationship between Black women and their own domestic space. Yet it is important to recognize the alienating aspects of things and space. The domestic sublime inheres in the alterity of things; this is not only found in the other that encounters the human but also in spaces and things that overwhelm and frustrate. As indicated in foregoing discussion, racist social organization and the intersection of racial, gendered and economic oppression can lead to a formation of space that undermines subjectivity.[90]

Although I welcome formulations of intersubjectivity, I also recognize the importance of boundaries for dignity. This has long been recognized by Black scholarship, as indicated here by Houston A. Baker, Jr: 'For place to be recognized by one as actually PLACE, as a personally valued locale, one must set and maintain the boundaries. If one, however, is constituted and maintained by and within boundaries set by a dominating authority, then one is not a setter of place but a prisoner of another's desire.'[91] We have seen in *Maud Martha* how the kitchenette apartment is both the place of Maud Martha's agency and also a place of alienation. Part of the struggle of the kitchenette is the lack of boundaries between households. In the shared garbage can, toilet and bathroom, through the thin walls which allow domestic conflict and intimacies to travel, the kitchenette building is a place that is both private and not-private (if still not quite public). In Brooks's poem 'kitchenette building' from *A Street in Bronzeville* the use of colour anticipates Maud Martha, who also finds her kitchenette building 'grayed in, and gray'.[92] The delicate colours and 'giddy sound' of a dream cannot compete with the urgency of accessing the lukewarm water in the shared bathroom. The presence of neighbours and competition for space and resources, the mingling of smells and sounds do not allow for the time 'to warm it [the dream], keep it very clean'.[93]

Public space is also fraught in Brooks's work. In 'a song in the front yard' the speaker associates freedom, sophistication and female sexuality with walking the streets in 'brave stockings of night Black lace'.[94] Here the stockings have their own sensibility, being 'brave' they confer courage on the speaker. The back yard 'where it's rough and untended and hungry weed grows' becomes a semi-private-semi-public space, a liminal zone in which the domestic leaks into the public space of the alley through the stolen back gate.[95] The speaker's mother wishes to keep her daughter safe, but as readers we are torn between sympathy for the mother's worldly wisdom and the daughter's bid for freedom.[96] I will explore the spiritual life of things in public space further in Chapter 5, but here I want to emphasize the significant relationship between aesthetics and social justice in the contemplation of domestic spaces. Bell hooks argues that domestic spaces could be safe places for Black people. These are places where a

Black aesthetic flourishes can be practiced and handed down the generations. Hooks's work yokes aesthetics to empowerment. The relationship between lively things, wonder, domestic ritual and Black female subjectivity in Brooks's poetry and prose provides resources for developing an aesthetics oriented towards justice.

5

Things in the city

All the authors in this volume share an interest in urban space. Paris, London and Chicago host a wide range of texts by Mary Butts, Virginia Woolf, H.D. and Gwendolyn Brooks. Like the domestic spaces and landscapes analysed in earlier chapters, the urban setting is anything but passive in its interaction with subjects and objects. This chapter brings my four writers together to chart how things move from domestic to public space, provoke wanderings, act as relics and sacred markers and generate the urban environment that moves subjects even as subjects move through it. The chapter begins with Mary Butts's urban short stories, 'Mappa Mundi' and 'From Altar to Chimney-Piece' in which objects provide a focus for the troubled journeys of young innocents in a Paris in which past and present, sacred and profane, ordinary and uncanny are layered.[1] In this analysis we consider how the city itself is a thing, with its own uncanny life. I then analyse how things and urban places (interior and exterior) organize affect in Woolf's London essay 'Street Haunting'. The chapter then turns to an analysis of bleaker, more painful engagements with public space. The war-torn streets of London are viewed starkly in H.D.'s short story collection *Within the Walls* as the threat of destruction brings a counter-apocalypse focused on resilience. Brooks's poem 'In the Mecca' (1968) charts a complex relationship between public and private space which confronts poverty and violence. Voices, bodies and things are brought together, leaving us to question the slippage between life and death and the animism of things. Here the chapter considers engagements with public space that are limned with fear, loss and oppression and asks what role things play in the mobilization of this affect and how the life of things contributes to the formation of communities of mourning.

There is a sense for all of these writers that the city is wounded or damaged in some way; whether by consequence of war, imperialism or economic and racial oppression. Butts, Woolf and H.D. wrote in the midst and aftermath of the First and Second World Wars and they consider the impact of these conflicts on urban spaces. While the Second World War touches Brooks's writing, she is more focused on charting the experience of poverty, racism and resilience in her exploration of Chicago's South Side at mid-century. Texts like Butts's Parisian short stories or Woolf's *Mrs Dalloway* explore the traumatic legacies of war through the psyches of their characters, yet the connections forged between individuals and their urban environment indicate the woundedness of the city itself. H.D.'s writing from the Second World War engages more explicitly with urban ruins, damaged landscapes and the threat inherent in inhabiting the city during wartime. Brooks's long poem, 'In the Mecca' not only confronts the poverty and violence inscribed in the slum apartment building but also invokes a spectral urban space in writing of a specific place that no longer exists.

Modernist cityscapes

Although rural and provincial places are beginning to draw more attention in modernist studies, the city continues to be seen as the 'quintessential modernist space' which 'celebrat[es] … impermanence, change, and the new'.[2] Writers concerned with literary geography create and explore an alternative city 'that is related to but distinct from the city of asphalt, brick, and stone, one that results from the interconnection of body, mind, and space, one that reveals the interplay of self/city identity. The writers adds other maps to the city atlas: those of social interaction but also of myth, memory, fantasy, and desire'.[3] Leonie Sandercock underlines the importance of different ways of apprehending the city: 'The city of memory, the city of desire, and the city of spirit: these are what animate life in cities, and they are also what animate urban conflicts (whose memories are respected? Whose desires are fulfilled? What spirit of place seduces us?)'.[4] I argue that things within the city, as well as its larger built environment, are crucial to the interplay of urban identities and I contend that the life of the city includes the animism of the material environment as well as the activities of human persons.

Part of the city's diversity is the numerous kinds of spaces it holds. The boundary between public and private spaces can be blurred, contested or sharply maintained as these different spaces tend to be in close proximity. Morag Shiach writes on the tendency in modernist criticism to emphasize the street as the premier space of urban modernist literature, at the expense of the domestic interior. She defends the room as an important locus for urban modernism, not only in the representation of urban life found in novels like Dorothy Richardson's

Pilgrimage but also in terms of the networks of cultural production.[5] Across our four authors we see a range of different engagements with the liminal zone between public and private and different modes of mapping these spaces. The city itself is frequently gendered female in literary and sociological discourses, but the right to access public space within it is traditionally a male prerogative and the place of women in the city is a contested one.[6]

Women's experience of the city in modernity has frequently been filtered through their role as consumers.[7] However, this analysis is limited by class boundaries and neglects the experience of women without sufficient means or leisure to pursue the middle-class phantasmagoria of the arcades.[8] Moreover, the emphasis on women as consumers loses sight of the alternative connections between human persons and things that we find in urban spaces. The authors studied here all offer complex constellations of women, urban spaces, materials and affects.

The secret matrix of Paris

In Chapter Two I considered Mary Butts's connection to rural landscapes in Dorset and Cornwall. Although she spent most of her life in cities (London and Paris), her attachment to Dorset made her relationship to urban centres 'complex, often contradictory'.[9] This complexity is seen sharply in her late Paris stories, 'Mappa Mundi' and 'From Altar to Chimney-Piece'. Sam Wiseman notes that in Butts's Dorset fiction, it is often the disaffected urbanites who are most sensitive to the 'strangeness and intensity' of the rural landscape. If 'the metropolitan outsider helps to generate a deeper awareness of our interconnected and interdependent relations with nonhuman objects and processes' this is also true in the Paris stories, which centre on expatriates and their experiences of both defamiliarization and recognition in the city.[10] For Butts, Paris is the source of both delight and horror: 'A sink of iniquity and a fountain of life at one and the same time; in the same quarter, in the same place, at the same hour, with the same properties – to even the same person.'[11] From her earliest stories, her work contains a thread of the uncanny and this is evident in the elusive sense of haunting and the inconclusive ending of 'Mappa Mundi'. In Butts, the uncanny is often indexed by nonhuman objects, processes and places. The Paris of 'Mappa Mundi' is an occult city, full of unexplained presences, enticement and mystery. In the story two expatriates come together through a shared exploration of Paris's occult presences. The American young man does not share the narrator's sense of caution and he traffics with the more sinister elements of the city, eventually becoming entangled with a ghost or demon and disappearing.

Butts follows tradition in seeing the city as female: 'Like all the great feminine places, behind its first dazzling free display, you come quickly upon profound reserves. After the spree a veil is drawn, a sober, *noli me tangere* veil' (279). For Butts the city is not just a place but a divine being, a goddess offering both joy and more austere mysteries. She describes urban material as divine: Isis, the goddess of Paris, is 'made of stone which is goddess's material' (279).[12] Here we have a *genius loci* which expresses Butts's familiar love of stone, not in pebbles or movable objects but in architecture: buildings and ruins.[13] The goddess is known in the physicality of the built environment but also in small, ephemeral objects and movements like the fluttering of a girl's scarf in the Tuileries (284).

The First World War is not overtly present in this story, but there is a hint at more recent destruction as well as the deep past of the city when the narrator describes 'the womb of Paris': 'Down the street where the broken bits of Julian's baths lie about, which he built when the legions occupied the little city of Parisii called Lutetia … All the Parises were about us, behind us, on our right and our left. Only before me, invisible behind the high roofs, stood the matrix of Isis' temple, the darkened shrine' (281). The city is described as sacred in a way that hearkens back to pre-Christian Roman paganism, with a protective *genius loci*.[14] The connection with fertility cults is drawn through frequent reference to Paris's matrix, or womb, and her fecundity. As with many of Butts's short stories, 'Mappa Mundi' is full of elliptical comments and is more about exploring mood and atmosphere then action. The story gives a sense of an inner sanctum, a hidden city only open to initiates, which reads as uncomfortably exclusionary. Butts never outlines explicitly what it takes to apprehend this hidden city but she suggests that it involves humility; it is open to those who 'had never boasted that we had seen her face' (285). The city is the body of the goddess but the material and spiritual are not completely interfused. They mingle but at times separate in unsettling ways. Paris/Isis is the source of creativity and change. The city creates her subjects, but in referring to the characters as phantoms, Butts suggests that not only does the spiritual become material, but the material may become ephemeral. The ghostliness of the modern city and its subjects are affirmed in a peculiar inversion in which the narrator's mental map of (ancient) Paris becomes more real than the material city: 'By now I had in my mind a chart of the place, of a Paris upon which the city of our time was no more than superimposed' (283).

The narrator repeatedly speaks of her understanding of the city in terms of exploration and maps: 'I had broken new country in the three great parallels along the river' (283). As she seeks after traces of Isis, the narrator describes a process of pondering and map-making that helps her to make sense of the historical layers of the city and the intensity of many emotions accumulated over time: 'A unique sense of all sorts of mixed pasts, a sense of the ancient city and all the fury of life that went to make it' (282). There are multiple kinds of maps in 'Mappa Mundi': both conceptual maps, held in the mind, and a physical map: 'a map of old Paris' that 'suddenly clattered on the wall' when the police agent is questioning the narrator about the disappearance of Currer Mileson (288). This physical map becomes a tangible representation of the occult Paris of the narrator and Mileson's wanderings. The mental maps are a way of stepping back from experience of a place and giving it a form. Crucially, these maps are formed in private space away from the public streets and buildings they explore: 'After such wandering you could go home, turn over in your mind what you had walked through' (283). The making of maps is a process of crossing the private/ public divide, as public spaces are brought within, both psychic and domestic interiors, in order to be understood.

The physical map harkens to the story's title, the mappa mundi that is a medieval map of the known world; in a sense old Paris recapitulates the world. The map on the wall moves with an uncanny life; like the girl's scarf, it is a trace, an incarnation of Isis. The narrator confesses to a feeling by the story's end that Isis 'began to be bored with me' and in her final encounter with the agent, 'the map on the wall was still' (290, 291). In 'Mappa Mundi' we have a city that is alive but with a capricious spirit that gives and withholds knowledge. For all of the story's occult dealings, there is sense of the darkness in the story as chthonic rather than evil. However, many of Butts's short stories have a troubling xenophobic edge in the way that they seem intent on distinguishing the initiated and their critique of those who occupy space in the wrong way. 'From Altar to Chimney-Piece' is frequently commented on for its stinging portrayal of Gertrude Stein and her salons. Although this story is less overtly occult than 'Mappa Mundi', it is in many ways more claustrophobic and the cruelty that the protagonist encounters is more discomforting. In 'Altar' the narrator is highly critical of the post-war influx of Americans and the changes they have brought with them. Paris's capacity to soothe traumatized survivors of the First World War is drained by those 'who think art synonymous with vice ... whose hell had not been occasioned by any dislocation of our society, but by the putrid state of their subconscious selves' (308–9). Butts draws a sharp line between those who appreciate the city, who respond to it and develop their own maps, and those who would spoil it. She critiques the salon for its privatization (contra the more open café), in which objects are on display and guests expected to act as if at a museum rather than a domestic space in which things are used and loved.[15]

The sense of sacrilege hovers across the whole story, as the hero, Vincent, a traumatized veteran, becomes the victim of cruel deception by a crowd of young Frenchmen and an American woman. The story has a brief moment of generosity, when Vincent senses a kinship with Miss Van Norden's visitors, recognizing that they all have been damaged by the violence of war and 'their sickness was part of the world's sickness' (329). Paris is personified less explicitly in this story than in 'Mappa Mundi' but the sinister side of the city is made more plain: Vincent meets Cherry 'at the end of the still noble part of a noble street, on the edge of the space in his map coloured "witchcraft"' (314). The story ends with sacred objects out of place. Vincent's eye is caught by Miss Van Nordan's unusual chimney pieces:

> About a foot high, of some common metal, gilt, rough, traditional. But the design was pure, the whole representing a flame or a star on fire, inset with a circular disk, rubbed silver-bright and painted on it in blue, the letter Chi. It was clear now that they were: they were frames, supports, stands for the ciborium, the box… to hold the wafers of the Host. The box taken away, they now made delightful chimney piece ornaments … The old pain was dry and cracked and the signature of Christ rubbed off at a touch. (330)

Rather than telling their own story and inviting intersubjectivity, these objects, outside the ritual context of rural Spanish churches for which they were made, are mute. They are unable to make themselves at home in their new urban setting, stifled by the depravity of Miss Van Norden's company and her insistence on a kind of formality which prohibits empathic connection with objects. As Rochelle Rives notes, Butts's critique here is for a failure of enabling, empathic sociality between persons and objects and her hero fails in this as much as the story's villains.[16]

In 'Altar', objects are wrenched out of place and this deadens their meaning. Unlike the stones of Dorset and Cornwall, and the jade cup in *Armed with Madness*, these objects cannot move between places without losing their stories and voices. Unlike the cup whose meaning oscillates and whose purpose is uncertain, the former altarpieces do not participate in the kind of sociality I have explored in earlier chapters, nor do they withhold their meaning, resisting human interpretation. They are seen only as impoverished in losing the Host and the painted Chi, not as liberated into a new way of demarcating the sacred. For Rives, what's crucial about Butts's understanding of things is the way they are placed and how this enables or inhibits intersubjectivity and empathy. While Butts's critique in 'Altar' may be apt, the story also holds an unsettling emphasis on purity, both in terms of the city itself and the desecrated altarpieces which are 'common' but 'pure'. If surrealism is presented as a demonic force, then the inventiveness of surrealism's engagement with everyday objects is lost. I am left wondering if there would be another way to engage the altar-now-chimney-piece ornaments to bring them to speech, to acknowledge their strangeness and to enable empathetic connection.

Although the narrator in 'Mappa Mundi' looks to the past, intent on excavating ancient and medieval Paris, the story's archaism is filtered through a modernist lens. It is a cosmopolitan text, narrated by and about expatriates. The traumatic legacy of the First World War is apparent in both stories. The liveliness of the city can be threatening as well as inviting. 'Mappa Mundi' shows how intersubjectivity can extend to the city, as subjects are shaped by places and hold places within themselves. 'From Altar to Chimney-Piece' presents a bleaker vision in which objects that traverse boundaries between public and private, rural and urban, sacred and profane fail to generate life. In her analysis of modernist 'theories of detachment and empathy', Rochelle Rives articulates one of Butts's concerns as 'the difficulty of carefully nourishing an empathic life with soluble boundaries without sacrificing the value of the object's discrete and independent being'.[17] In 'Mappa Mundi' we see how the lively, material city, personified as Isis yet still clearly made of stone and articulated spaces shaped by streets and buildings, carries on its independent being. In 'Altar' the liveliness of the altarpieces is lost, as they become mere symbols, and empty, decaying symbols at that.

Affect, interiors and urban wandering in Virginia Woolf's 'Street Haunting'

Mary Butts's claimed that 'if Paris is a lovely salon displayed for conversation, London is a lumber-room to be foraged for junk, rubbish, white elephants, treasure.'[18] So we turn now from Paris to London, where Woolf and H.D. find treasure in the junk heap that proves more lively than Butts's rubbished altarpieces. Many critics have emphasized the importance of London to

Virginia Woolf's writing and Woolf is frequently included in accounts of urban modernism.[19] While Woolf's writing largely celebrates the possibilities for creativity, connection and freedom found in urban space, her work also attends to the associations of the city with 'violence and alienation', particularly those related to the 'economic and gendered politics of space'.[20] I want to consider a text frequently read as emblematic of Woolf's London, 'Street Haunting', and to think about how the humble pencil contributes to the liveliness of the city. The gender politics of capitalism and the commodification of women's bodies are evident in the need the narrator feels for the excuse of shopping to indulge in her desire to wander the city streets.[21] Yet the smallness of the object sought and the negligible profit represented by the pencil suggests that the role of shopper is a mask for other ways of being in the city. The final exchange moves closest to the gift economy as the pencil, 'representing only a minimal investment in the capitalist system … reveals a resistance to the acquisitive ethos of this economy'.[22] The pencil marks the unstable boundary between gift and market economies. It partakes in capitalist exchange yet also is bound up in the affective domain of the gift economy. In the gift economy the gift must always move, and this circulation enables the formation and maintenance of social bonds.[23] Rebecca Colesworthy argues that Woolf (among others) centres the gift in metropolitan spaces like London: 'In fostering unlikely connections and stretching the bounds of altruism in strange and surprising ways, these urban centers play home to expansive webs of give and take.'[24]

The pencil is also described as 'the only spoil we have retrieved from all the treasures of the city.'[25] Kathryn Simpson argues that this association with theft also undermines the pencil's status as a commodity, but I would argue that theft is also structured in opposition to the generosity of the gift economy. I would rather note the resonance here with London as a 'junkyard' in which treasures are to be found rather than stolen. The pencil is not quite rubbish, the discarded remains of production that Benjamin sees as so crucial for the creative activity of children (and surrealists), but its low exchange value brings it closer to such remnants.[26] Robin Kimmerer notes that in Indigenous worldviews, the gift gives itself, locating agency with the object.[27] Movement is crucial but not only movement between individuals but also one involving a larger spiritual domain. As discussed in Chapter One, Adelaide Morris points to the Moari *hau* or 'spirit of things' which is 'alive and active'.[28] The circulation of gifts involves ritual processes to include the third term, the spirit of the environment that participates in the gift economy and is the source of the liveliness of things (in Butts's short story the altarpieces cease moving and, therefore, lose their generativity).

Critical engagements with disruptions to commodity culture often turn to Walter Benjamin's cultural critique. In his interest in situating objects otherwise, Benjamin attends to their liveliness. While Benjamin's work (especially latterly) is insistently materialist, his materialism remains inflected with his earlier engagement with mysticism and metaphysics. In her analysis of Benjamin, Susan Buck-Morss affirms the resonances of Jewish Kabbalah with Benjamin's materialism. As a metaphysical system, 'Kabbalism avoided the split between spirit and matter … and it rejected the notion that redemption was an antimaterial, otherworldly concern.'[29] In Kabbalah, divine being is broken and spilled into the world; the task of gathering together 'divine sparks' engenders the renewal of the world. Therefore, 'Even in its fallen state … material nature is the sole source of divine knowledge.'[30] The liveliness of matter as it participates in divinity underwrites Benjamin's interest in the speech of things: 'There is no event or thing in either animate or inanimate nature that does not in some way partake of language, for it is in the nature of all to communicate their mental meanings.'[31] Mick Smith argues that for Benjamin, language's origin is in expression: 'All material things (all things) express themselves in various ways, and whatever of this expression is potentially communicable to other things *is* language as such.'[32]

In 'Street Haunting', the speech of things is achieved in relation to affect and the essay demonstrates how places are crucial to the organization of affect. The pencil allows the narrator to take on the role of shopper (even if only superficially) and wanderer and to move in and out of shops. Thus we see how the city is both 'a network of rooms' and a pattern of streets.[33] The shop rooms are not private to the same extent as a domestic interior, but they are also not as public and exposed as the city streets. Shops are shaped by objects and a dynamic relation with the pattern of affects and movements of the lives of those within them. The dwarf woman participates in a fantasy of bodily perfection within the shoe shop, and the transition from shop to street causes the chimera of bodily transformation to vanish.[34] Simpson reads this section of Woolf's essay as a critique of the grotesque fragmentation of women's bodies effected by the false lack and desires created by marketing in a capitalist economy.[35] I sympathize with Simpson's reading but I am troubled by Woolf's language. I find it hard not to read her word choices such as 'deformity' and 'grotesque' as abjecting the dwarf woman and her uneven movements. However, the woman does display a fierce agency in her transformation of the urban scene. She provokes a change of perspective for the narrator who writes, 'All joined in the hobble and tap of the dwarf's dance' (74). Woolf's narrator attempts a reckoning with her own privilege, firstly imagining that her prosperity does not evoke bitterness but then faced with the stark cruelties of poverty, 'A question is asked which is never answered' (74). 'Street Haunting' cannot answer this question as the narrator struggles to transcend the limitations of her perspective.

The stationer's shop presents another liminal space between public and private as the husband and wife who run the shop move in and out of the depths of a more private space in 'the back room': a space where the narrator imagines they will retire after her departure, with sewing, a newspaper and a canary (80). As in the domestic interiors in *Maud Martha*, affect is a significant aspect of the material dimensions of the space: 'It is always an adventure to enter a new room; for the lives and characters of its owners have distilled their atmosphere into it, and directly we enter it we breast some new wave of emotion. Here, without a doubt, in the stationer's shop people had been quarrelling. Their anger shot through the air' (80). The pencil colludes with the narrator in holding the space for the resolution of the quarrel; it resists the husband's search and enables the wife's. The narrator and the pencil give time and this 'act of kindness and generosity' moves the exchange into the realm of gift.[36] To return to Benjamin, if the pencil speaks, one of its registers is affect.

The affect that is mobilized by the different thingly exchanges in the essay not only indicates a movement away from commodity exchange and towards a gift economy but also generates intersubjectivity. This is evident in the connections between the dwarf woman and others after she leaves the shoe shop, between the narrator and the stationers, between the narrator and past selves: 'Into each of these lives one could penetrate a little way, far enough to give oneself the illusion that one is not tethered to a single mind, but can put on briefly for a few minutes the bodies and minds of others' (81). The variability of the self as seen in 'Street Haunting' is an affirmation of intersubjectivity: 'For Woolf … the potential for multiple selves is not a neutral description, but generally valued as an affirmative sign of people's (usually women's) versatility and variation.'[37] The multiplicity of selves allows for numerous points of connection and divergence. Jessica Berman notes: 'Woolf's focus on the mosaic of inter-relationship can be read as an attempt to create a political community without resurrecting a suffocating unity.'[38] Here we can see how the diversity of the city enables a 'cosmopolitanism from below' that considers ways in which fragments from the junkyard can enable connection that does not stifle difference.[39] Intersubjectivity in Woolf is generally considered in terms of other human persons, but 'Street Haunting' demonstrates the centrality of lively objects to these formulations.

At the close of 'Street Haunting' we see that the narrator has experienced her excursion as 'recuperation'; she no longer feels stifled by her domestic environment and possessions but is able to rejoice in being 'sheltered' (80).[40] The essay closes, not with reflection on the self 'which has battered like a moth at the flame of so many inaccessible lanterns', but with the humble lead pencil itself (81). While Woolf's narrator ponders the wilderness of the mysteries of human personality (and its likeness to 'wild beasts'), she concludes with the other-than-animal: 'Let us touch it with reverence ... a lead pencil' (81).[41] Reverence and intimacy suggest that the pencil is not as much of a flimsy pretext as first suggested but is rather a partner in crime, enabling theft and generating alternatives to exchange value. Looking at the way the pencil structures the narrator's wandering through the city, we can see it as a relic: the goal of pilgrimage, a material fragment that mobilizes affect, is generative and inspires reverence. The narrator's touch emphasizes the importance of embodied experience in movements through the city and in human relations with things. Reverence also suggests the pencil's alterity. It cannot be fully known, absorbed or owned. It disrupts commodification of material, remaining stubbornly on the boundary between exchange and gift economies.

Things in the war-torn city

In Chapter One I explored the significance of gift-giving in H.D.'s nonfiction and poetry during the Second World War. The circulation of practical items alongside expressions of gratitude and care suggest the gift economy as outlined by Cixous. In H.D.'s Blitz-writing, we see a profound change from Woolf's writing of the 1920s as the London streetscape becomes a theatre of war rather than a place of invitation and exploration. The risk of travelling after dark, under the blackout, was significant. The claustrophobia of the domestic interior also increased, although, as H.D. put it in a letter to Marianne Moore, 'every day one is so grateful for the wall about one, the roof, the unbroken windows'.[42] H.D.'s writing during and after the Second World War reflects both the trauma of the fractured city and her tenacious affection for London.

H.D.'s short story collection, *Within the Walls*, documents her experiences living in London during the Blitz. Many of the stories are short, more what we might consider vignettes or meditations than plot-driven narratives. Taken together they explore alternate conceptions of time and space. They contain both philosophical musings and practical descriptions of the mundane realities of wartime life and consider how the two are related: 'The dream-state, the romantic 4th dimensional stage … the actual life dimension or actual realities of life all merge and flow along together.'[43] The '4th dimension'. as H.D. calls it, is represented in myriad ways across the sequence: dream, writing, unconscious, literature, theatre, film. One of the most evocative descriptions of the merging of this dream-space and more concrete reality is given in 'Escape' where the narrator goes to see a war film but then becomes disoriented when the snow of the film is repeated in London, an extraordinary event:

> I, in life, walk straight out of the Empire Theatre, Leicester Square into a snowy street scene. Real snow lies on the pavement, real snow powders the trees … snow is so rare in London, that this Square and this street become completely unreal. Yes, this is Leicester Square, but my eyes have been adjusted to the film-sequence and there was snow in many of those sets. I walk into a film-set … It is as if the news-reel had got mixed up with the romance. (115–16)

The theatre also gives H.D. images for representing different modes of consciousness and mapping them on the more pragmatic ways boundaries are disrupted by the war: 'I was thinking of a dream I had a few nights ago, during my fever. The side of a room, my own room, seemed to have slid away … It was suggested no doubt, by the houses we see, with rooms open to the street like stage-rooms, some are neatly sliced off with furniture still standing' (127). Not only is the house open to the street, but the outside comes in, with snow again appearing and crossing boundaries: 'Now snow swirls and drifts and to my surprise as the snow whirls into the room, in a soft living cloud, I realize that the snow is not cold. It has all the qualities of snow, the whiteness, the lightness, the softness, the beauty' (127–8).[44] Snow also occurs in 'Dream of a Book', but here it is only in the mind of the narrator as she describes putting wax in her ears during an air raid and shifting the sound of gunfire to 'snow falling' (113).[45]

Things out of place, whether natural phenomena or domestic objects, both display their ordinariness and suggest alterity. Ordinary objects appear frequently in *Within the Walls*, providing an anchor for philosophical musings, or giving material detail to the depiction of wartime London. 'Warehouse' describes the journey undertaken by H.D. and Bryher to the warehouse in Battersea where Bryher stored her parents' china and pictures in order to unearth some pieces to furnish Robert Herring's house. The Victorian associations with the paintings and furniture contrasts with the damaged city outside: 'The city is desolate … there are the usual gaps in our rows of houses, we notice them more in unfamiliar districts, we so soon grow accustomed to our own ruins' (123). The cheerful colours of the paintings and their evocations of earlier European travels contrast with the 'desolation' of the broken glass and newspapers on the floor of the warehouse, thus highlighting the ever-present threat of damage and death. However, this leads to a sense that the personal, material history held in objects and images is important: 'Perhaps that is why, in the dampness, standing in old newspapers, straw and broken glass, the clock released in me some spring of consciousness, some watch-spring or clock-spring. There *is* new-time of course, to be established, but let us stick to our old time as well' (126). Throughout H.D.'s wartime writing she wrestles with questions of history (both her own and that of the wider society), revisiting old traumas and indicting the current generation with repeating past violence. In her post-war writing she is more ambivalent about the possibilities for redeeming the time.[46]

Across the stories we see the significance of objects; privations and danger encourage attachment in a way that recognizes the unique being of things and acknowledges their fragility. *Within the Walls* includes particular things that work across real time and dream space. For the narrator of 'Dream of a Book' typewritten pages are objects to be protected and worried over: 'if I am blitzed, the house will go with me and the stack of papers will go, too. This, that I now write will go with it, and why does one type pages that only have the slightest chance of survival?' (114). But the writing is also a dream book that returns again and again in a variety of forms: 'The substance of the dream was the book, over and over. But this book had to be alive' (114). This dream book contains a sense of urgency: 'I must let go my critical faculty, I can not afford to criticize or re-consider these words. They are the words of a spell … they are the words that in a sense … *keep me alive*' (114). The narrator goes on to play with the connotations of words, magic spells and spelling: 'This spell-book must be related to my first book, my first spelling-book. The book to live, must go back to the first book, the first spell or spell-ing … The real spell must relate and derive from the pre-spelling book days' (114). The conflation of typed words on paper, magical words and an ineffable book that relates time present to time past suggests the tangibility of words, their life and substance a means of connecting material and spiritual realities. This is reminiscent of the relation H.D. drew between her writing and stitching in her letter to Viola Jordan referring to 'typestry'.[47] The other object to link visionary, creative consciousness with daily life is the blue light, which is both a flame in the skull and the electric torch used in the blackout:

> We have a blue-flame in our skull, rather like the blue-slide of my blackout lantern … I write because the little blue flame in my skull, needs me in order to burn … this flame must meet another flame, other flames, as the electric-torch picks out, in the damp and dank and murk of our London streets at night, the distant steady, strange little gleam of another distant electric torch, coming or going or crossing a street or climbing onto a bus. (120)

Here we see the material inspiration for the 'companions / of the flame' of *The Walls Do Not Fall*.[48] For H.D., the esoteric blue psychic light and the mundane electric torch signify each other.

Apocalypse when?

Trilogy, H.D.'s epic poem from the late war years, largely takes place in the dream-space invoked in *Within the Walls*. However, the material details of wartime London inform the text. In her work on modernism, trauma and mourning, Madelyn Detloff critiques the apocalyptic language of *Trilogy*, arguing that despite the poem's 'resilient message … it redescribes loss as something triumphant, character-building, transformative'.[49] Detloff reads *Trilogy* as partaking of the same ideology as texts that embrace self-sacrifice as a way of making meaning out of confusion and loss, such as W. B. Yeats's 'The Second Coming' and T. S. Eliot's *Four Quartets*.[50] The triumphal conclusion of 'Little Gidding' has potentially violent consequences; by describing an ending as a beginning, the poem 'risks overlook[ing] … actions that result in the ends of others'.[51] Detloff argues that *Trilogy* employs a similar rhetoric in its use of Revelations and the imagery of the 'New Jerusalem'.[52] She contrasts *Trilogy* to the greater sense of particularity, embodiment and refusal to ignore unremarked deaths in H.D.'s wartime autobiographical novel *The Gift*. Detloff crafts a powerful critique of triumphalism but I would argue for a greater congruence between *Trilogy* and *The Gift*, supported by the connections we can draw between these texts and *Within the Walls*.[53] I suggest that the persistent presence of material things in H.D.'s texts and her attention to the damaged city across her war-writing work against an ideal of death-denying rebirth. Moreover, I suggest that further exploration of the rhetorics of apocalypse can help us here.

The theologian Catherine Keller shares Detloff's anxiety about the dangers of apocalyptic discourse; she outlines how it has underwritten imperialist gestures across the centuries and into the third millennium of the Common

Era.[54] Keller argues that the way biblical stories of beginnings and endings are subordinated to a 'linear order moving from an absolute origin to an absolute closure' has always been a power play that is destructive to the text as well as to bodies, human and planetary. Keller argues that John's biblical apocalypse includes anti-imperialist strains and she notes how the intensities of apocalyptic rhetoric have fired numerous liberation movements in their passion for the transformation of injustice (what she calls 'dissident apocalypses').[55] She defines counter-apocalypse as one that refuses the violent dichotomies of apocalypse, instead hoping to 'convert emergency into emergence, "second coming" into a sustainable be-coming'.[56] This counter-apocalypse would be oriented towards 'a *living* earth and sky ... the great recycling and renewing project called the "new heaven and earth"'.[57] Keller picks up on Joyce's neologism *chaosmos* as a name for the ongoing becoming of creation.[58]

Keller's counter-apocalypse of creative becoming resonates with the liveliness of things that we see in H.D.'s work. Detloff suggests that apocalyptic narratives provide a coping strategy for those who have survived cataclysm, however it's important to remember that *Trilogy*, like *Within the Walls*, was written during the war, when H.D.'s status as survivor was in question. *Within the Walls* contains numerous oblique references to the potential for annihilation at any moment. While the opening section of *The Walls Do Not Fall* indicates current survival – 'the frame held / we passed through the flame' – the poem includes no guaranteed future. The questions 'what saved us? what for?' are those of confusion and hope rather than triumphalism.[59] *Trilogy* is a visionary poem yet as Susan Edmonds argues, 'H.D. insists on locating this space of epiphany in the repetitive flow of earthly time.'[60] This is evident in the sequence where the Lady – a figure of wisdom, creativity and feminine divinity – appears in an ordinary but liminal place, in a hallway, at the 'turn of the stair'.[61] *Tribute to the Angels* contains numerous visionary moments and ritual practices that are situated in the places of London: from the flowers blossoming in the rubble to the half-burnt out tree blossoming. The poet emphasizes the everydayness of this tree and its place: 'It was an ordinary tree / in an old garden square.'[62] This imagery indicates the hope for renewal but does not erase the signs of destruction and loss. The final image of the poem suggests the Christian nativity but not as an other-worldly telos.[63] By recasting the Christ child as a bundle of fragrant myrrh, H.D. gives us a sensual, living image for the sacred.[64] Intangible but not insensible, fragrance drifts between transcendence and immanence, in the interstices between persons, embodying both bitterness and hope. In H.D.'s war writing, the liveliness of the city shapes a place of encounter and witness to both life and death, destruction and resilience.

Roses in the Mecca: Liveliness and loss in Gwendolyn Brooks's urban epic

The previous chapter analysed Brooks's Black domestic aesthetic and began to consider the relationship between private and public spaces in poems like 'a song in the front yard'. I now turn to one of Brooks's later works, 'In the Mecca' (1968), to explore how material spirituality shapes the relationship between domestic and public space. 'In the Mecca' describes the life of the Mecca, an apartment building in Chicago, in the late 1940s. The Mecca began its life in the late nineteenth century as luxury homes for Chicago elites, however, by mid-century it had become a run-down and crowded tenement largely housing working class and poor African Americans.[65] The Mecca became an iconic symbol of urban decline and the racist representations imbricated in such discourse within and beyond Chicago. A *Life* photo essay in 1950 suggested that the building's decay was an inevitable result of African Americans moving in, rather than a result of poverty, structural inequalities, the impact of the Depression on African American employment and overcrowding due to segregated housing.[66] Brooks herself had contact with the Mecca when she worked there as a sales assistant for a 'spiritual advisor' who sold 'love charms'.[67] The building was torn down in 1952 so the poem is an oblique elegy for a place as well as a person.

At over eight hundred lines, 'In the Mecca' is a long poem, an epic; many critics have commented on the polyvocality of the poem and the democratization of forms and voices it enacts.[68] The poem focuses on the character of Mrs Sallie Smith, a mother of nine who discovers the disappearance of her youngest child. A search for Pepita ensues, and at the poem's close she is discovered, murdered under the bed of 'Jamaican / Edward'.[69] Interspersed with the overarching narrative of the quest for Pepita are the multiple stories of the Mecca. Many individual portraits the poem contains provide a link to Brooks's earlier work.[70] While the poems of *A Street in Bronzeville*, *Annie Allen* and *The Bean Eaters* (1960) employ irony to indicate the impact of poverty and racism on the lives of urban African Americans, 'In the Mecca' presents the realities of urban Black experience in the mid-twentieth century more starkly.

The Mecca building presents a different urban space from those previously considered. As an apartment building, the stairs and passages are publicly accessible, while the many domestic interiors – 'small hells/ small semi-heavens' – hold the host of stories that make up the counter-history of 'In the Mecca' (422). In her reading of the speaker of 'In the Mecca' as an example of Black *flânerie*, Kirsten Bartholomew Ortega emphasizes the way the building crosses the public/private divide. She explores how mapping race and gender onto *flânerie* gives us a *flâneuse* who 'moves women's urban strolling out of artificial urban shopping spaces and back into the actual city spaces, but she is also confined inside the Mecca's walls, her movement limited by gender, race, and class.'[71] Daniela Kukrechtová argues that both the modernist architectural style of the building and its vulnerability to the depredations of poverty, neglect and overcrowding erode public trust and inforce a privacy that is unchosen and undermines community cohesion.[72]

The contradictions of the Mecca are evident within the second stanza as it is introduced as the home of Mrs Sallie Smith. However, to reach her place of 'marvelous rest' she must traverse public space and climb the 'sick and influential stair' (407), which 'suggest[s] how the physiological and psychological effects of poverty are interwoven.'[73] On her climb up the stairs towards her children, Mrs Sallie is inundated by all the other lives and stories within the building. The intermingling of private and public also resonates with the larger social implications of Mrs Sallie's labor: 'Within the Black community historically, Black women have never had the leisure to conceive of motherhood as a privatized activity that takes place apart from labor.'[74] As Courtney Thorsson puts it, for Black women motherhood is 'always already public'.[75] This is evident in the juxtaposition of Mrs Sallie's ruminations on the luxuries of her employer's child and her realization that her own daughter, Pepita, is missing. Even while she searches for Pepita, Mrs Sallie is aware that 'the ham hocks are burning at the bottom of the pan' (419). Her anxiety at her child's disappearance mingles with her anxiety about the need to feed her other children.

Kukrechtová argues that the dynamic of public/private effects the Smith siblings' attitude towards their neighbours as they search for Pepita: 'Suddenly / ever one in the world is Mean. / Could that old woman, passively passing, mash a child? / Has she a tot's head in that shiny bag?' (420) Thus we see how 'the discourse on urban decline that hides facts of segregation and poverty has systematically eliminated public trust among Meccans.'[76] This mistrust means that despite overcrowding and lack of privacy, the Meccans are isolated: their monologues rarely indicate true interpersonal connection, either with the other residents or the reader.[77] However, there are moments in the Smiths's search that work against this mistrust and the Meccans do connect with each other through voicing their own stories and witnessing those of others, including Great-great Gram's memories of slavery and Loam Norton's recollections as a Holocaust survivor (417).[78] Pepita's death indicates the cost of enforced privacy and isolation: 'Only if the private loss is rearticulated as a public loss can the violence committed against Pepita and the conditions causing it be illuminated.'[79] This insistence on the public nature of loss is echoed in Sheila Hassell Hughes's contention that Pepita's death ruptures the walls of the Mecca building (prefiguring its destruction) as well as the community itself: 'Her loss is thus both a radical dismemberment of the Meccan "community" and the sign of a needed re-membering and re-imagining of a more powerfully self-identified Black community.'[80]

The importance of the domestic interiors is emphasized by the ubiquity of objects across the poem. Ortega notes how '*flânerie* is steeped in the complex exchange of producer and product in the city' and argues that the Meccans 'are defined by the things (tangible and intangible) that they consume'.[81] Yet I would argue that Brooks resists the embrace of commodity culture in the way that she engages with things. One of the epigraphs to 'In the Mecca' comes from an article on the building that participates in the racist discourses around urban decline. It notes the rubbish discarded in the liminal space outside the building: 'The dirt courtyard is littered with newspapers and tin cans, milk cartons and broken glass.'[82] Brooks, in contrast, details the significance of domestic objects from Mrs Sallie's 'bird-hat' to Aunt Dill's 'crocheted doilies' and 'old mahogany, / polished till it burns with a smothered glow' (420, 432).[83] As we saw earlier in Woolf's 'Street Haunting', in 'In the Mecca', objects organize affect. Marian who remains unseen, even by her husband, stirs a gumbo in which 'fury and violent imaginings are ingredients'.[84] Her desire to be seen leads to a desire for another kind of thing, not a meal but an action:

> Crime: her murder, her deep wounding, or
> a leprosy so lovely as to pop
> the slights and sleep of her community,
> her Mecca.
> A Thing. To make the people heel and stop
> and See her.

Marian's desperation and rage run so deep that even the distortions of leprosy appear 'lovely' if they will rouse those around her.

The connection between things and affect is also seen in Mrs Sallie's apartment, where the liveliness of things is immediately evident. 'Mrs. Sallie's apartment is a space where things can jump to life; where stoves can be "cruel," where mustard can be "mesmerized".'[85] However, Mrs Sallie is propelled from this lively space to wander through the apartment building searching for her child.[86] After the first frantic search, the Smiths return to their home only to be faced with interrogative doors: 'The / door says, "What are you doing here?" And where / is Pepita the puny – the halted, glad-sad child?' (419) The home itself cries out for the lost daughter.

The poem closes with the discovery of Pepita's dead body juxtaposed to her voice speaking of roses. The confined space beneath the cot where she is found indicates a connection between violence and the crowded space of the Mecca: 'her confinement echoing both burial and the constricting size of overcrowded apartments'.[87] Yet Pepita's voice lingers as a ghostly revenant after death: ' "I touch" – she said once – "petals of a rose. / A silky feeling through me goes!" ' (433) Kukrechtová suggests that Pepita's lyrical rhyming couplet provides a space of innocence within the free verse of the rest of the poem. Here we see how a girl coming to subjectivity is brought into greater awareness of her own being by the petals of the rose. Pepita frames this insight into her sensory experience with poetic diction. The insight into Pepita's developing sense of self in relation to things (roses) comes to the reader only after her death, underlining the void she leaves behind. The poem's roses bring together the creativity and sensual subjectivity of a young Black girl, roses and a mother's determination to bear witness. Mrs Sallie discards the impotence she feels in the face of decorating her kitchen, in her commitment to 'try for roses' for her daughter (433).[88] Pepita's death ruptures the walls of the Mecca: 'by bringing the roses to Pepita's funeral, Sallie will make Pepita's private story public … Sallie's public recognition of the power of her daughter's private poetry functions as a way to identify an interconnectedness between private and public suffering.'[89]

Despite Pepita's posthumous voicings, there is no bodily resurrection and we are returned to Mrs Sallie's grief. Her commitment to 'try for roses' is both provisional (she can only try; there are no guarantees) and also a sign that the roses will signify un-assuageable loss and the need to transform the space of Pepita's death through a more radical material transformation than razing the Mecca and evicting the residents. There is a trace of counter-apocalypse in the demand for social justice evident in 'In the Mecca'. Sheila Hassell Hughes reads

Alfred's transformation from failed poet to prophet when he witnesses Pepita's death and absence.[90] Hughes sees an apocalyptic trajectory in which the telling of the tale is necessary to move forward with integrity:

> Something, something in Mecca
> continues to call! Substanceless; yet like mountains,
> like rivers and oceans too; and like trees
> with wind rustling through them. And steadily
> an essential sanity, Black and electric,
> builds to reportage and redemption.
>   A hot estrangement.
>   A material collapse
> that is construction. (433)

This so-called substanceless thing that continues to call is immediately given form. The form is of a wide ecology: mountains, water, trees, wind. This wind in the trees calls forth sanity out of chaos and gives the impetus for the poet's work. The collapse of the building will not preclude the construction of telling the story in order to rebuild community. However, Brooks makes space in the poem's final words for Pepita's lost voice: 'The chopped chirpings oddly rising' (433).

Thorsson argues that however bleak we may find the Mecca, 'it houses hope as well as decay.' She locates this hope in 'a diverse, polyvocal community [which] finds the Mecca into coherence in the context of social injustice'.[91] She points to the 'Second Sermon on the Warpland', in the 'After Mecca' section of *In the Mecca* where the poet claims that 'the whirlwind is our commonwealth' (454). The poem opens with an exhortation: 'This is the urgency: Live! / and have your blooming in the noise of the whirlwind' (453). This response to the 'chopped chirpings' of Pepita continues the call for material transformation, while also claiming the whirlwind, the chaosmos, as the location for life and growth. In Pepita and Mrs Sallie's roses we see the 'the divinity of small things' that is essential to coalitions that have room for both the living and the dead, folded into the material, living world.[92]

The spiritual lives of things

The street has been seen as the pre-eminent urban space for the modernist writer.[93] However, this chapter shows how other places, including shop interiors, cinemas and apartment stairwells, alongside streets themselves, can offer a more textured, complex view of the city. We have seen how the movements of human persons and objects organize affect in the city and provoke wonder, from the interventions of a pencil to the electric torches in a blackout, or the liveliness of the built environment itself when conceived as an ancient goddess, revealing and concealing hidden dimensions of urban space. In these texts, objects are at their most powerful when they participate in intersubjectivity. The 'silky feeling' of 'In the Mecca' emerges between Pepita and the rose she touches. I have considered texts confronting war and death, yet even in these texts, life-shaking experiences are folded into the everyday. The quest for the missing daughter involves the hamhocks burning in a pan. In the war-torn city, an ordinary stairway becomes a space of visionary encounter. This fascination with the everyday was central to the surrealists and their 'hermeneutics of wonder', through which 'the mundane world became the privileged site of revelation, mystery and the poetic'.[94] The authors in this study were not associated with the surrealist movement. Their engagement with the ordinary is more prosaic and domestic than surrealist art, but it is no less engaged with wonder and wildness.

This is the point of the book where I believe I am meant to draw my threads carefully together, to stand back, and, as Delia does in *The Sword Went Out to Sea*, declare the pattern complete. Yet I resist this call to closure. For across this volume my aim has been to explore details and differences, to develop a richly textured collage of the spiritual lives of things from a range of textual genres, styles, locations. I am reluctant to claim a completed tapestry but prefer to stay with the messy underside where threads snarl or hang loose, images blur and this tripartite sentence refuses to go anywhere. The writers considered in this study are not homogenous; they speak from different geographic, racial, economic and religious positions. The spiritual paths traced by lively things in their texts also resist being ordered into a singular narrative or explanatory framework. In this project I have considered 'the lives', not 'the life', of things.

Christoph Lindner argues that in Victorian fiction we see things as subjects of production and exchange as the novels portray the early days of consumer capitalism, but that modernist texts present things in a more jaded light, as indicative of suspicion of consumption. Both commodities and consumer take on 'an air of decay'.[95] However, I argue that in the texts explored here we see a less constrained celebration of things, one that seeks to evade commodity fetishism and relate to things otherwise. Our paradoxical desire and disregard for things have brought the planetary community to a perilous point as we continually seek to evade facing 'the truly catastrophic consequences of inappropriate manifestations of desire'.[96] The texts I have considered here suggest there is much to be gained from paying closer attention to things, to their agency, their alterity and their intimacy. The power of things in themselves, their resistance to interpretation and co-option provokes a decentring of the sovereign subject that helps us to see ourselves otherwise: as intricately bound up in 'the mysteries that beat in the heart of the world'.[97] As Bennett argues, 'Part of the energy needed to challenge injustice comes from the reservoir of enchantment – including that derived from commodities.'[98] Enchantment comes alongside critique to generate the passion needed to intervene in matters of justice.

I write these inconclusive words while sitting at my desk at the University of Aberdeen. The sun and clouds are playing hide–and-seek across the sky, as they so often do in springtime in Scotland (or in any season, really). My desk is alternately bathed in light that dazzles my computer screen and plunged into shadow. My desk reveals how my love of orderly, hospitable spaces is all too often overwhelmed by the exigencies of daily life. My precious stoneware mug and my coaster – with its beautiful, if somewhat sentimental, image of trees and old stone buildings – jostle with drifts of papers, library books, post-its, bookmarks, lip gloss, conkers, cough drops, boxes of tea, tissues. I write with my knitting in my lap, making a few stitches now and then when the words stall. It has only just occurred to me that I am knitting a green shawl like Mrs Ramsay's (although mine is not cashmere) and it feels apt to begin this slow craft project as I draw an even slower intellectual project to a close. Tomorrow, children and young people across the world will protest the lack of significant government action in the face of the climate crisis. They know to hold tight to this world. They know the importance of phenomena.

Notes

Introduction

1 Katherine Mansfield, *Selected Stories*, ed. Angela Smith (Oxford: Oxford University Press, 2008), 93.

2 Maurizia Boscagli, *Stuff Theory: Everyday Objects, Radical Materialism* (New York: Bloomsbury, 2014), 20.

3 A brief note on terminology: Lara Vetter notes the proliferation of terms dealing with matters of ultimate concern, including 'esoteric, otherworldly, metaphysical, paranormal, spiritual, mystical, spiritualist, supernatural, magical, psychical, occult' in addition to 'religion'. I follow her choice of the word 'religion', as most inclusive of this broad semantic field, noting her emphasis on its connotations of 'structure, order, and some degree of mainstream acceptance': *Modernist Writings and Religio-Scientific Discourse: H.D., Loy, and Toomer* (Basingstoke: Palgrave Macmillan, 2010), 23. However, I also use 'sacred' and 'spirituality' when religion's connection to traditions, structures and institutions becomes contextually inappropriate. As Stephen Pattison and John Swinton argue, spirituality as a performative term that speaks to a range of contexts and contingencies is helpfully capaciousness: 'Moving Beyond Clarity: Towards a Thin, Vague, and Useful Understanding of Spirituality in Nursing Care', *Nursing Philosophy* 11 (2010): 226–9.

4 Andrew Thacker, *Moving through Modernity: Space and Geography in Modernism* 2003 (Manchester: Manchester University Press, 2009), 13.

5 Doreen Massey, *For Space* (London: Sage, 2005), 9.

6 Michel de Certeau, *The Practice of Everyday Life*, trans. Steven Rendall (London: University of California Press, 1988), 117.

7 bell hooks, *Yearning: Race, Gender, and Cultural Politics* (Boston: South End Press, 1990), 152.

8 Tatiana Kontou, *Spiritualism and Women's Writing: From the Fin De Siècle to the Neo-Victorian* (Basingstoke: Palgrave Macmillan, 2009); Timothy Materer, *Modernist Alchemy: Poetry and the Occult* (Ithaca, NY: Cornell University Press, 1995); Alex Owen, *The Place of Enchantment: British Occultism and the Culture of the Modern* (Chicago, IL: University of Chicago Press, 2004); Leigh Eric Schmidt, *Hearing Things: Religion, Illusion and the American Enlightenment* (Cambridge, MA: Harvard University Press, 2000); Helen Sword, *Ghostwriting Modernism* (Ithaca, NY: Cornell University Press, 2002); Pamela Thurswell, *Literature,*

Technology and Magical Thinking, 1880–1920 (Cambridge: Cambridge University Press, 2001); Vetter, *Modernist Writings and Religio-Scientific Discourse*; Leigh Wilson, *Modernism and Magic: Experiments with Spiritualism, Theosophy and the Occult* (Edinburgh: Edinburgh University Press, 2012).

9 For further discussion of the significance of transnational cultural exchange for modernist poetry, see Jahan Ramazani, *A Transnational Poetics* (Chicago, IL: University of Chicago Press, 2009), 23–49.

10 Pericles Lewis, *Religious Experience and the Modernist Novel* (Cambridge: Cambridge University Press, 2010), 20.

11 Suzanne Hobson, *Angels of Modernism: Religion, Culture, Aesthetics 1910–1960* (Basingstoke: Palgrave Macmillan, 2011), 1, 5.

12 Judaism and modernism remain an under-researched area. In *Modernism, Feminism, and Jewishness* (2011), Maren Tova Linnett analyses the complex negotiations between Feminism and Jewishness in the work of several modernist women writers but her work considers Jewishness as a cultural marker constructed by outsiders rather than those who identify with Judaism as a religion: Maren Tova Linett, *Modernism, Feminism, and Jewishness* (Cambridge: Cambridge University Press, 2007).

13 Houston A. Baker, Jr, *Workings of the Spirit: The Poetics of Afro-American Women's Writing* (Chicago, IL: University of Chicago Press, 1991); Judylyn Ryan, *Spirituality as Ideology in Black Women's Film and Literature* (Charlottesville: University of Virginia Press, 2005); Mark A. Sanders, 'African American Folk Roots and Harlem Renaissance Poetry', in *The Cambridge Companion to the Harlem Renaissance*, ed. George Hutchinson (Cambridge: Cambridge University Press, 2007); Jean E. Snyder, *Harry T Burleigh: From the Spiritual to the Harlem Renaissance* (Champaigne: University of Illinois Press, 2016); Elizabeth J. West, *African Spirituality in Black Women's Fiction: Threaded Visions of Memory, Community, Nature, and Being* (Plymouth: Lexington Books, 2011).

14 See Margot K. Louis, *Persephone Rises, 1860–1927: Mythography, Gender, and the Creation of a New Spirituality* (Farnham: Ashgate, 2009); Eileen Gregory, *H.D. And Hellenism: Classic Lines* (Cambridge: Cambridge University Press, 1997); Cathy Gere, *Knossos and the Prophets of Modernism* (Chicago, IL: University of Chicago Press, 2009); Martha C. Carpentier, *Ritual, Myth, and the Modernist Text: The Influence of Jane Ellen Harrison on Joyce, Eliot, and Woolf* (Amsterdam: Gordon and Breach, 1998); Dennis Denisoff, 'The Dissipating Nature of Decadent Paganism from Pater to Yeats', *Modernism/Modernity* 15, no. 3 (2008): 431–46.

15 Margot K. Louis, 'Gods and Mysteries: The Revival of Paganism and the Remaking of Mythography through the Nineteenth Century', *Victorian Studies* 47, no. 3 (2005): 330.

16 Ibid., 351.

17 Scott Freer, *Modernist Mythopoeia: The Twilight of the Gods* (Basingstoke: Palgrave Macmillan, 2015), 7. Freer presents compelling readings, but his analysis is oddly free-floating; for example, he neglects to situate his reading of H.D. in the context of the substantial body of criticism on feminist revisioning and myth in H.D.'s writing.

18 There are also numerous single author studies that contribute to the nuance of this growing field: Jane de Gay, *Virginia Woolf and Christian Culture* (Edinburgh: Edinburgh University Press, 2018); Jenny Hyest, ' "Born with God in the House": Feminist Vision and Religious Revision in the Works of Zora Neale Hurston', *Legacy* 35, no. 1 (2018): 25–47; Luke Ferretter, *The Glyph and the Gramophone: D. H. Lawrence's Religion* (London: Bloomsbury, 2013); Matte Robinson, *The Astral H.D.: Occult and Religious Sources and Contexts for H.D.'S Poetry and Prose* (London: Bloomsbury, 2016); Mimi Winick, 'Modernist Feminist Witchcraft: Margaret Murray's Fantastic Scholarship and Sylvia Townsend Warner's Realist Fantasy', *Modernism/modernity* 22, no. 3 (2015): 565–92.

19 Elizabeth Anderson, Andrew Radford and Heather Walton, eds, *Modernist Women Writers and Spirituality: A Piercing Darkness* (London: Palgrave Macmillan, 2016). For more wide-ranging studies on twentieth-century women writers and spirituality see Kristina K. Groover, *The Wilderness Within: American Women Writers and Spiritual Quest* (Fayetteville, NC: University of Arkansas Press, 1999); Heather Ingman, *Women's Spirituality in the Twentieth Century: An Exploration through Fiction* (Bern: Peter Lang, 2004).

20 Cassandra Laity, 'Editor's Introduction: Toward Feminist Modernisms', *Feminist Modernist Studies* 1, nos 1–2 (2018): 1.

21 Anne E. Fernald, 'Women's Fiction, New Modernist Studies, and Feminism', *MFS: Modern Fiction Studies* 59, no. 2 (2013): 230. Although they point to the neglect of feminist concerns in the field as a whole, both Fernald and Laity emphasize the significant scholarship on the recovery of women writers and on gender as central to understanding modernism and modernity: Ann L. Ardis and Leslie W. Lewis, eds, *Women's Experience of Modernity, 1875–1945* (London: Johns Hopkins University Press, 2003); Shari Benstock, *Women of the Left Bank: Paris, 1900–1940* (London: Virago, 1986); Rita Felski, *The Gender of Modernity* (Cambridge, MA: Harvard University Press, 1995); Bonnie Kime Scott, ed., *The Gender of Modernism: A Critical Anthology* (Bloomington: Indiana University Press, 1990); *Gender in Modernism: New Geographies, Complex Intersections* (Urbana: University of Illinois Press, 2007); Urmila Seshagiri, 'Mind the Gap! Modernism and Feminist Praxis', *Modernism/modernity Print Plus Forum* 2, no. 2 (2017), https://doi.org/10.26597/mod.0022. Numerous single author studies, perhaps most especially Susan Stanford Friedman's *Psyche Reborn* (1987) on H.D. and Jane Marcus's *Virginia Woolf and Languages of Patriarchy* (1987) shifted

scholarly reception of these writers and enabled much feminist scholarship in the following decades.

22 Vetter, *Modernist Writings and Religio-Scientific Discourse*. Vetter's work is one of a few that considers race in the context of modernism and religion, see also: Jenny Hyest, 'Anne Spencer's Feminist Modernist Poetics', *Journal of Modern Literature* 38, no. 3 (2015): 96–130; 'Feminist Vision'; Alexandra Peat, *Travel and Modernist Literature: Sacred and Ethical Journeys*(London: Routledge, 2011).

23 For an overview of new directions in modernist studies taken in the 1990s and early 2000s, see Douglas Mao and Rebecca L. Walkowitz, 'The New Modernist Studies', *PMLA* (2008): 737–48. The turn to the material is also reflected in other periods, see, for example: Paula Findlen, ed. *Early Modern Things: Objects and Their Histories, 1500–1800* (London: Routledge, 2012); Julie Park, *The Self and It: Novel Objects and Mimetic Subjects in Eighteenth-Century England* (Stanford, CA: Stanford University Press, 2009); Mary Jacobus, *Romantic Things: A Tree, a Rock, a Cloud* (Chicago, IL: University of Chicago Press, 2012); Elaine Freedgoode, *The Ideas in Things: Fugitive Meaning in the Victorian Novel* (London: University of Chicago Press, 2006).

24 Douglas Mao, *Solid Objects: Modernism and the Test of Production* (Princeton, NJ: Princeton University Press, 1998), 4.

25 Bill Brown, *Other Things* (London: University of Chicago Press, 2015), 5.

26 Brown's usage correlates with W. J. T. Mitchell's claim that 'objects are the way things appear to a subject – this is, with a name, an identity, a gestalt … Things … [signal] the moment when the object becomes the Other, when the sardine can look backs … when the subject experiences the object as uncanny'; W. J. T. Mitchell qtd. in Jane Bennett, *Vibrant Matter: A Political Ecology of Things* (London: Duke University Press, 2010), 2. I would suggest that the slippage between object and thing can be so rapid as to allow things/objects to be simultaneously known and unknown. Moreover, both definitions still define the object in terms of the subject, either comfortable or discomforting. The thing-in-itself continues to resist interpretation.

27 Brown, *Other Things*, 22.

28 Ibid., 155–74. In his analysis of Latour, Brown is particularly concerned that the 'new democracy of persons and things' elides the fact that democracy of persons remains incomplete (168).

29 Mao, *Solid Objects*, 258.

30 Rochelle Rives, 'Problem Space: Mary Butts, Modernism, and the Etiquette of Placement', *Modernism/modernity* 12, no. 4 (2005): 607–27.

31 Mao explicitly states that his analysis is more focused around production and class issues than analysis of gender and race: *Solid Objects*, 24.

32   Colleen McDannell, *Material Christianity: Religion and Popular Culture in America* (London: Yale University Press, 1995).

33   David Morgan, 'Introduction: The Matter of Belief', in *Religion and Material Culture: The Matter of Belief*, ed. David Morgan (London: Routledge, 2010), 3; Manuel A. Vásquez, *More than Belief: A Materialist Theory of Religion* (Oxford: Oxford University Press, 2011), 7.

34   Edward B. Tylor, *Primitive Culture: Researches into the Development of Mythology, Philosophy, Religion, Art, and Custom*, vol. 1 (London: John Murray, 1871), 383–5. Tylor in turn borrowed the term from Georg Ernst Stahl, who used it to describe the 'vital principle and soul' in his eighteenth-century text *Theoria Medica Vera*: ibid., 384–5n1. For a critique of the way in which ethnocentric hierarchy is built into Tylor's explanation of culture, see George W. Stocking, Jr, *Race, Culture, and Evolution: Essays in the History of Anthropology* 1968 (Chicago, IL: University of Chicago Press, 1982), 81–2. For a critique of the logical problems of Tylor's distinctions between religion and magic, see Wouter Hanegraaff, 'The Emergence of the Academic Science of Magic: The Occult Philosophy in Tylor and Frazer', in *Religion in the Making*, ed. Arie L. Molendijk and Peter Pels (Leiden: Brill, 1998), 253–75.

35   Martin D. Stringer, 'Building on Belief: Defining Animism in Tylor and Contemporary Society', in *The Handbook of Contemporary Animism*, ed. Graham Harvey (Abingdon: Routledge, 2015), 66, 72.

36   Juanita Sundberg defines Indigenous as referring to 'groups with ancestral ties/ claims to particular lands prior to colonization by outside powers and "whose nations remain submerged within the states created by those powers"': W. S. Shaw, R. D. K. Herman and G. R. Dobbs qtd. in Sundberg, 'Decolonizing Posthumanist Geographies', *Cultural Geographies* 21, no. 1 (2014): 33–47.

37   Graham Harvey, *Animism: Respecting the Living World* (London: Hurst, 2005), xi.

38   Harry Garuba, 'Explorations in Animist Materialism: Notes on Reading/Writing African Literature, Culture, and Society', *Public Culture* 15, no. 2 (2003): 267.

39   Ibid., 265–7.

40   Robin Wall Kimmerer, *Braiding Sweetgrass* (Minneapolis, MN: Milkweed Editions, 2013), 55. For more work on Indigenous worldviews and animism, see Deborah Bird Rose, 'Connectivity Thinking, Animism, and the Pursuit of Liveliness', *Educational Theory* 67, no. 4 (2017): 491–508; Linda Hogan, 'We Call It Tradition', in *The Handbook of Contemporary Animism*, ed. Graham Harvey (London: Routledge, 2015), 17–26; Linda Hogan, *Dwellings: A Spiritual History of the Living World* (New York: W. W. Norton, 2007).

41   Peter Pels, 'The Spirit of Matter: On Fetish, Rarity, Fact, and Fancy', in *Border Fetishisms: Material Objects in Unstable Spaces*, ed. Patricia Spyer (New York: Routledge, 1998), 64.

42   Ibid., 98.

43   Tim Ingold, *Being Alive: Essays on Movement, Knowledge and Description* (Abingdon: Routledge, 2011), 29; Emma Restall Orr, *The Wakeful World: Animism, Mind and the Self in Nature* (Winchester: Moon Books, 2012), 188.

44   Caroline Walker Bynum, *Christian Materiality: An Essay on Religion in Late Medieval Europe* (New York: Zone Books, 2015), 20.

45   Gerard Manley Hopkins, *The Major Works* (Oxford: Oxford University Press, 2002), 129. Richard Kearney explores the connection between Scotus and Hopkins, describing Hopkins's work as 'revisit[ing] the "inscape" of the sacred in every passing particular': Richard Kearney, 'Epiphanies of the Everyday: Toward a Micro-Eschatology', in *After God: Richard Kearney and the Continental Turn in Contemporary Philosophy*, ed. John Panteleimon Manoussakis (New York: Fordham University Press, 2006), 4.

46   John Chryssavgis, 'The Earth as Sacrament: Insights from Orthodox Christian Theology and Spirituality', in *The Oxford Handbook of Religion and Ecology*, ed. Roger S. Gottlieb (Oxford: Oxford University Press, 2006), 95–7.

47   Catherine Keller, *Cloud of the Impossible: Negative Theology and Planetary Entanglement* (New York: Columbia, 2015).

48   Ibid., 191.

49   Mayra Rivera, *The Touch of Transcendence: A Postcolonial Theology of God* (London: Westminster John Knox Press, 2007), 2.

50   Hermeticism, the quest for hidden wisdom, arose in Hellenic Egypt and was popularized in the European Renaissance (when occult scholars believed Hermetic texts to be of ancient provenance). It indicates a worldview that sees the divine as permeating the material world: Ernest Lee Tuveson, *The Avatars of Thrice Great Hermes* (London: Associated University Presses, 1982), xiv. For exploration of the early modern Hermeticist Giordano Bruno and his formulation of the 'world soul' see Orr, *Wakeful World*, 116; Frances Yates, *Giordano Bruno and the Hermetic Tradition* 1964 (London: Routledge and Kegan Paul, 1971), 130–43.

51   See Zoe Todd, 'An Indigenous Feminist's Take on the Ontological Turn: "Ontology" Is Just Another Word for Colonialism', *Journal of Historical Sociology* 29, no. 1 (2016): 9; Vanessa Watts, 'Indigenous Place-Thought & Agency amongst Humans and Non-Humans (First Woman and Sky Woman go on a European World Tour!)', *Decolonization: Indigeneity, Education & Society* 2, no. 1 (2013): 28–33.

52   Juanita Sundberg, 'Decolonizing posthumanist geographies', *Cultural Geography* 21, no. 1 (2014): 33–42; Todd, 'Indigenous Feminist', 4–19.

53   Ibid., 9, 17–18.

54   Brown, *Other Things*, 306n37.

55   Kyla Wazana Tompkins, 'New Materialisms', *Lateral* 5, no. 1 (2016), https://doi.org/10.25158/L5.1.8. Juanita Sundberg critiques the way Bennett's rejection

of animism 'calls forth the [superstitious] non-modern Other as … *incapable* of producing knowledge relevant to theorizing materialism': 'Decolonizing Posthumanist Geographies', 37–8. See also Todd, 'Indigenous Feminist', 6–9, 17–19.

56 Bennett, *Vibrant Matter*, viii.

57 Ibid., xii.

58 Ibid., 19, 10.

59 Ibid., 13.

60 The distinction between object-oriented ontology and new materialism is the latter's attention to dynamic relations between things which attends to difference instead of flattening it: Catherine Keller and Mary-Jane Rubenstein, 'Introduction: Tangled Matters', in *Entangled Worlds: Religion, Science, and New Materialisms*, ed. Catherine Keller and Mary-Jane Rubenstein (New York: Fordham University Press, 2017), 2.

61 Lara Vetter examines early twentieth-century precursors to new materialist concerns in physics as the mechanistic, positivist nineteenth-century position that eroded belief and advanced secularism began to give way to the more mysterious relativism of Einstein and thus was often referred to in religious terms: Vetter, *Modernist Writings and Religio-Scientific Discourse*, 3–7.

62 Karen Barad, *Meeting the Universe Halfway: Quantum Physics and the Entanglement of Matter and Meaning* (London: Duke University Press, 2007), 33.

63 Ibid., 210.

64 Ibid., 333, 336.

65 Karen Barad, ' "Matter Feels, Converses, Suffers, Desires, Yearns and Remembers": Interview with Karen Barad', in *New Materialism: Interviews and Cartographies*s, ed. Rick Dolphijn and Iris van der Tuin (Ann Arbor, MI: Open Humanities Press, 2012), http://dx.doi.org/10.3998/ohp.11515701.0001.001.

66 Keller, *Cloud of the Impossible*, 122.

67 Serenella Iovino and Serpil Oppermann, 'Introduction: Stories Come to Matter', in *Material Ecocriticism*, ed. Serenella Iovino and Serpil Oppermann (Bloomington: Indiana University Press, 2014), 1.

68 Brown reminds us that we don't 'yet enjoy democracy of persons': *Other Things*, 168. This critique is made particularly by scholars defending the sovereignty of Indigenous tribes and nations subjected to settler colonization: Adam Burke Carmichael, 'Post-National Foundation of Judith Butler's and Rosi Braidotti's Relational Subjectivity', *Atlantis* 37, no. 2 (2016): 134–44.

69 Barad, *Meeting the Universe Halfway*, 155.

70 Keller, *Cloud of the Impossible*, 228.

71 Judith Butler and Athena Asanasiou qtd. in ibid.

72 Barad, 'Matter Feels'.

73   Bennett, *Vibrant Matter*, xiii; Keller, *Cloud of the Impossible*, 164. For additional
     dialogue between new materialism and theology and religious studies see: Clayton
     Crockett and Jeffrey W. Robbins, eds, *Religion, Politics, and the Earth: The New
     Materialism* (New York: Palgrave Macmillan, 2012); Catherine Keller and Mary-
     Jane Rubenstein, eds, *Entangled Worlds: Religion, Science, and New Materialisms*
     (New York: Fordham University Press, 2017); Joerg Rieger and Edward
     Waggoner, eds, *Religious Experience and New Materialism: Movement Matters*
     (New York: Palgrave Macmillan, 2016).

74   Keller, *Cloud of the Impossible*, 164.

75   Bennett, *Vibrant Matter*, 119.

76   Ibid., 63.

77   Jane Bennett, *The Enchantment of Modern Life: Attachments, Crossings, and Ethics*
     (Princeton, NJ: Princeton University Press, 2001), 5, 162.

78   Marc Schnieder qtd. in John Eade, 'Introduction to the Illinois Paperback', in
     Contesting the Sacred: The Anthropology of Christian Pilgrimage, ed. John Eade and
     Michael J. Sallnow (Chicago: University of Illinois Press, 2000), xv.

79   For a discussion of Weber in relation to modernism, see Lewis, *Religious
     Experience*, 145–53.

80   Roger Griffen in John Bramble, *Modernism and the Occult* (Basingstoke: Palgrave
     Macmillan, 2015), xii.

81   Lewis, *Religious Experience*, 3.

82   Matthew Arnold, 'Dover Beach', in *The Norton Anthology of Poetry*, ed. Alexander
     W. Allison, et al. (New York: W. W. Norton, 1983), 794; Lewis, *Religious Experience*,
     19–22. See also Lara Vetter, 'Afterword: Modernist Women Writers and Spirituality',
     in *Modernist Women Writers and Spirituality: A Piercing Darkness*, ed. Elizabeth
     Anderson, Andrew Radford and Heather Walton (London: Palgrave Macmillan,
     2016), 238–9.

83   Peat, *Travel and Modernist Literature*, 10–11.

84   Lewis, *Religious Experience*, 26; Talal Asad, *Formations of the Secular: Christianity,
     Islam, Modernity* (Stanford, CA: Stanford University Press, 2003), 25.

85   See Rosi Braidotti, Bolette Blaagaard, Tobin De Grand and Eva Midden,
     eds, *Transformations of Religion and the Public Sphere: Postsecular Publics*
     (Basingstoke: Palgrave Macmillan, 2013); Asad, *Formations of the Secular*; William
     Connolly, *Why I Am Not a Secularist* (Minneapolis: University of Minnesota Press,
     1999); Nicholas Howe, *Landscapes of the Secular: Law, Religion, and American
     Sacred Space* (Chicago, IL: University of Chicago Press, 2016); Gordon Lynch, *The
     Sacred in the Modern World: A Cultural Sociological Approach* (Oxford: Oxford
     University Press, 2012).

86   McDannell, *Material Christianity*, 4.

87 Saba Mahmood, 'Sexuality and Secularism', in *Religion, the Secular, and the Politics of Sexual Difference*, ed. Linell E. Cady and Tracy Fessenden (New York: Columbia University Press, 2013); Joan Wallach Scott, 'Secularism and Gender Equality', in *Religion, the Secular, and the Politics of Sexual Difference*, ed. Linell E. Cady and Tracy Fessenden (New York: Columbia University Press, 2013). I would like to thank Jenny Hyest for introducing me to feminist post-secularism.

88 Rosi Braidotti, 'Conclusion: The Residual Spirituality in Critical Theory: A Case for Affirmative Postsecular Politics' in Transformations of Religion and the Public Sphere: Postsecular Publics, ed. Rosi Braidotti, et al. (Basingstoke: Palgrave Macmillan, 2013), 252.

89 Ibid., 256–63.

90 de Certeau, *Everyday Life*, xiii–xiv. See also Heather Walton, *Writing Methods in Theological Reflection* (London: SCM Press, 2014), 181–3.

91 Madelyn Detloff, *The Persistence of Modernism: Loss and Mourning in the Twentieth Century* (Cambridge: Cambridge University Press, 2010), 3–11; Susan Friedman, *Planetary Modernisms: Provocations on Modernity across Time* (New York: Columbia University Press, 2015), 1–10, 83–93; Mao and Walkowitz, 'The New Modernist Studies', 738.

1 Threads and silver paper: Spirituality of gift and process in H.D.'s war writing

1 H.D., *Tribute to Freud* 1956 (New York: New Directions, 2012), 99.

2 The separation between Freud and his antiquities is undermined elsewhere in his writings, when he notes that patients would often confess to be considering the objects in the room, and Freud saw this as a projection of thoughts about the analyst: Diana Fuss, *The Sense of an Interior: Four Rooms and the Writers That Shaped Them* (London: Routledge, 2004), 43. I am primarily interested in the spiritual and creative resonances of the relationship between persons and things. For a more psychoanalytic reading of the complex connections and identifications between humans and objects (largely drawing on the object relations models developed by Melanie Klein and D. W. Winnicott), see Anne Anlin Cheng, *The Melancholoy of Race: Psychoanalytic Assimilation, and Hidden Grief* (Oxford: Oxford University Press, 2001), 75–6; Barbara Johnson, *Persons and Things* (Cambridge, MA: Harvard University Press, 2008), 94–105.

3 For a psychoanalytic reading of the placement of objects, furniture and persons in Freud's study, see Fuss, *Sense of an Interior*, 33–43.

4 Some of the antiquities may well have been objects of everyday use in their time, but their survival across the centuries confers on them a degree of value that removes them from the realm of the ordinary.

5 Tim Ingold, 'Being Alive to a World without Objects', in *The Handbook of Contemporary Animism*, ed. Graham Harvey (London: Routledge, 2014), 215.

6 For further discussion of H.D. and Hermeticism, see Elizabeth Anderson, *H.D. and Modernist Religious Imagination: Mysticism and Writing* (London: Bloomsbury, 2013), 2–4, 73–83. See also Demetres Tryphonopoulos, 'Introduction', in *Majic Ring*, ed. Demtres Tryphonopoulos (Gainesville: University Press of Florida, 2009), xxiii–xxvii, xxxvii-xxxi.

7 See Dianne Chisholm, *H.D.'s Freudian Poetics: Psychoanalysis in Translation* (Ithaca, NY: Cornell University Press, 1992), 34–6; Diana Collecott, *H.D. and Sapphic Modernism, 1910 – 1950* (Cambridge: Cambridge University Press, 1999), 254; Susan Stanford Friedman, *Penelope's Web: Gender, Modernity, H.D.'s Fiction* (Cambridge: Cambridge University Press, 1990), 299, 304.

8 See also Douglas Mao, *Solid Objects: Modernism and the Test of Production* (Princeton, NJ: Princeton University Press, 1998), 3–4.

9 H.D., *Tribute*, 11.

10 Ibid., 9.

11 Rebecca Colesworthy argues that the distinctions between gift and market economies are inevitably blurred, a sign of modernity that she sees in both Mauss and H.D., among others: *Returning the Gift: Modernism and the Thought of Exchange* (Oxford: Oxford University Press, 2018), 204. I will return to this point in the final chapter.

12 Adalaide Morris, *How to Live/What to Do: H.D.'s Cultural Poetics* (Chicago, IL: University of Illinois Press, 2003), 127.

13 Ibid., 128.

14 Ibid., 130.

15 Colesworthy, *Returning the Gift*, 8. For a full discussion of Mauss as a modernist, concerned with 'thinking about the gift in response to contemporary crises and changes with metropolitan market society', see Colesworthy, 8–11, 21–62.

16 Harvey, *Animism*, 12–13.

17 T. P. Tawhai, 'Maori Religion' in *Readings in Indigenous Religons*, ed. Graham Harvey (London: Continuum, 2002), 244.

18 Cixous is not advocating a simple correlation between the feminine and women in an 'anatomy equals destiny' kind of argument, rather, she argues that women have a greater (though not exclusive) degree of access to such an economy because of their social positioning.

19 Hélène Cixous and Catherine Clément, *The Newly Born Woman*, trans. Betsy Wing La Jeune Née, Paris: Union Générale d'Editions, 1975 (London: I. B. Tauris, 1996), 87.

20 Ibid., 86–7.

21 Sal Renshaw, 'Graceful Gifts: Hélène Cixous and the Radical Gifts of Other Love', in *Women and the Gift: Beyond the Given and the All-Giving*, ed. Morny Joy (Bloomington: Indiana University Press, 2013), 131–3.

22 Cixous qtd. in ibid., 133.

23 Morris, *How to Live*, 128. H.D.'s notes from the time of analysis are included in the 'Advent' section of *Tribute to Freud*. There is more understated instance of gift economy in this text. The third partner in 'Advent' is Bryher. She supported H.D.'s analysis financially and emotionally through letters and gifts. H.D. frequently mentions flowers appearing on her desk. Like the gardenias, these gifts were unsigned, but the recipient knew the giver's identity.

24 I have discussed this in more depth in Elizabeth Anderson, *H.D. and Modernist Religious Imagination: Mysticism and Writing* (London: Bloomsbury, 2013), 48–56.

25 Colesworthy, *Returning the Gift*, 201–19.

26 Edith Sitwell, "Letter to H.D., Undated, 1942–44?," in *H.D. Papers, Yale Collection of American Literature* (New Haven, CT: Beinecke Rare Book and Manuscript Library, Yale University,). For further discussion of the significance of tea and nationality in H.D.'s writing, see Bryony Randall, ' "Funny, but No Hybrid': H.D., Tea and Expatriate Identity', *Symbiosis* 13, no. 2 (2009): 189–210.

27 H.D., "Letter to Bryher, 2 March, 1938," in *Bryher Papers, Yale Collection of American Literature* (New Haven, CT: Beinecke Rare Book and Manuscript Library, Yale University).

28 William Shakespeare, 'The Winter's Tale', in *The Norton Shakespeare: Based on the Oxford Edition*, ed. Stephen Greenblatt, et al. (New York: W. W. Norton 1997), IV: 4, 119.

29 Bryher legally adopted Perdita and Perdita referred to Bryher and H.D. as her 'two mothers': Perdita Schaffner, 'Running', *The Iowa Review* 16, no. 3 (1986): 9.

30 H.D. was fond of exchanging Christmas cards and many of her letters refer to them. For more on the development of Christmas cards as hybrid objects that bridge fine art and everyday aesthetics, see Patricia Zakreski, 'The Victorian Christmas Card as Aesthetic Object', *Journal of Design History* 29, no. 2 (2015): 120–32.

31 The poems in *What Do I Love?* were published in the 'Uncollected Poems' section of the *Collected Poems* where their positioning underplays the significance of H.D.'s original placement. They have recently been made available as H.D. ordered them in *Within the Walls and What Do I Love?*, a critical edition edited by Annette Debo and published by the University Press of Florida in 2014. *Within the Walls* is a collection of short stories about wartime London, written in the early 1940s. In her introduction to the volume, Debo notes that H.D. viewed the poems of *What Do I Love?* as a coda to this collection: Annette Debo, 'Introduction', in *Within the Walls and What Do I Love*, ed. Annette Debo (Gainesville: University Press of

Florida, 2014), 5. Susan Schweik compares 'Christmas 1944' with *The Flowering of the Rod*, the final volume of *Trilogy*, and H.D.'s 'disrupted and disruptive New Testament Narrative': *A Gulf So Deeply Cut: American Women Poets and the Second World War* (Madison: University of Wisconsin Press, 1991), 244–5.

32 In his reading of H.D., Robert Duncan defines poetry not only as a gift to the reader but to the universe more broadly: *The H.D. Book* (Berkeley: University of California Press, 2011), 267–8. My thanks to Lara Vetter for bringing this to my attention.

33 Here we see a connection with *Trilogy* as angels are a significant presence in the second volume, *Tribute to the Angels*. For more on angels in H.D.'s mature work, see Suzanne Hobson, *Angels of Modernism: Religion, Culture, Aesthetics 1910–1960* (Basingstoke: Palgrave Macmillan, 2011), 141–81.

34 H.D., *Within the Walls and What Do I Love* (Gainesville: University Press of Florida, 2014), 173.

35 Ibid., 174. In the bombings of July 1944, the home of friends of H.D. and Bryher was hit. Bryher commented that she and other friends had an hour to salvage what they could from the ruined building: Debo, 'Introduction', 91.

36 H.D., *Walls*, 174.

37 Ibid., 174–5.

38 The text was written between 1941 and 1943, with a later section of notes added in 1944. It remained unpublished in her lifetime; an abridged version was published by New Directions in 1982 with the full version appearing from the University Press of Florida in 1998.

39 H.D., *The Gift by H.D.: The Complete Text*, ed. Jane Augustine (Gainesville: University Press of Florida, 1998), 85.

40 Ibid.

41 Ibid., 88–9.

42 Tim Ingold, *Making: Anthropology, Archaeology, Art and Architecture* (New York: Routledge, 2013), 31.

43 Ibid., 29.

44 For discussion of alchemy in *Trilogy*, see Anderson, *H.D. and Modernist Religious Imagination*, 77–81; Morris, *How to Live*, 110–16.

45 Ingold, 'World without Objects', 215.

46 Renshaw, 'Graceful Gifts', 138.

47 H.D., *The Gift*, 89.

48 Dorothee Soelle qtd. in Ann Pedersen, 'Creativity, Christology and Science: A Process of Composition and Improvisation', in *Creating Women's Theology: A Movement Engaging Process Thought*, ed. Monica A. Coleman, Nancy R. Howell and Helene Tallon Russell (Eugene, OR: Pickwick, 2011), 167.

49 Walter Benjamin, *One-Way Street and Other Writings*, trans. Edmund Jephcott and Kingsley Shorter (London: Verso, 2006), 52–3. This way of creating also suggests

the practice of patchwork that has lent important imagery to many feminist and womanist theologians and theorists, see bell hooks, *Belonging: A Culture of Place* (New York: Routledge, 2009), 154–68; Kwok Pui-lan, *Postcolonial Imagination & Feminist Theology* (London: SCM Press, 2005), 46; Adrienne Rich, *The Dream of a Common Language: Poems 1974–1977* (London: W. W. Norton, 1978), 76–7.

50 Pedersen, 'Creativity, Christology and Science', 168.

51 The connection between divinity and beauty is most explicit in the 1943 poem 'Ancient Wisdom Speaks from the Mountain'.

52 Debo notes the 'Books for Battle' campaign which saw many books used for munitions production; H.D. was ambivalent about the campaign, recognizing the military need but worrying about the loss of interesting books: 'Introduction', 24.

53 H.D., *Trilogy* (New York: New Directions, 1998), 16.

54 H.D., *The Gift*, 215.

55 Catherine Keller, *Face of the Deep: A Theology of Becoming* (London: Routledge, 2003), xvii.

56 For further discussion of H.D.'s craft practice as a means to heal psychic traumas, see Amy Elkins, 'A Stitch in Time: H.D.'S Craft Modernism as Transhistoric Repair', *The Space Between: Literature and Culture 1914–1945* 12 (2016), http://scalar.usc.edu/works/the-space-between-literature-and-culture-1914-1945/vol12_2016_elkins.

57 H.D., "Letter to Viola Baxter Jordan, 5 September, 1947?,"(Viola Baxter Jordan Papers, Yale Collection of American Literature, Beinecke Rare Book and Manuscript Library).

58 H.D.'s mature work resonates with Pound's *Cantos* as both writers deploy occult sources as part of their densely layered mythic projects. For further discussion of the occult in H.D. and Pound see Matte Robinson, *The Astral H.D.: Occult and Religious Sources and Contexts for H.D.'S Poetry and Prose* (London: Bloomsbury, 2016), 96–156; Demetres P. Tryphonopoulos, *The Celestial Tradition: A Study of Ezra Pound's the Cantos* (Waterloo: Wilfred Laurier University Press, 1992); Leon Surette, *The Birth of Modernism: Ezra Pound, T.S. Eliot, W.B. Yeats, and the Occult* (Montreal: McGill-Queens University Press, 1994).

59 H.D., 'H.D. By *Delia Alton*', *Iowa Review* 16, no. 3 (1986): 190.

60 H.D., *The Hirslanden Notebooks: An Annotated Scholarly Edition* (Victoria: ELS Editions, 2015), 5. PAGE

61 H.D., *End to Torment: A Memoir of Ezra Pound* (Manchester: Carcanet, 1980), 22.

62 The designs of verdure tapestries emphasized plants rather than figures: Ronald Rees, *Interior Landscapes: Gardens and the Domestic Environment* (Baltimore, MD: Johns Hopkins University Press, 1993), 33–4.

63 Images of H.D.'s embroideries indicate that the patterns were H.D.'s own, containing flowers, fruit, trees and animals in designs strongly reminiscent of the medieval patterns that were so compelling to Morris and other Arts and Crafts designers.

The natural objects are highly stylized in their representation, as in medieval and
Morris designs. For images of H.D.'s tapestries, see Elkins, 'H.D.'S Craft Modernism'.

64   Most of the tapestries produced by Morris & Co. that feature figures were designed
     by Morris and Edward Burne-Jones, the latter supplying the figures and the former
     the backgrounds. Morris travelled to France and the Low Countries in the 1850s
     where he would have seen numerous examples of medieval tapestries, including
     those held at the Hôtel (later Musée) de Cluny in Paris which was established in
     the 1840s. Morris saw his work as new yet inspired by past forms: Jennifer Harris,
     'William Morris and the Middle Ages', in *William Morris and the Middle Ages*,
     ed. Joanna Banham and Jennifer Harris (Manchester: Manchester University
     Press, 1984), 11; Imogen Hart, *Arts and Crafts Objects* (Manchester: Manchester
     University Press, 2010), 122.

65   H.D., "Letters to Bryher, 2 January, 10 November, 15 November, 1947" (Bryher
     Papers, Beinecke Rare Book and Manuscript Libary, Yale University).

66   "Letters to Bryher, 10 and 16 February, 1947" (Bryher Papers, Beinecke Rare Book
     and Manuscript Libary, Yale University, 19).

67   "Letter to Viola Baxter Jordan, April 28, 1942" (Viola Baxter Jordan Papers,
     Yale Collection of American Literature, Beinecke Rare Book and Manuscript
     Library, 1942).

68   Anna Fisk, ' "To Make, and Make Again': Feminism, Craft and Spirituality', *Feminist
     Theology* 20, no. 2 (2012): 161–2; Beverly Gordon, *Textiles: The Whole Story*
     (London: Thames and Hudson, 2011), 248; Joanne Turney, *The Culture of Knitting*
     (Oxford: Berg, 2009), 152–60.

69   Rozsika Parker, *The Subversive Stitch* (London: I. B. Tauris, 2010), 174–8; Glen
     Adamson, *The Invention of Craft* (London: Bloomsbury, 2013), 215–21.

70   Parker, *The Subversive Stitch*, 148–52. See also Talia Schaffer, *Novel Craft: Victorian
     Domestic Handicraft and Nineteenth-Century Fiction* (Oxford: Oxford University
     Press, 2011), 23–4; Deborah Wynne, "Charlotte Brontë's Frocks and Shirley's Queer
     Textiles', in *Literary Bric-À-Brac and the Victorians*, ed. Jen Harrison and Jonathan
     Shears (Farnham: Ashgate, 2013), 147–62.

71   Parker, *The Subversive Stitch*, 9–10.

72   Fiona Hackney, 'Quiet Activism and the New Amateur: The Power of Home and
     Hobby Crafts', *Design and Culture* 5, no. 2 (2013): 169–94; Parker, *The Subversive
     Stitch*, 214.

73   See Adamson, *The Invention of Craft*, 210–32; Fiona Hackney, 'Home Craft and
     Make-Do-and-Mend in British Women's Magazines of the 1920s and 1930s', *Journal
     of Design History* 19, no. 1 (2006): 23–38.

74   Constance Howard, *Twentieth-Century Embroidery in Great Britain to 1939*
     (London: Batsford, 1981), 135–9.

75   Hackney, 'Quiet Activism', 179.

76 For further discussion of the development of craft as a profession for women and the interrelationship of amateur and professional craft practices and discourses see Kyiaki Hadjiafxendi and Patricia Zakreski, eds, *Crafting the Woman Professional in the Long Nineteenth Century: Artistry and Industry in Britain* (London: Routledge, 2013).

77 Parker, *Subversive Stitch*, 181.

78 May Morris, qtd. in Hilary Laucks Walter, 'Another Stitch to the Legacy of William Morris: May Morris's Designs and Writings on Embroidery', in *William Morris in the Twenty-First Century*, ed. Phillippa Bennett and Rosie Miles (Bern: Peter Lang, 2010), 77.

79 Parker, *The Subversive Stitch*, 181.

80 Hackney, 'Quiet Activism', 179.

81 Constance Howard, *Twentieth-Century Embroidery in Great Britain 1940–1963* (London: Batsford, 1983), 8–9.

82 Ibid., 10–11.

83 In her post-war correspondence H.D. frequently reflects on the privileges afforded her in Switzerland in contrast to the deprivations facing her friends in England.

84 H.D., *The Sword Went out to Sea: (Synthesis of a Dream), by Delia Alton* (Gainesville: University Press of Florida, 2007), 90. Subsequent references will be given in the text.

85 Elizabeth K. Helsinger, *Poetry and the Pre-Raphaelite Arts: Dante Gabriel Rossetti and William Morris* (New Haven, CT: Yale University Press, 2008), 2–3, 22.

86 Talia Schaffer and Kathy Alexis Psomiades, 'Introduction', in *Women and British Aestheticism*, ed. Talia Schaffer and Kathy Alexis Psomiades (Charlottesville: University Press of Virginia, 1999), 11; Vincent Sherry, *Modernism and the Reinvention of Decadence* (Cambridge: Cambridge University Press, 2015).

87 Cassandra Laity has explored H.D.'s affiliations with the Pre-Raphaelite and Decadent poets and painters at length, however she only briefly touches on H.D.'s late prose. See also Alison Halsall, 'H.D. And the Victorian Spectres of *White Rose and the Red*', *College Literature* 38, no. 4 (2011): 115–33.

88 Morris's association with the Pre-Raphaelites weakened after Jane Morris and Rossetti began their affair and waned further after Rossetti's death. Anna Vaninskaya argues that Morris literary reputation improved when he was seen to depart from his earlier Pre-Raphaelite style, however, his ongoing and productive association with Burne-Jones indicates that this picture is more complex and it can be argued that the association between Morris and the Pre-Raphaelites was never completely closed: *William Morris and the Idea of Community: Romance, History and Propaganda 1880–1914* (Edinburgh: Edinburgh University Press, 2010), 136–7.

89 Wendy Parkins, 'Jane Morris's Art of Everyday Life at Kelmscott', in *William Morris and the Art of Everyday Life*, ed. Wendy Parkins (Newcastle: Cambridge Scholars, 2010), 146.

90 H.D., *Tribute*, 146.

91 Jan Marsh, *Dante Gabriel Rossetti: Painter and Poet* (London: Phoenix, 2005), 201, 337; Elizabeth Miller, *Slow Print: Literary Radicalism and Late Victorian Print Culture* (Stanford, CA: Stanford University Press, 2013), 313n11; Dante Gabriel Rossetti, *The Correspondence of Dante Gabriel Rossetti*, vol. IV (Cambridge: Brewer, 2004), 50, 54.

92 For further discussion of H.D.'s spiritualism, see Anderson, *H.D. and Modernist Religious Imagination*, 31–39; Rachel Connor, *H.D. And the Image* (Manchester: Manchester University Press, 2004), 152; Sword, *Ghostwriting Modernism*, 103–31.

93 Whilst travelling in Greece, H.D. saw a series of visions, what she called 'pictures on the wall'. For a description of this experience see H.D., *Tribute*, 44–56.

94 H.D., "Letter to Bryher, November 8, 1947" (Bryher Papers, Beinecke Rare Book and Manuscript Libary, Yale University).

95 Caroline Arscott, *William Morris and Edward Burne-Jones: Interlacings* (New Haven, CT: Yale University Press, 2008), 35. Arscott refers to wallpaper but the same can be said for printed fabric.

96 H.D., "Letter to Bryher, November 8, 1947."

97 Caroline Zilboorg, ed. *Richard Aldington & H.D.: Their Lives in Letters 1918–61* (Manchester: Manchester University Press, 2003), 270.

98 The pilots are also associated with Lord Howell, Delia's name for Lord Hugh Dowding, the chief Air Marshall responsible for the British success in the Battle of Britain, a spiritualist and an important figure in the novel. H.D.'s key to the characters includes an annotation 'indicating that both the RAF pilots and Delia's companions are considered "goldwings"'; Cynthia Hogue and Julie Vandivere, 'Introduction', in *The Sword Went out to Sea: (Synthesis of a Dream), by Delia Alton* (Gainesville: University Press of Florida, 2007), xlii.

99 Phillippa Bennett, 'Rejuvenating Our Sense of Wonder: The Last Romances of William Morris', in *William Morris in the Twenty-First Century*, ed. Phillippa Bennett and Rosie Miles (Bern: Peter Lang, 2010), 226.

100 Hogue and Vandivere, 'Introduction', xxxvii.

101 Ibid., xxxvii, xliii.

102 Ibid., xlii.

103 William Morris, *The Defense of Guinevere, and Other Poems* (London: Bell and Daldy, 1858), 207.

104 Ibid., 213, 12.

105 For discussion of Morris's anti-war writing, see Florence Saunders Boos, 'Dystopian Violence: William Morris and the Nineteenth-Century Peace Movement', *Journal of Pre-Raphaelite Studies* 14 (2005): 15–35.

106 Morris, *Defense*, 202, 14.

107 H.D., *Collected Poems: 1912–1944* (New York: New Directions, 1983), 561.

108 H.D. "Letter to Viola, April 28, 1942".

109 Fiona MacCarthy, *William Morris: A Life for Our Time* (London: Faber and Faber, 1994), 262.

110 Sandra M. Gilbert and Susan Gubar, *The Madwoman in the Attic* (New Haven, CT: Yale University Press, 1984), 45–83.

111 Kathryn R. King, 'Of Needles and Pens and Women's Work', *Tulsa Studies in Women's Literature* 14, no. 1 (1995): 77–93.

112 See hooks, *Belonging*, 153–68.

113 Virginia Woolf, *A Room of One's Own* (London: Penguin, 2004), 103.

114 Annette Debo, *The American H.D.* (Iowa City: University of Iowa Press, 2012), 54.

115 H.D., 'Writing on the Wall', in *Tribute to Freud* (New York: New Directions, 2012), 153.

116 Friedman, *Penelope's Web*, 87.

117 The significance of textile crafts and their natural counterparts is anticipated in H.D.'s earlier text, *Palimpsest* (1926), with mention of webs, weaving, the spinning and cutting of the Fates and so on: Rebecca Bowler, *Literary Impressionism: Vision and Memory in Dorothy Richardson, Ford Maddox Ford, H.D. And May Sinclair* (London: Bloomsbury, 2016), 121–2.

118 Lara Vetter, *A Curious Peril: H.D.'S Late Modernist Prose* (Gainesville: University Press of Florida, 2017), 9.

119 H.D., *Tribute*, 9.

120 Adamson, *Invention of Craft*, xv-xvii, 182–4.

121 See also Arscott, *Morris and Burne-Jones*, 29.

122 Adamson, *Invention of Craft*, 184.

123 Ibid., 222–5.

124 Ibid., 227.

125 For additional readings of H.D. and trauma, see Anderson, *H.D. and Modernist Religious Imagination*, 26–39; Madelyn Detloff, *The Persistence of Modernism: Loss and Mourning in the Twentieth Century* (Cambridge: Cambridge University Press, 2010), 88–101; Miriam Fuchs, *The Text Is Myself: Women's Life Writing and Catastrophe* (Madison: University of Wisconsin Press, 2003), 78–108; Sarah H. S. Graham, 'Falling Walls: Trauma and Testimony in H.D.'S *Trilogy*', *English* 56, no. Autumn (2007): 299–319.

126 Donna Krolik Hollenberg, ed., *Between History & Poetry: The Letters of H.D. & Norman Holmes Pearson* (Iowa City: University of Iowa Press, 1997), 104.

127 For a reading of *Sword* as a text that challenges notions of historical authenticity by placing a greater emphasis on ethics than truth claims, see Vetter, *A Curious Peril*, 82–100.

128 Virginia Woolf, *To the Lighthouse* (Oxford: Oxford University Press, 2008), 74.

129 Catherine Keller, *Cloud of the Impossible: Negative Theology and Planetary Entanglement* (New York: Columbia, 2015), 189.

130 Mariana Ortega, 'Gift of Being, Gift of Self', in *Women and the Gift: Beyond the Given and the All-Giving*, ed. Morny Joy (Bloomington: Indiana University Press, 2013), 113.

2 'The pebbles were each one alive': Animism and Anglo-Catholicism in Mary Butts's writing

1 Mary Butts, *The Crystal Cabinet: My Childhood at Salterns* (Manchester: Carcanet, 1988), 1–3.

2 Jed Esty, *A Shrinking Island: Modernism and National Culture in England* (Princeton, NJ: Princeton University Press, 2004), 118; Jane Garrity, *Step-Daughters of England: British Women Modernists and the National Imaginary* (Manchester: Manchester University Press, 2003), 188–241.

3 Mary Butts, *The Journals of Mary Butts* (New Haven, CT: Yale University Press, 2002), 186.

4 qtd. in Nathalie Blondel, *Mary Butts: Scenes from the Life* (Kingston, NY: McPherson, 1998), 174. For a further discussion of the knight's move as a narrative strategy in Butts's fiction, see Elizabeth Anderson, ' "The Knight's Move": Fluidity of Identity and Meaning in Mary Butt's *Armed with Madness*', *Women: A Cultural Review* 18, no. 3 (2007): 245–56.

5 The exact time of Butts's conversion is unclear, on 7 December 1934 she first mentions St Hilary's Church, Marazion – 'The discovery of Father Walke, & a place to pray', while in February 1935 she wrote to Ellis Roberts: 'Have you noticed I'm a Christian again?': Butts, *Journals*, 438; qtd. in Blondel, *Mary Butts*, 361. St Hilary's will become increasingly important to Butts; as ever, place is significant in her sense of spiritual identity and belonging.

6 Garrity, *Step-Daughters of England*, 194; Andrew Radford, *Mary Butts and British Neo-Romanticism: The Enchantment of Place* (London: Bloomsbury, 2014), 193–4; Patrick Wright, 'Coming Back to the Shores of Albion: The Secret England of Mary Butts (1890–1937)', in *On Living in an Old Country*, ed. Patrick Wright (London: Verso, 1985), 124.

7 John Sheail, *Rural Conservation in Interwar Britain* (Oxford: Oxford University Press, 1981), 7–8.

8 David Evans, *A History of Nature Conservation in Britain* (London: Routledge, 1992), 59–62.

9 Sam Wiseman, *The Reimagining of Place in English Modernism* (Clemson, SC: Clemson University Press, 2015), 5.

10 Butts, *Journals*, 142.

11 Butts, *Crystal Cabinet*, 221.

12 Butts, *Journals*, 350.

13 Unusually for an Edwardian upper-class girl, Butts was sent to a school which gave girls the same education as boys, followed by a stint at Westfield College: Nathalie Blondel, 'Introduction', in *The Journals of Mary Butts*, ed. Nathalie Blondel (New Haven, CT: Yale University Press, 2002), 9–11.

14 A full evaluation of the significance of the Grail (the sacred object extraordinaire) in Mary Butts's work is beyond the scope of this chapter, for further discussion, see Roslyn Reso Foy, *Ritual, Myth, and Mysticism in the Work of Mary Butts: Between Feminism and Modernism* (Fayetteville, NC: University of Arkansas Press, 2000), 51–71; Garrity, *Step-Daughters of England*, 208–24; Andrew Radford, 'A "Fine, Mysterious, Almost Sacred Fable?" Retelling the Grail Quest in Mary Butts' *Armed with Madness*', *Literature and Theology* 29, no. 3 (2015): 298–322.

15 Several scholars have noted Harrison's influence on Butts. Ruth Hoberman defines Butts's 'mythical method' as structured by ritual and mana, derived from Harrison's work on ancient religion: Ruth Hoberman, *Gendering Classicism: The Ancient World in Twentieth-Century Women's Historical Fiction* (Albany: State University of New York, 1997), 47–8.

16 Louis, *Gods and Mysteries*, 329, 330.

17 Ibid., 351.

18 Mary Butts, *Armed with Madness* 1928 (London: Penguin, 2001), 15. Subsequent references given in the text.

19 Butts, *Journals*, 263.

20 Wiseman, *Reimagining of Place*, 78.

21 Writers as varied as David Jones, John Cowper Powys, Evelyn Underhill and Charles Williams wrote about the Grail in differing styles and genres.

22 Butts, *Crystal Cabinet*, 33.

23 Mimi Winick, 'Scholarly Enchantment', *Nineteenth-Century Literature* 73, no. 2 (2018): 203.

24 Ibid., 215. Winick also notes how Butts places Weston (along with Jane Harrison) firmly at the centre of a literary history 'in which readers of fiction and scholarship alike are on the same quest for magic': 220.

25 Corrine Saunders, 'Religion and Magic', in *The Cambridge Companion to the Arthurian Legend*, ed. Elizabeth Archibald and Ad Putter (Cambridge: Cambridge University Press, 2009), 206–7.

26 Stephen Heath, 'Introduction: Chances of the Sacred Game', in *Armed with Madness*, ed. Mary Butts (London: Penguin, 2001), xxii.

27 Rochelle Rives, 'Problem Space: Mary Butts, Modernism, and the Etiquette of Placement'. *Modernism/modernity* 12, no. 4 (2005): 624.

28 Ibid., 608.

29 Ibid., 624.

30 Mary Butts, *Ashe of Rings and Other Writings* (Kingston, NY: McPherson, 1998), 47.

31 Jane Ellen Harrison, *Themis: A Study of the Social Origins of Greek Religion*, 2nd ed.,
    1912 (Cambridge: Cambridge University Press, 1927), 67. Harrison participates
    in the casual racism of her time, referring to Indigenous peoples as 'savages' and
    drawing distinctions between such cultures as childlike, and what she calls 'the
    mature and civilized mind': ibid., 68. Yet elsewhere in her work she refuses the
    developmental model that reinforces racist hierarchies, depended on by Tylor and
    Frazer, as she privileges the chthonic deities over the Olympian, ritual over myth
    and does not see a disconnect between ancient worldviews and modern life.

32 Ibid., 67–8.

33 Hoberman, *Gendering Classicism*, 47.

34 Anon., 'Mana', Oxford University Press, www.oed.com. In *Themis*, Harrison refers
    to Robert Henry Codrington's study *The Melanesians*, published in 1891.

35 William James, *Some Problems of Philosophy* 1911 (Cambridge, MA: Harvard
    University Press, 1979), 15. While it is not certain that Butts read *Some Problems of
    Philosophy*, she was familiar with James's earlier work: Butts, *Journals*, 245. James
    goes on to connect mana with the idea of 'sympathetic magic' which would have
    appealed to Butts's interest in the occult and the hermetic lore of correspondences
    found in the Emerald Tablet. There is evidence in Butts's papers that she was
    familiar with the Emerald Tablet: "Coda," in *Papers of Mary Butts, Box 13, folder
    184* (Beinecke Rare Book and Manuscript Library, Yale University, 1929).

36 Peter J. Mataira, '*Mana* and *Tapu*: Sacred Knowledge, Sacred Boundaries', in
    Indigenous Religions: A Companion, ed. Graham Harvey (London: Bloomsbury,
    2000), 99–102. Numerous scholars, including Mataira, have noted the difficulty of
    properly translating 'mana'. It has also been defined as 'the driving force to ensure
    the happiness and good existence of the tribal nation': Pat Hohepa qtd. in Angela
    Middleton, *Te Puna – a New Zealand Mission Station: Historical Archaeology in
    New Zealand* (New York: Springer, 2008), 48.

37 Mataira, '*Mana* and *Tapu*', 111. See also, Harvey, *Animism*, 50–1, 56. Mataira rejects
    the appellation of animism, indicating that Maori distinguish between 'the essence
    of inanimate and animate objects' although 'the natural order is not a closed
    system [and] it is subject to infiltration and interpretation by higher order spirits'.
    However, he goes on to say that all things 'possessed mauri by which they cohere in
    nature': Mataira, '*Mana* and *Tapu*', 111. *Mauri* is the 'life principle, life force … the
    essential quality and vitality of a being or entity': Anon., 'Mauri', *Māori Dictionary*
    (2003–18), www.maoridictionary.co.nz. It appears that Maori worldview refuses
    animism as defined by Tylor but is more closely aligned with the new animism that
    sees the life particular to things in themselves.

38 An important distinction between a modern, European writer like Butts and an Indigenous worldview is that she is writing outwith the mainstream of her culture, in an attempt to restore what she perceives as damaged, while for Indigenous peoples, concepts like mana are embedded in their culture and are a source of social cohesion.

39 Butts, *Journals*, 407–10.

40 Ibid., 427.

41 Butts, *Crystal Cabinet*, 61. Subsequent references given in the text. For further discussion of the relationship between the Virgin Mary and Graeco-Roman goddesses, see Anne Baring and Jules Cashford, *The Myth of the Goddess: Evolution of an Image* (London: Penguin, 1993), 547–608; Stephen Benko, *The Virgin Goddess: Studies in the Pagan and Christian Roots of Mariology* (Leiden: Brill, 2004), 20–82.

42 Mary Butts, qtd. in Blondel, *Mary Butts*, 290.

43 Mary Butts, "Progress in the West," (Mary Butts Papers, Beinecke Rare Book and Manuscript Libary, Yale University, n.d.).

44 "Notebooks," (Mary Butts Papers, Beinecke Rare and Manuscript Library, Yale University, 1936).

45 Clinton Gardner, 'Vladimir Solov̆ev: From Theism to Panentheism', in *Vladimir Solov̆ev: Reconciler and Polemicist*, ed. Wil van den Bercken, Manon de Courten and Evert van der Zweerde (Leuven: University of Nijmegen, 2001), 112.

46 Oliver Smith argues that Soloviev ties the process of theosis more closely with historical time and wordly affairs than earlier theologians: Oliver Smith, *Vladimir Soloviev and the Spiritualization of Matter* (Brighton, MA: Academic Studies Press, 2011), 2. Soloviev was interested in a broad range of mystical and occult traditions from Kabbalah to Hermeticism and Neoplatonism: ibid., 28.

47 John Chryssavgis, 'The Earth as Sacrament: Insights from Orthodox Christian Theology and Spirituality', in *The Oxford Handbook of Religion and Ecology*, ed. Roger S. Gottlieb (Oxford: Oxford University Press, 2006), 96.

48 Rosemary Radford Ruether traces the history of this tradition from its origins in the Christian syncretism of Hebraic, Greco-Roman and Eastern thought to the possibility of its development in a feminist ecotheology: Rosemary Radford Ruether, *Gaia and God: An Ecofeminist Theology of Earth Healing* (London: SCM Press, 1992), 229–53.

49 Sallie McFague stresses the value of things in and for themselves, 'the value of huckleberries as huckleberries': Sallie McFague, *The Body of God: An Ecology Theology* (London: SCM Press, 1993), 184. See also Richard Kearney, 'Epiphanies of the Everyday: Toward a Micro-Eschatology', in *After God: Richard Kearney and the Continental Turn in Contemporary Philosophy*, ed. John Panteleimon Manoussakis (New York: Fordham University Press, 2006), 4.

50 Ivone Gebara, *Longing for Running Water: Ecofeminism and Liberation* (Minneapolis, MN: Fortress Press, 1999), 105.

51 Soloviev was accused of pantheism: Smith, *Soloviev*, 50.

52 Catherine Keller, *Face of the Deep: A Theology of Becoming* (London: Routledge, 2003), 218–20.

53 Gebara, *Running Water*, 124. See also Chryssavgis, 'Earth as Sacrament', 103; McFague, *Body of God*, 149–50.

54 Grace Jantzen, *Becoming Divine: Towards a Feminist Philosophy of Religion* (Manchester: Manchester University Press, 1998), 271. See also Mayra Rivera's relational model of transcendence discussed in the introduction and third chapter: *The Touch of Transcendence: A Postcolonial Theology of God* (London: Westminster John Knox Press, 2007), 2.

55 Mary-Jane Rubenstein, 'The Matter with Pantheism: On Shepherds and Goat-Gods and Mountains and Monsters', in *Entangled Worlds: Religions, Science, and New Materialisms*, ed. Catherine Keller and Mary-Jane Rubenstein (New York: Fordham University Press, 2017), 164–5. This is not to argue that pantheism, and, indeed, panentheism, are always immune to the problems of unity. Theologians such as Soloviev that tend towards Neoplatonism and its assertion of an ideal unity, warrant this critique.

56 In the mid-1930s Mary Butts began a correspondence with the writer Charles Williams, she was drawn to his Christian Neoplatonism, evident in novels like *The Place of the Lion* (1931), in which the true forms of creatures emerge. The Neoplatonic emphasis on ideal forms over particulars undercuts the material spirituality found elsewhere in Butts.

57 Butts, 'Notebooks'.

58 Ibid. According to legend, Corbenic was the castle that held the Grail. Jessie Weston links the Grail castle (traditionally close to water) to the 'Nature worship' evident in the cult of Adonis: *From Ritual to Romance* 1920 (Princeton, NJ: Princeton University Press, 1993), 50–1.

59 Butts, *Journals*, 437.

60 Blondel, *Mary Butts*, 397, 436.

61 The dispersal and sale of the house and contents caused ill feeling between Butts and her family; she blamed her mother in particular for emotional and financial loss: ibid., 18–20; Foy, *Ritual, Myth, and Mysticism*, 130n.10. See also correspondence between Mary Butts and her brother, which details their shared sadness at the sale of family heirlooms at Sotheby's, although Tony implies that Mary's distress is somewhat excessive: Anthony Butts, 'Letter to Mary Butts' (Beinecke Rare Book and Manuscript Library, Yale University, 1932?).

62 Foy, *Ritual, Myth, and Mysticism*, 15–29; Joel Hawkes, 'Inside *the Crystal Cabinet*: Truth, Lies and Vision in Mary Butts's Autobiography of Place', *Creative Spaces* 1 (2010): 36–41.

63 Butts, *Crystal Cabinet*, 55. Subsequent references given in the text.

64 She also elides much of the dissidence, including counter-cultural socialism, of her younger self.

65 Blondel, *Mary Butts*, 16.

66 For further discussion of the influence of Blake in Mary Butts's writing, see Hawkes, 'Inside *the Crystal Cabinet*', 31–8; Radford, *Mary Butts and British Neo-Romanticism*, 96–100.

67 Heather Walton, *Not Eden: Spiritual Life-Writing for This World* (London: SCM Press, 2015), 12.

68 Her earlier texts, *Ashe of Rings*, the Taverner novels and some of her short stories also engage with the spiritual significance of the Dorset landscape and the struggle over inheritance and home ownership, however, all these texts are oblique, fictionalized accounts.

69 Butts, *Journals*, 390.

70 It should be noted that she had help, her day maid Lucy came in from a nearby village to prepare meals: Blondel, *Mary Butts*, 288.

71 Butts, *Journals*, 444.

72 Ibid., 407.

73 Ibid., 397.

74 Ibid., 388.

75 Daniel Miller, *The Comfort of Things* (London: Polity Press, 2009), 287.

76 Isobel Armstrong, 'Circumventing the Subject-Object Binary', in *Bodies and Things*, ed. Katharina Boehm (Basingstoke: Palgrave Macmillan, 2012), 23.

77 Ibid.

78 Edward B. Tylor, *Primitive Culture: Researches into the Development of Mythology, Philosophy, Religion, Art, and Custom*, vol. 2 (London: John Murray, 1871), 132.

79 Peter Pels, 'The Spirit of Matter: On Fetish, Rarity, Fact, and Fancy', in *Border Fetishisms: Material Objects in Unstable Spaces*, ed. Patricia Spyer (New York: Routledge, 1998), 94. In common parlance, 'to fetishize' is usually used negatively, following Marx and Freud. It is generally used to indicate human agency but objectifying another thing, person, idea (often bringing commerce and sexuality together), giving undue or insincere value in an attempt to assert mastery. This usage elides the ability of fetishes to provoke subjects, to assert their own uncanny agency.

80 William Pietz, 'The Problem of the Fetish, I', *RES: Anthropology and Aesthetics* 9 (1985): 5–6.

81 Pels, 'Spirit of Matter', 97. See also Arjun Appadurai, *The Social Life of Things: Commodities in Cultural Perspective* (Cambridge: Cambridge University Press, 1986), 50–4. Pietz notes that the Portuguese traders were predominantly Catholic and that as the term migrated, we see Dutch, French and English

Protestant capitalists lumping Catholic sacramental objects and African religious objects together as degraded 'fetishes': Pietz, 'The Problem of the Fetish, I', 14.

82   Michael Taussig, 'Crossing the Face', in *Border Fetishisms: Material Objects in Unstable Spaces*, ed. Patricia Spyer (New York: Routledge, 1998), 224–5.

83   Pels, 'Spirit of Matter', 99.

84   In Tylorian terms, animism 'project[s] anthropomorphous attributes onto phenomena in the human environment' while the 'new theoretical use of the term animism takes as its starting point that those other persons are not at all characterized by any human form': Tord Olsson, 'Animate Objects: Ritual Perception and Practice among the Bambara in Mali', in *The Handbook of Contemporary Animism*, ed. Graham Harvey (London: Routledge, 2015), 229.

85   Here Butts avoids the common trope of equating Indigenous cultures with an early developmental stage. For Butts, animism presents a sophisticated level of understanding that is not part of a developmental model.

86   Matthew 5:3-4, New Revised Standard Version.

87   Walter Benjamin, *One-Way Street and Other Writings*, trans. Edmund Jephcott and Kingsley Shorter (London: Verso, 2006), 52–3.

88   Bruno Latour describes such objects thus: 'They trace networks. They are real, quite real, and we humans have not made them. But they are collective because they attach us to one another, because they circulate in our hands and define our social bond by their very circulation. They are discursive, however; they are narrated, historical, passionate, and people with actants of autonomous forms': *We Have Never Been Modern*, trans. Catherine Porter (Cambridge, MA: Harvard University Press, 1993), 89.

89   W. J. T. Mitchell, 'Romanticism and the Life of Things', *Critical Inquiry* 28, no. 1 (2001): 182.

90   This place, too, holds grief and loss, as the home becomes the witness of the painful disintegration of her marriage to Gabriel Atkin, Butts, *Journals*, 438.

3 Darkness and dirt: Virginia Woolf's material mysticism

1   Pericles Lewis, *Religious Experience and the Modernist Novel*, (Cambridge: Cambridge University Press, 2010), 142–69.; Mark Gaipa, 'An Agnostic's Daughter's Apology: Materialism, Spiritualism and Ancestry in Woolf's *to the Lighthouse*', *Journal of Modern Literature* 26, no. 2 (2003): 1–41.

2   For discussion of the influences of such traditions on Woolf's work, see Sheela Banerjee, 'Spectral Poetics in Virginia Woolf's the Waves', in *Modernist Women Writers and Spirituality: A Piercing Darkness*, ed. Elizabeth Anderson, Andrew Radford and Heather Walton (Basingstoke: Palgrave Macmillan, 2016), 153–68;

Julie Kane, 'Varieties of Mystical Experience in the Writings of Virginia Woolf', *Twentieth Century Literature* 41 (1995): 328–49.

3   For a substantial history of Western Christian Mysticism, see Bernard McGinn's four volume history: *The Presence of God: A History of Western Christian Mysticism* (New York: Crossroads, 1992–2006). For a discussion of the development of the understanding of mysticism in the late nineteenth and early twentieth centuries, see Grace Jantzen, *Power, Gender and Christian Mysticism* (Cambridge: Cambridge University Press, 1995), 305–21; Leigh Eric Schmidt, 'The Making of Modern "Mysticism"', *Journal of the American Academy of Religion* 71, no. 2 (2003): 273–302.

4   Jane Marcus, *Virginia Woolf and the Languages of Patriarchy* (Bloomington: Indiana University Press, 1987), 115–35; Val Gough, 'With Some Irony in Her Interrogation: Woolf's Ironic Mysticism', in *Virginia Woolf and the Arts: Selected Papers from the Sixth Annual Conference on Virginia Woolf*, ed. Diane F. Gillespie and Leslie K. Hankins (New York: Pace University Press, 1997), 85–90; Kane, 'Mystical Experience', 328–49; Lewis, *Religious Experience*, 142–69.

5   See, for example Jane Goldman, *The Feminist Aesthetics of Virginia Woolf: Modernism, Post-Impressionism and the Politics of the Visual* (Cambridge: Cambridge University Press, 2001), 23–4, 46, 187–9.

6   Donna Lazenby, *A Mystical Philosophy: Transcendence and Immanence in the Works of Virginia Woolf and Iris Murdoch* (London: Bloomsbury, 2014), 199.

7   For exploration of the liveliness of holy matter in late medieval Europe, see Caroline Walker Bynum, *Christian Materiality: An Essay on Religion in Late Medieval Europe* (New York: Zone Books, 2015), 21–36.

8   Denys Turner, *The Darkness of God: Negativity in Christian Mysticism* (Cambridge: Cambridge University Press, 1995), 19–22.

9   Beverly J. Lanzetta, *The Other Side of Nothingness: Toward a Theology of Radical Openness* (Albany: State University of New York Press, 2001), 70.

10   Amy Hollywood, *The Soul as Virgin Wife: Mechthild of Magdeburg, Marguerite Porete and Meister Eckhart* (Notre Dame, IN: University of Notre Dame Press, 1995), 17–19.

11   John D. Caputo, *The Prayers and Tears of Jacques Derrida: Religion without Religion* (Bloomington: Indiana University Press, 1997), 26–56; Harold Coward, ed., *Derrida and Negative Theology* (Albany: State University of New York, 1992).

12   Catherine Keller, 'The Apophasis of Gender: A Fourfold Unsaying of Feminist Theology', *Journal of the American Academy of Religion* 76, no. 4 (2008): 907.

13   Catherine Keller, *Cloud of the Impossible: Negative Theology and Planetary Entanglement* (New York: Columbia, 2015), 3.

14   Lazenby, *A Mystical Philosophy*, 7.

15   Marianna Torgovnick, *Primitive Passions: Men, Women and the Quest for Ecstasy* (Chicago, IL: University of Chicago Press, 1996), 5.

16 Rachel Blau Duplessis, *Writing beyond the Ending: Narrative Strategies of Twentieth-Century Women Writers* (Bloomington: Indiana University Press, 1985), 164.

17 Virginia Woolf, *Moments of Being* (San Diego, CA: Harcourt, 1985), 72.

18 Lorraine Sim, *Virginia Woolf: The Patterns of Ordinary Experience* (Abingdon: Routledge, 2010), 162.

19 Mayra Rivera, *The Touch of Transcendence: A Postcolonial Theology of God* (London: Westminster John Knox Press, 2007), 2.

20 Rachel Bowlby, *Feminist Destinations and Further Essays on Virginia Woolf* (Edinburgh: Edinburgh University Press, 1997), 100–8.

21 Gough, 'Woolf's Ironic Mysticism', 68–9; Kane, 'Mystical Experience', 333.

22 Virginia Woolf, *To the Lighthouse* (Oxford: Oxford University Press, 2008), 52–3. Subsequent references given in the text.

23 Lazenby, *A Mystical Philosophy*, 72.

24 Here it appears to beat out rhythms for an impersonal subjectivity, but we must remember that the recurring strokes of light were designed to lead sailors to safe passage. As we see so often in Woolf, the social and the metaphysical are layered together.

25 Lazenby, *A Mystical Philosophy*, 113.

26 Ibid., 109. Plotinus is associated with Neoplatonism, which, as I discussed in Chapter Two, has an anti-materialist strain in its affirmation of ideals and quest for transcendence. However, the Plotinian sense of the connectedness of all things and an inspired phenomenal world accords with the liveliness of matter we see in Woolf's work.

27 Davidson, qtd. in ibid., 108. Val Gough notes that Woolf's depiction of Mrs Ramsay is not without irony, as there is an element of self-dramatization but also self-awareness in Mrs Ramsay's reverie. However, as Gough argues, such irony itself participates in an unsaying that is part of Woolf's apophatic discourse: 'Woolf's Ironic Mysticism', 68.

28 Woolf, *Moments of Being*, 133.

29 Lazenby, *A Mystical Philosophy*, 110–8.

30 Here we have a linkage between Mrs Ramsay's domestic craft and Woolf's exploration into women's creativity in the form of Lily Briscoe's painting.

31 For discussion of the history of Kashmiri shawls in the nineteenth century in relation to British imperialism and European fashion, see Nupur Chaudhuri, 'Shawls, Jewelry, Curry, and Rice in Victorian Britain', in *Western Women and Imperialism: Complicity and Resistance*, ed. Nupur Chaudhuri and Margaret Strobel (Bloomington: Indiana University Press, 1992), 234–6; Michelle Maskiell, 'Consuming Kashmir: Shawls and Empires, 1500–2000', *Journal of World History* 13, no. 1 (2002): 35–43.

32 Caroline Walker Bynum explores a similar set of objects from the Middle Ages that live and die but in death retain a kind of liveliness and agency: relics, the often fragmentary bodily remains of the saints: *Christian Materiality*, 20–2.

33 Alfred Gell notes that a group of interconnected things can be seen as a unit when the relationships between them are stressed and the boundaries between them blurred: *Art and Agency: An Anthropological Theory* (Oxford: Oxford University Press, 1998), 139.

34 Arjun Appadurai, 'The Thing Itself', *Public Culture* 18, no. 1 (2006): 15.

35 Daniel Miller, *The Comfort of Things* (London: Polity Press, 2009), 282–97; Gaston Bachelard, *The Poetics of Space*, trans. Maria Jolas 1958 (Boston, MA: Beacon Press, 1994), xxxvi–xxxviii.

36 See Sophie Bowlby, Susan Gregory and Linda McKie, ' "Doing Home": Patriarchy, Caring, and Space', *Women's Studies International Forum* 20, no. 3 (1997): 343–7; Victor Buchli, 'Households and "Home Cultures"', in *The Oxford Handbook of Material Culture Studies*, ed. Dan Hicks and Mary C. Beaudry (Oxford: Oxford University Press, 2010), 510; Wendy Gan, *Women, Privacy and Modernity in Early Twentieth-Century British Writing* (Basingstoke: Palgrave Macmillan, 2009), 8; Linda McDowell, *Gender, Identity and Place: Understanding Feminist Geographies* (Cambridge: Polity Press, 1999), 75–6; Roberta Rubenstein, *Home Matters: Longing and Belonging, Nostalgia and Mourning in Women's Fiction* (New York: Palgrave, 2001), 2; Anna Snaith, *Virginia Woolf: Public and Private Negotiations* (New York: Palgrave Macmillan, 2003), 8–12. The relationship between domesticity and labour is more complex for poor women and women of colour who often have limited choice about work, both within and outwith the home, and for whom the relationship between public and private space is much more fraught, a point I will explore further in Chapter Four.

37 Virginia Woolf, *The Essays of Virginia Woolf*, vol. VI 1933–1941 & Additional Essays 1906–1924 (London: Hogarth Press, 2011), 481.

38 For critical discussion of domestic space in Woolf's work, see Victoria Rosner, *Modernism and the Architecture of Private Life* (New York: Columbia University Press, 2005), 15–16, 120–6; Wendy Gan, 'Solitude and Community: Virginia Woolf, Spatial Privacy and *a Room of One's Own*', *Literature and History* 18, no. 1 (2009): 69–78; Terri Mullholland, *British Boarding Houses in Interwar Women's Literature: Alternative Domestic Spaces* (London: Routledge, 2017), 151–62.

39 Rosner, *Private Life*, 4.

40 Thomas Foster, *Transformations of Domesticity in Modern Women's Writing: Homelessness at Home* (Basingstoke: Palgrave Macmillan, 2002), 10.

41 Bachelard, *Poetics of Space*, xxxvi–xxxvii.

42 Ibid., 6. Jennifer Reek offers perceptive suggestions for how we might read Bachelard against the grain, finding in his mode of reverie a way of approaching

imagined spaces for those 'dispersed beings' whose experiences of house and home may be unhomely and alienating: Jennifer Reek, *A Poetics of Church: Reading and Writing Sacred Spaces of Poetic Dwelling* (Abingdon: Routledge, 2018), 48–9.

43 For critique of Bachelard's correlation of domestic space with maternity, see Susan Fraiman, *Extreme Domesticity: A View from the Margins* (New York: Columbia University Press, 2017), 34–5; Sharon Haar and Christopher Reed, 'Coming Home: A Postscript on Postmodernism', in *Not at Home: The Suppression of Domesticity in Modern Art and Architecture*, ed. Christopher Reed (London: Thames and Hudson, 1996), 258.

44 Bill Brown, *Other Things* (London: University of Chicago Press, 2015), 5.

45 The house as holding a mysterious inner life finds a parallel in Woolf's short story 'The Haunted House'. The house has a pulse that beats 'softly', 'gladly' and 'wildly': Virginia Woolf, *The Mark on the Wall and Other Short Fiction* (Oxford: Oxford University Press, 2008), 30–1.

46 Bachelard, *Poetics of Space*, 98.

47 Ibid., 136–7.

48 bell hooks, *Wounds of Passion: A Writing Life* (London: Women's Press, 1998), 180–1.

49 'Unhomely' is another translation for 'unheimlich' most often translated as 'uncanny': Hugh Haughton, 'Introduction', in *Sigmund Freud: The Uncanny* (London: Penguin, 2003), xlii.

50 Bachelard, *Poetics of Space*, 66.

51 Bonnie Kime Scott, *In the Hollow of the Wave: Virginia Woolf and the Modernist Uses of Nature* (Charlottesville: University of Virginia Press, 2012), 216.

52 Ibid.

53 Virginia Woolf, *Mrs Dalloway*, The Cambridge Edition of the Works of Virginia Woolf 1925 (Cambridge: Cambridge University Press, 2015), 59.

54 Scott, *In the Hollow of the Wave*, 216–17.

55 Ibid., 202. Tracey Hargreaves describes her as 'an isolated, poetic voice in a text that is otherwise committed to realism': 'I Should Explain He Shares My Bath: Art and Politics in *the Years*', *English* 50, no. 198 (2001): 188.

56 Virginia Woolf, *The Years*. The Cambridge Edition of the Works of Virginia Woolf (Cambridge: Cambridge University Press, 2012), 118. Subsequent references given in the text.

57 Maren Tova Linett, *Modernism, Feminism, and Jewishness* (Cambridge: Cambridge University Press, 2007), 55. Sara's anxiety about entering the world of work is particularly marked in racial terms as her creative freedom is described in terms of whiteness: 'And I said, "Must I join your conspiracy? Stain the hand, the unstained hand," – he could see her hand gleam as she waved it in the half-light of the sitting-room' (307).

58 Ibid., 53. This reading accords with Tracey Hargreaves's analysis of the published novel alongside the manuscript versions in which the Jew in the bath comes to represent both the thwarting of the woman writer and the upholding of creative integrity. But in focusing on Woolf's ambivalence around how to accommodate both the political and the poetic in her writing, Hargreaves mutes the significance of antisemitic discourse in Woolf's text: Hargreaves, 'Art and Politics', 188–97. Both Linett and Hargreaves emphasize how Woolf, among other modernist writers, uses Jewishness as a cultural referent that has everything to do with cultural stereotypes and little to do with actual Jews. For a broader discussion of the way Jews and Jewishness could be 'constructed to represent both sides of a political or social or ideological divide' in nineteenth and twentieth-century English literature, see Bryan Cheyette, *Constructions of 'the Jew' in English Literature and Society: Racial Representations, 1975-1945* 1993 (Cambridge: Cambridge University Press, 1995), 9; Mia Spiro, *Anti-Nazi Modernism: The Challenges of Resistance in 1930s Fiction* (Evanston, IL: Northwestern University Press, 2013), 144–7.

59 I follow Linett's use of antisemitism without an –S: this usage is drawn from social science research that rejects 'Semite' as a racial category: 'Introduction: Modernism's Jews/Jewish Modernism', *MFS: Modern Fiction Studies* 51, no. 2 (2005): 256n1. Linett draws upon a wide range of Woolf's private writings to demonstrate how she 'adapted for her private use a prevalent antisemitic discourse that associated Jews with the sexual, the material, the bodily' in order to express her own discomfort with embodiment and sexuality: *Modernism, Feminism, and Jewishness*, 183. See also Leena Kore Schröder, 'Tales of Abjection and Miscegenation: Virginia Woolf's and Leonard Woolf's "Jewish" Stories', *Twentieth Century Literature* 49, no. 3 (2003): 303. Hargreaves notes Elvira/Sara's distaste of a wider range of bodily experiences, including Rose's lesbianism and Maggie's breastfeeding, in earlier drafts of the novel: 'Art and Politics', 186. For further discussion of antisemitism, Jews and the body, see Mayra Rivera, *Poetics of the Flesh* (Durham, NC: Duke University Press, 2015), 40, 154; Paul R. Mendes-Flohr and Jehuda Reinharz, eds, *The Jew in the Modern World: A Documentary History*, 2nd ed. (Oxford: Oxford University Press, 1995), 340.

60 Foster, *Transformations of Domesticity*, 106.

61 Ibid. Foster suggests that the 'Jew in the bath' passage 'deliberately thematises the virulently anti-Semitic attitudes of the time' and that Sara struggles to work through these attitudes: Ibid., 111–12. Yet I fail to see the textual evidence that Sara engages in self-critique, and Foster doesn't fully explore Woolf's failure to make space for the subjectivity of the other in this passage. As Phyllis Lassner argues, it is difficult to read Woolf's positioning as an outsider when she provides no 'positive identification with that other outsider, the Jew' and no 'narrative distance' from

the negative connotations of his depiction in Sara and North's dialogue: Phyllis Lassner, '"The Milk of Our Mother's Kindness Has Ceased to Flow": Virginia Woolf, Stevie Smith, and the Representation of the Jew', in *Between 'Race' and Culture: Representations of 'the Jew' in English and American Literature*, ed. Bryan Cheyette (Stanford, CA: Stanford University Press, 1996), 135.

62 Mullholland, *British Boarding Houses*, 156.

63 Ibid., 160–1.

64 Mullholland, *British Boarding Houses*, 161. Linett argues that *The Years* doesn't clearly demonstrate that Woolf (or Sara) sees the connection between public and private modes of antisemitism: 'The chalked symbols do show Woolf's awareness of the danger Jews faced from the BUF in the East End where Sara lives; but they do not mean she understood her complicity or Sara's in the antisemitism of fascism': *Modernism, Feminism, and Jewishness*, 54. For further discussion of the relation between antisemitism and anti-fascism in Woolf's work, see Spiro, *Anti-Nazi Modernism*, 14–16; 42–58; 174–86. David Bradshaw reads this passage in concert with the fascist graffiti that North passes on his way to Sara's boarding house. He argues for a disruption between inside and outside that yokes the public threat of the British Union of Fascists with Sara's private antisemitic tirade. He goes on to suggest that the multiple invocations of blue and white (colours associated with Judaism through the tallit, the traditional prayer shawl, and the Zionist flag) mark Woolf's insistence on the place of Jews in English life, in sharp distinction to the antisemitism of both Mosley's fascists and the more genteel Pargiters: 'Hyam's Place: *The Years*, the Jews and the British Union of Fascists', in *Women Writers of the 1930s: Gender, Politics, and History*, ed. Maroula Joannou (Edinburgh: Edinburgh University Press, 1999), 179–91. While the place of blue and white objects in Bradshaw's argument is compelling for a project centred on things, I still find it too subtle a critique of grotesquely offensive language that reinforces common stereotypes.

65 Woolf, *The Years*, 306.

66 Mary Douglas, *Purity and Danger* 1966 (London: Routledge, 2006), 44.

67 Daniel Boyarin, *Unheroic Conduct: The Rise of Heterosexuality and the Invention of the Jewish Man* (Berkeley, LA: University of California Press, 1997), 3–4.

68 Ibid., 2.

69 Ibid., 11.

70 Ibid., 239–40.

71 Daniel Boyarin, *Sparks of the Logos: Essays in Rabbinic Hermeneutics* (Leiden: Brill, 2003), 43. See also Elliot R. Wolfson, 'Circumcision and the Divine Name: A Study in the Transmission of Esoteric Doctrine', *Jewish Quarterly Review* 78, no. 1–2 (1987): 78–85.

72 Rivera, *Poetics of the Flesh*, 2.

73 bell hooks, *Belonging: A Culture of Place* (New York: Routledge, 2009), 40. See also Karen Baker-Fletcher, *Sisters of Dust, Sisters of Spirit* (Minneapolis, MN: Fortress Press, 1998), 16–20.

4 Radiant dandelions: Gwendolyn Brooks's domestic sublime

1 Steven Tracy, 'Introduction', in *Writers of the Black Chicago Renaissance*, ed. Steven Tracy (Chicago: University of Illinois Press, 2011), 2. The Chicago Renaissance occurred between the mid-1930s and early 1950s: Yomna Mohamed Saber, *Brave to Be Involved: Shifting Positions in the Poetry of Gwendolyn Brooks* (Oxford: Peter Lang, 2010), 16.

2 Tracy, 'Introduction', 2.

3 James Smethurst, *The African American Roots of Modernism: From Reconstruction to the Harlem Renaissance* (Chapel Hill: University of North Carolina Press, 2011), 145–6.

4 Gary Smith, 'Paradise Regained: The Children of Gwedolyn Brooks's Bronzeville', in *A Life Distilled: Gwendolyn Brooks, Her Poetry and Fiction*, ed. Maria K. Mootry and Gary Smith (Chicago: University of Illinois Press, 1987), 129.

5 Steven Caldwell Wright, 'Gwendolyn Brooks', in *Writers of the Black Chicago Renaissance*, ed. Steven Tracy (Chicago: University of Illinois Press, 2011), 99.

6 Ibid., 97.

7 Smith, 'Paradise Regained', 129. See also, Maria K. Mootry, ' "Tell It Slant": Disguise and Discovery as Revisionist Poetic Discourse in *the Bean Eaters*', in *A Life Distilled: Gwendolyn Brooks, Her Poetry and Fiction*, ed. Maria K. Mootry and Gary Smith (Chicago: University of Illinois Press, 1987), ibid., 178.

8 For discussion of the influence of the Harlem Renaissance on modernism more broadly, see Houston A. Baker, Jr, *Modernism and the Harlem Renaissance* (Chicago, IL: Chicago University Press, 1987); Jeremy Braddock, 'Race: Tradition and Archive in the Harlem Renaissance', in *A Handbook of Modernism Studies*, ed. Jean-Michel Rabaté (Hoboken, NJ: John Wiley, 2013), 87–106; Hyest, 'Anne Spencer's Feminist Modernist Poetics', *Journal of Modern Literature* 38, no. 3 (2015):131; Smethurst, *Roots of Modernism*, 2–3 ff.

9 Gertrude Reif Hughes, 'Making It Really New: Hilda Doolittle, Gwendolyn Brooks, and the Feminist Potential of Modern Poetry', *American Quarterly* 42, no. 3 (1990): 376–9.

10 Barbara Christian, 'Nuance and the Novella: A Study of Gwendolyn Brooks's *Maud Martha*', in *A Life Distilled: Gwendolyn Brooks, Her Poetry and Fiction*, ed. Maria K. Mootry and Gary Smith (Urbana: University of Illinois Press, 1987), 239–53;

A. Yemisi Jimoh, 'Double Consciousness, Modernism, and Womanist Themes in Gwendolyn Brooks's "the Anniad"', *MELUS* 23, no. 3 (1998): 167–86; Patricia H. Lattin and Vernon E. Lattin, 'Dual Vision in Gwendolyn Brooks's *Maud Martha*', *Critique* 25, no. 4 (1984): 180–8; Mootry, 'Tell It Slant', 167–92; Mary Helen Washington, '"Taming All That Anger Down" Rage and Silence in Gwendolyn Brooks' *Maud Martha*', *Massachusetts Review* 24, no. 2 (1983): 453–66.

11 Hortense J. Spillers, '"An Order of Constance"': Notes on Brooks and the Feminine', in *Reading Black, Reading Feminist*, ed. Jr Henry Louis Gates (New York: Penguin, 1999), 254.

12 Henry Louis Gates, Jr analyses the importance of Black self-representation in writing for undermining the construction of enslaved persons as objects or commodities: *Signifying Monkey: A Theory of African-American Literary Criticism* [1988] (OUP: Oxford University Press, 2014), 140–1. For analysis of the way racism continues the commodification and objectification of Black bodies beyond abolition, see Toni Morrison, *Mouth Full of Blood: Essays, Speeches, Meditations* (London: Chatto & Windus, 2019), 74–8. For analysis of the representation of Black women as commodities in imperialist discourse, see Urmila Seshagiri, *Race and the Modernist Imagination* (Ithaca: Cornell University Press, 2010), 188.

13 Will Coleman, *Tribal Talk: Black Theology, Hermeneutics, and African/American Ways of "Telling the Story"* (University Park: Pennsylvania State University Press, 2000), 32.

14 Harry Garuba, 'Explorations in Animist Materialism: Notes on Reading/Writing African Literature, Culture, and Society', *Public Culture* 15, no. 2 (2003): 267.

15 Ibid.

16 Coleman, *Tribal Talk*, 27–8. For further discussion of the connection between West African religious traditions and African American Christianity, see Karen Baker-Fletcher, *Sisters of Dust, Sisters of Spirit* (Minneapolis, MN: Fortress Press, 1998), 18, 110–16; Yvonne Patricia Chireau, *Black Magic: Religion and the African-American Conjuring Tradition* (Berkeley: University of California Press, 2003), 25–8, 54; Theophus H. Smith, *Conjuring Culture: Biblical Formations of Black America* (New York: Oxford University Press, 1994), 36–45 ff.

17 Critics have also explored Christian forms in Brooks's work. Gayle Jones notes that Brooks deploys biblical imagery and Black Christian rhetorical devices in her poetry, including the spiritual, the sermon and the proverb: Gayle Jones, 'Community and Voice: Gwendolyn Brooks's "in the Mecca"', in *A Life Distilled: Gwendolyn Brooks, Her Poetry and Fiction*, ed. Maria K. Mootry and Gary Smith (Urbana: University of Illinois Press, 1987), 196.

18 James Haskins, qtd. in Coleman, *Tribal Talk*, 34.

19 Dwight N. Hopkins, *Down, Up, and Over: Slave Religion and Black Theology* (Minneapolis, MN: Fortress Press, 2000), 111.

20 Coleman, *Tribal Talk*, 4.

21 Ibid., 31.

22 Ibid. We can see here a correlation with the animist, Hermetic worldviews underpinning the writing of Mary Butts and H.D. Hermeticism traversed the Mediterranean region to impact on the development of occult movements in Europe. See Introduction, note 49 for a definition of Hermeticism.

23 Houston A. Baker, *Workings of the Spirit: The Poetics of Afro-American Women's Writing* (Chicago, IL: University of Chicago Press, 1991), 39.

24 Hopkins, *Down, Up, and Over*, 115.

25 Baker, *Workings of the Spirit*, 66. For further discussion of traditional African religions as a framework for reading a spirituality of interconnection in African American women's writing, see Anne Dalke, 'Spirit Matters: Re-Possessing the African-American Women's Literary Tradition', *Legacy: A Journal of American Women Writers* 12, no. 1 (1995): 3, Judylyn Ryan, *Spirituality as Ideology in Black Women's Film and Literature* (Charlottesville: University of Virginia Press, 2005), 2–3; Elizabeth J. West, *African Spirituality in Black Women's Fiction: Threaded Visions of Memory, Community, Nature, and Being* 2011 (Plymouth: Lexington Books, 2013), 11.

26 Chireau, *Black Magic*, 3–4, 12.

27 Garuba, 'Animist Materialism', 265. Garuba's emphasis.

28 Wright, 'Gwendolyn Brooks', 103.

29 Washington, 'Rage and Silence', 453.

30 Gwendolyn Brooks, *Maud Martha* 1953 (Chicago, IL: Third World Press, 1993), 1. Subsequent references given in the text.

31 Hopkins, *Down, Up, and Over*, 116.

32 Zora Neale Hurston, *Their Eyes Were Watching God* 1937 (London: Virago Press, 2018), 13–14; Nella Larsen, *Quicksand and Passing* 1928–29 (New Brunswick, NJ: Rutgers University Press, 1998), 59; Toni Morrison, *Beloved* 1987 (New York: Alfred A. Knopf, 2006), 105.

33 West, *African Spirituality in Black Women's Fiction*, 161.

34 Ibid. West draws on the work of Michael A. Gomez: *Exchanging Our Country Marks: The Transformation of African Idenitites in the Colonial Antebellum South* (Chapel Hill: University of North Carolina Press, 1998), 112.

35 Ibid.

36 Larry R. Andrews, 'The Aliveness of Things: Nature in *Maud Martha*', in *Gwendolyn Brooks' Maud Martha*, ed. Jacqueline Bryant (Chicago, IL: Third World Press, 2002), 69.

37 In the story, Brooks makes brief reference to the Great Migration and white flight.

38 Alice Walker, *In Search of Our Mother's Gardens: Womanist Prose* 1967 (New York: Harcourt Brace Jovanovich, 1983), 241.

39   Baker, *Workings of the Spirit*, 52.

40   Ibid., 66.

41   Gwendolyn Brooks, "Gladys the Gladiolus"(Bancroft Library, Gwendolyn Brooks Papers, n.d.).

42   Ibid.

43   Rivera draws upon the work of Gayatri Chakravorty Spivak here: Mayra Rivera, *The Touch of Transcendence: A Postcolonial Theology of God* (London: Westminster John Knox Press, 2007), 105.

44   Tamra Wright, Peter Hughes and Alison Ainley, 'The Paradox of Morality: An Interview with Emannuel Levinas', in *The Provocation of Levinas: Rethinking the Other*, ed. Robert Bernasconi and David Woods (London: Routledge, 1988), 169.

45   Susan Fraiman, *Extreme Domesticity: A View from the Margins* (New York: Columbia University Press, 2017), 25.

46   Ibid., 123.

47   Thomas Foster, *Transformations of Domesticity in Modern Women's Writing: Homelessness at Home* (Basingstoke: Palgrave Macmillan, 2002), 147.

48   Henry Louis Gates, *Signifying Monkey: A Theory of African-American Literary Criticism*, 1988 (Oxford: Oxford University Press, 2014), 196.

49   Foster, *Transformations of Domesticity*, 148.

50   Thadious M. Davis, *Southscapes: Geographies of Race, Region, and Literature*, (Chapel Hill: University of North Carolina Press, 2011), Chapter Two: Poverty and Porches; Susan Stanford Friedman, *Mappings: Feminism and the Cultural Geographies of Encounter* (Princeton, NJ: Princeton University Press, 1998), 128–29.

51   bell hooks, *Yearning: Race, Gender, and Cultural Politics* (Boston: South End Press, 1990), 41–2.

52   Ibid., 42.

53   Ibid., 103.

54   Ajuan Maria Mance makes a similar point about domestic activities being a form of skilled labour that must be learned and practiced in her analysis of nineteenth-century African American women's writing: *Inventing Black Women: African American Women Poets and Self-Representation, 1877–2000* (Knoxville: University of Tennessee Press, 2007), 28.

55   hooks, *Yearning*, 104.

56   Ibid.

57   Tracy Floreani, *Fifties Ethnicities: The Ethnic Novel and Mass Culture at Midcentury* (New York: State University of New York Press, 2013), 61. See also Bill V. Mullen, *Popular Fronts: Chicago and African-American Cultural Politics, 1935–56* (Urbana: University of Illinois Press, 1999), 149.

58   Floreani, *Fifties Ethnicities*, 62–64.

59 Ibid., 55.

60 Margo Natalie Crawford, ' "Perhaps Buddha Is a Woman": Women's Poetry in the Harlem Renaissance', in *The Cambridge Companion to the Harlem Renaissance*, ed. George Hutchinson (Cambridge: Cambridge University Press, 2007), 127–8.

61 Brooks, "Gladys."

62 Nora Blakely Brooks, 'Of Mama and Maud: A Forward', in *Gwendolyn Brooks' Maud Martha: A Critical Collection*, ed. Jacqueline Bryant (Chicago, IL: Third World Press, 1993), x-xi.

63 Tracy Floreani discusses how travel as consumption can work to 'reinforce the constructed boundaries of 'whiteness''' as an imperial gesture: *Fifties Ethnicities*, 56.

64 Ibid., 65.

65 GerShun Avilez, 'Housing the Black Body: Value, Domestic Space, and Segregation Narratives', *African American Review* 42, no. 1 (2008): 135.

66 Ibid., 136.

67 Kathleen Stewart, 'Afterword: Worlding Refrains', in *The Affect Theory Reader*, ed. Melissa Gregg and Gregory J. Seigworth (Durham: Duke University Press, 2010), 342.

68 Ibid., 353.

69 Fraiman, *Extreme Domesticity*, 14.

70 Catherine Bell, *Ritual Theory, Ritual Practice* 2002 (Oxford: Oxford University Press, 2009), 197–204.

71 Jonathan Z. Smith qtd. in ibid., xiv.

72 Ibid., 208.

73 Not all threats to the beloved family home come from oppressive housing policy and restricted access to financing. The flourishing of the homespace is also threatened by more subliminal racism. In anticipating a visit from a white classmate, the teenage Maud Martha's view of her home alters: 'Three or four straight chairs that had long ago given up the ghost of whatever shallow dignity they may have had in the beginning and looked completely disgusted with themselves and with the Brown family' (16). Maud Martha resents the way in which her perceptions and emotions are altered by unequal status: 'What was she feeling now? Not fear, not fear. A sort of gratitude! It sickened her to realize it. As though Charles, in coming, gave her a gift' (18). We are left with Maud Martha's disgust at her own internalized oppression that would rate Charles as a benefactor. Despite the pernicious encroachment of white supremacy, Maud Martha's perceptions, emotions and judgement are centred here. We see both Maud Martha's unwilling investment in racial hierarchy and her resistance to this investment. The disgust that Maud Martha feels forms between her and the chairs in her home and as the disgust circulates, she can recognize and resist the effects of this emotion.

74   In a different essay, 'Again – Segregation Must End', hooks discusses issues of
     housing, ownership, segregation and anti-racism: *Belonging*, 69–88. For analysis
     of racist and classist in post-war housing policy in Chicago, see Preston H. Smith,
     Racial Democracy and the Black Metropolis: Housing Policy in Postwar Chicago
     (Minneapolis: University of Minnesota Press, 2012).

75   This passage is part of Brooks's sustained critique of colourism throughout the
     novel. Helen is consistently preferred over Maud Martha because she is seen to
     be more beautiful, in part because of her lighter skin. Colourism hurts Maud
     Martha within her childhood home, in her interactions with her peers and later her
     marriage.

76   Jacqueline Bryant, 'Home', in *Gwendolyn Brooks' Maud Martha: A Critical
     Collection*, ed. Jacqueline Bryant (Chicago, IL: Third World Press, 2002), 8.

77   Sara Ahmed, *Queer Phenomenology: Orientations, Objects, Others* (Durham: Duke
     University Press, 2006), 164. Ahmed's discussion is in context of developing a queer
     phenomenology. Brooks's work privileges heterosexuality, although she does expose
     its failures.

78   Ibid. This pledge of return is reminiscent of the social bonds nurtured by the gift
     economy explored in Chapter One.

79   Mary Douglas qtd. in Joe Moran, 'Houses, Habit and Memory', in *Our House: The
     Representation of Domestic Space in Modern Culture*, ed. Gerry Smyth and Jo Croft
     (Amsterdam: Rodopi, 2006), 41.

80   It is notable that Maud Martha's most difficult encounters around domestic spaces
     and things are with white women. Here Brooks emphasizes the failure of white
     women to recognize female solidarity across racial lines.

81   Heather Walton, *Literature, Theology and Feminism* (Manchester, NH: Manchester
     University Press, 2007), 180.

82   Ibid.

83   Rivera, *Touch of Transcendence*, 2.

84   Walton, *Literature, Theology and Feminism*, 183.

85   Spillers, '"An Order of Constance": Notes on Brooks and the Feminine', 263–4.

86   Sara Ahmed, *The Cultural Politics of Emotion*, 2nd ed. 2004 (Edinburgh: Edinburgh
     University Press, 2014), 179.

87   Ibid., 180.

88   Ibid.

89   Jane Bennett, *The Enchantment of Modern Life: Attachments, Crossings, and Ethics*
     (Princeton, NJ: Princeton University Press, 2001), 5.

90   Kimberlé Crenshaw coined the term 'intersectionality' to address how multiple
     oppressions are compounded, with specific reference to the subordination of Black
     women: 'Demarginalizing the Intersection of Race and Sex: A Black Feminist

Critique of Antidiscrimination Doctrine, Feminist Theory and Antiracist Politics',
University of Chicago Legal Forum (1989): 140.

91 Baker, *Workings of the Spirit*, 104.

92 Gwendolyn Brooks, *Blacks* (Chicago, IL: Third World Press, 1994), 20.

93 Ibid.

94 Ibid., 28.

95 Ibid.

96 For further discussion of the challenges for young Black women negotiating public
urban space in which they are simultaneously erased and scrutinized, see Aimee
Cox, 'The Body and City Project: Young Black Women Making Space, Community,
and Love in Newark, New Jersey', *Feminist Formations* 26, no. 3 (2014): 5; Feminista
Jones, *Reclaiming Our Space: How Black Feminists Are Changing the World from the
Tweets to the Streets* (Boston, MA: Beacon Press, 2019), 23–4.

5 Things in the city

1 These stories both appeared in the posthumous volume, *Last Stories*, published in
1938 by Bryher's publishing house, Brendin Publishing: Mary Butts, *The Complete
Stories* (Kingston, NY: McPherson, 2014), 15.

2 Kathryn Simpson, ' "Street Haunting," Commodity Culture, and the Woman
Artist', in *Woolf and the City*, ed. Elizabeth F. Evans and Sarah E. Cornish
(Liverpool: Liverpool University Press, 2010), 47.

3 Deborah L. Parsons, *Streetwalking the Metropolis: Women, the City and Modernity*
(Oxford: Oxford University Press, 2000), 1.

4 Leonie Sandercock, *Cosmopolis II: Mongrel Cities of the 21st Century*
(New York: Continuum, 2003), 221.

5 Shiach explores Pound's connections with established writers like Ford Madox
Ford and W. B. Yeats, largely established in private rooms: 'Modernism, the City
and the "Domestic Interior" ', *Home Cultures* 2, no. 3 (2005): 262–5. To Pound's
networking we could add the Hogarth Press, operated out of Leonard and Virginia
Woolf's home.

6 Barbara Hooper critiques Haussmann and other urban reformers of the nineteenth
and early twentieth centuries for developing a model of urban planning that
frames the unruly aspects of city life in terms of female body: qtd. in Sandercock,
Cosmopolis II, 30–31.

7 See, for example, Rita Felski, *The Gender of Modernity* (Cambridge, MA: Harvard
University Press, 1995), 61–90; Krista Lysack, *Come Buy, Come Buy: Shopping and
the Culture of Consumption in Victorian Women's Writing* (Athens: Ohio University
Press, 2008).

8   Walter Benjamin's writings popularized the image of the Parisian arcades as the space of urban wandering par excellence. For analysis of the arcades in Benjamin's work, see Susan Buck-Morss, 'The Flâneur, the Sandwichman and the Whore: The Politics of Loitering', in *Walter Benjamin and the Arcades Project*, ed. Beatrice Hanssen (London: Bloomsbury, 2006), 33–65.

9   Sam Wiseman, 'Cosmopolitanism and Environmental Ethics in Mary Butts's *Dorset*', *Twentieth Century Literature* 61, no. 3 (2015): 376.

10 Ibid., 278.

11 Butts, *The Complete Stories*, 279. Subsequent references will be given in the text.

12 In her late poetry, H.D. also reads Paris in occult terms and as allied with Isis: H.D., *Hermetic Definition* (Oxford: Carcanet Press, 1972), 5–8; Matte Robinson, *The Astral H.D.: Occult and Religious Sources and Contexts for H.D.'s Poetry and Prose* (London: Bloomsbury, 2016), 87.

13 'From Altar to Chimney-Piece' was written a couple of years before *The Crystal Cabinet* and 'Mappa Mundi' soon after; all three texts are products of Butts's Cornwall years.

14 For further discussion on the spirit of a place in relation to literary geography, see Robert T. Tally, *Spatiality* (London: Routledge, 2013), 78–81.

15 Rochelle Rives, 'Problem Space: Mary Butts, Modernism, and the Etiquette of Placement', *Modernism/modernity* 12, no. 4 (2005): 622.

16 Ibid., 623–4.

17 Ibid., 619.

18 Mary Butts, *Armed with Madness*, 1928 (London: Penguin, 2001), 114.

19 See Rachel Bowlby, *Feminist Destinations and Further Essays on Virginia Woolf*, (Edinburgh: Edinburgh University Press, 1997); Elizabeth F. Evans and Sarah E Cornish, eds, *Woolf and the City* (Liverpool: Liverpool University Press, 2010); Lisbeth Larsson, *Walking Virginia Woolf's London* (Cham, Switzerland: Palgrave Macmillan, 2017); Shiach, 'Modernism, the City and the "Domestic Interior"; Andrew Thacker, *Moving through Modernity: Space and Geography in Modernism*, 2003 (Manchester: Manchester University Press, 2009).

20 Jessica Berman, *Modernist Fiction, Cosmopolitanism, and the Politics of Community* (Cambridge: Cambridge University Press, 2001), 47; Kathryn Simpson, ' "Street Haunting", Commodity Culture, and the Woman Artist', in *Woolf and the City*, ed. Elizabeth F. Evans and Sarah E. Cornish (Liverpool: Liverpool University Press, 2010), 47.

21 Both 'Street Haunting' and *Mrs Dalloway* are frequently discussed in terms of *flânerie* in analyses of urban experience: Bowlby, *Feminist Destinations*, 204–19; Parsons, *Streetwalking*, 200. The *flâneur* is a figure popularized by Walter Benjamin in his writing on the nineteenth-century French poet Charles Baudelaire. For Benjamin, the *flâneur* wanders the city, observing the spectacle and display and

eventually transforming his [he is also white, and of sufficient leisure to spend time in such wandering] observations into art. Feminist scholars have debated to what extent women can participate in *flânerie*. Parsons summarizes the argument neatly, pointing out that critics such as Janet Wolff and Griselda Pollock argue that a *flâneuse*, or female *flâneur*, is impossible because women do not have the same freedom to walk and gaze in urban space, while others such as Rachel Bowlby and Judith Walkowitz detail women's presence and mobility in the modern city. Parsons points out that 'the concept of the *flâneur* itself contains gender ambiguities that suggest the figure to be a site for the contestation of male authority rather than the epitome of it': ibid., 4–7.

22 Kathryn Simpson, *Gifts, Markets and Economies of Desire in Virginia Woolf* (Basingstoke: Palgrave Macmillan, 2008), 27.

23 For Derrida, any hint of obligation of return is a demand that renders the gift void (even acknowledging the gift indicates gratitude that is a return and, therefore, the gift as such is impossible) while for Mauss, gift exchange is preliminary to capitalism as the gift stands in for something else (exchange of commodities and power). However, I would argue that the social bonds created by the gift economy (or even gestures towards it) are not rooted in closure but rather a generativity that opens out: a spiral, rather than a circle and hence evades the notion of return that so troubles Derrida: Jacques Derrida, *Given Time: 1, Counterfeit Money*, trans. Peggy Kamuf 1991 (Chicago, IL: Chicago University Press, 1992), 12; Marcel Mauss, *The Gift; Forms and Functions of Exchange in Archaic Societies*, trans. Ian Cunnison (London: Cohen & West, 1954), 45.

24 Rebecca Colesworthy, *Returning the Gift: Modernism and the Thought of Exchange* (Oxford: Oxford University Press, 2018), 16.

25 Virginia Woolf, 'Street Haunting', in *The Crowded Dance of Modern Life: Selected Essays: Volume Two*, ed. Rachel Bowlby (London: Penguin, 1993). Subsequent references given in the text.

26 Walter Benjamin, *One-Way Street and Other Writings*, trans. Edmund Jephcott and Kingsley Shorter (London: Verso, 2006), 55. See discussion of the gift in Chapter One.

27 Robin Wall Kimmerer, *Braiding Sweetgrass* (Minneapolis, MN: Milkweed Editions, 2013), 22–32. In a later chapter Kimmerer distinguishes between gifts of the natural world that carry vibrancy, and manufactured products that contribute to deadening rampant consumption: 197–99.

28 Adalaide Morris, *How to Live/What to Do: H.D.'s Cultural Poetics* (Chicago: University of Illinois Press, 2003), 130.

29 Susan Buck-Morss, *The Dialectics of Seeing: Walter Benjamin and the Arcades Project* (London: MIT Press, 1999), 230.

30 Ibid., 235.

31 Benjamin qtd. in Mick Smith, 'Lost for Words? Gadamer and Benjamin on the Nature of Language and the 'Language' of Nature', *Environmental Values* 10 (2001): 63.

32 Ibid., 64.

33 Shiach, 'Modernism, the City and the "Domestic Interior"', 255.

34 For further discussions of issues of stereotyping and marginalized figures in 'Street Haunting', see Phyllis Lassner and Mia Spiro, 'A Tale of Two Cities: Virginia Woolf's Imagined Jewish Spaces and London's East End Jewish Culture', *Woolf Studies Annual* 19 (2013): 59–60.

35 Simpson, 'Street Haunting', 50–1.

36 Ibid., 52.

37 Bowlby, *Feminist Destinations*, 258–9.

38 Berman, *Modernist Fiction*, 122–3.

39 Pheng Cheah, 'Introduction Part II: The Cosmoplitical-Today', in *Cosmopolitics: Thinking and Feeling Beyond the Nation*, ed. Bruce Robbins and Pheng Cheah (Minneapolis: University of Minnesota Press, 1998), 21. See also: Christine W. Sizemore, 'Cosmopolitanism from Below in *Mrs. Dalloway* and "Street Haunting"', ed. Sarah E. Cornish and Elizabeth F. Evans, *Woolf and the City* (Liverpool: Liverpool University Press, 2016). 107.

40 Bowlby, *Feminist Destinations*, 259.

41 Woolf also suggests interpenetration of natural and built environment in her contemplation of urban intersubjectivity: 'Those footpaths that lead beneath brambles and thick tree trunks into the heart of the forest where live those wild beasts, our fellow men': Virginia Woolf, 'Street Haunting', in *The Crowded Dance of Modern Life: Selected Essays: Volume Two*, ed. Rachel Bowlby (London: Penguin, 1993), 81.

42 H.D. qtd. in Debo, 'Introduction', 21. Debo's introduction provides a detailed biographical analysis of H.D.'s experience in London during the war.

43 H.D., *Within the Walls and What Do I Love* (Gainesville: University Press of Florida, 2014), 116. Subsequent references given in the text.

44 This image is echoed in *The Sword Went Out to Sea* where H.D. indicates that the bombs turn an ordinary street into the transitory world of theatre 'the debris … sometimes left a half-house open, like a … stage-set': *The Sword Went out to Sea: (Synthesis of a Dream), by Delia Alton* (Gainesville: University Press of Florida, 2007), 67.

45 This connection of snow to dream-space indicates the significance of the image in H.D.'s poetry of the period. Snow appears in a poem H.D. performed for a gala organized by the Sitwells in 1943 in which the figure of Ancient Wisdom stands as witness 'the snow on her blue hood: / winter and summer, /… never forgetting/ but remembering/ our peculiar desolation'. Snow is also important to *The Flowering of*

the Rod, where H.D. declares it linked to love: 'I go where I love and where I am loved, / into the snow': H.D., *Collected Poems: 1912–1944* (New York, 1983), 483–4; *Trilogy*, 115.

46 Lara Vetter argues that H.D. takes a more pessimistic view in *Sword*, which Vetter reads as insisting on the inescapability of historical repetition: *A Curious Peril: H.D.'s Late Modernist Prose* (Gainesville: University Press of Florida, 2017), 80–82.

47 H.D., "Letter to Viola Jordan, April 28, 1942" (Viola Baxter Jordan Papers, Yale Collection of American Literature, Beinecke Rare Book and Manuscript Library, 1942).

48 H.D., *Trilogy*, 21.

49 Madelyn Detloff, *The Persistence of Modernism: Loss and Mourning in the Twentieth Century* (Cambridge: Cambridge University Press, 2010), 80.

50 Ibid., 84.

51 Ibid., 85.

52 Ibid., 87.

53 I have argued elsewhere that *Trilogy* and *Four Quartets* are very different in their investments, despite the similarities between the texts. *Trilogy* embraces a material mysticism while *Four Quartets* aims for other-worldly transcendence: Elizabeth Anderson, 'Burnt and Blossoming: Material Mysticism in *Trilogy* and *Four Quartets*', *Christianity and Literature* 62, no. 1 (2012): 121–42.

54 For further discussion of the way apocalyptic narratives are mapped onto imperial conquest and resistance to such discourse, see Rita Nakashima Brock and Rebecca Ann Parker, *Saving Paradise: How Christianity Traded Love of This World for Crucifixion and Empire* (Boston, MA: Beacon Press, 2008), 272–73, 322; Catherine Keller, *Apocalypse Now and Then: A Feminist Guide to the End of the World*, 1996 (Minneapolis, MN: Fortress Press, 2005), 140–80.

55 Catherine Keller, *God and Power: Counter-Apocalyptic Journeys* (Minneapolis, MN: Fortress Press, 2005), 4.

56 Ibid., xi.

57 Ibid., x.

58 Ibid., 127.

59 H.D., *Trilogy*, 4. For a reading of bodies in *Trilogy* as sites of abjection, survival and desire, see Cassandra Laity, *H.D. And the Victorian Fin De Siècle: Gender, Modernism, Decadence* (Cambridge: Cambridge University Press, 1996), 170–83.

60 Susan Edmonds, *Out of Line: History, Psychoanalysis, & Montage in H.D.'s Long Poems* (Stanford, CA: Stanford University Press, 1994), 65.

61 H.D., *Trilogy*, 89.

62 Ibid., 83.

63   Detloff argues that in ending with a nativity scene, *Trilogy* encodes a 'Christian telos … [which] suggests a traditional conclusion to the redemptive trajectory of the poem'. However, she also notes the woman-identified ending: the bundle of myrrh appearing with Mary signifies the recuperation of the daughter (earlier in the poem myrrh is identified with Mary Magdalene and Mary of Bethany): *Persistence of Modernism*, 104.

64   For further discussion of H.D.'s biblical revision, see Alicia Ostriker, *Writing Like a Woman* (Ann Arbor: University of Michigan Press, 1983), 32–7.

65   Daniela Kukrechtová, 'The Death and Life of a Chicago Edifice: Gwendolyn Brooks's "in the Mecca"', *African American Review* 43, no. 2–3 (2009): 458; John Lowney, *History, Memory, and the Literary Left: Modern American Poetry, 1935–1968* (Iowa City: University of Iowa Press, 2006), 128–9; Kirsten Bartholomew Ortega, 'The Black Flaneuse: Gwendolyn Brooks's "in the Mecca"', *Journal of Modern Literature* 30, no. 4 (2007): 143.

66   Lowney, *History, Memory, and the Literary Left*, 138–9. See also Kukrechtová, 'Chicago Edifice', 457–59.

67   Gwendolyn Brooks, *Report from Part One* (Detroit, MI: Broadside Press, 1972), 162.

68   See Gayle Jones, 'Community and Voice: Gwendolyn Brooks's "in the Mecca"', in *A Life Distilled: Gwendolyn Brooks, Her Poetry and Fiction*, ed. Maria K. Mootry and Gary Smith (Urbana: University of Illinois Press, 1987), 194; Lowney, *History, Memory, and the Literary Left*, 129; Courtney Thorsson, 'Gwendolyn Brooks's Black Aesthetic of the Domestic', *MELUS* 40, no. 1 (2015): 151. Elizabeth Alexander comments on the fractured community in 'In the Mecca' but argues that the 'choral voice' emerges in the later poems in the volume: Elizabeth Alexander, *The Black Interior* (Saint Paul, MN: Graywolf Press, 2004), 54.

69   Gwendolyn Brooks, *Blacks* (Chicago, IL: Third World Press), 433. Subsequent references given in the text.

70   Alexander, *Black Interior*, 47.

71   Ortega also notes the crucial aspect of flanerie performed by the speaker: 'She makes the city legible through poetic response': Ortega, 'Black Flaneuse', 146. Critics have also noted how the poetic form of 'In the Mecca' recapitulates the space itself: 'The lack of aeration – the poem is not sectioned – emphasizes the claustrophobia of the world Brooks portrays': Alexander, *Black Interior*, 49.

72   Kukrechtová, 'Chicago Edifice', 458–9.

73   Lowney, *History, Memory, and the Literary Left*, 143.

74   Betsy Erkkila, *Wicked Sisters: Women Poets, Literary History, and Discord* (Oxford: Oxford University Press, 1992), 196–7.

75   Thorsson, 'Black Aesthetic', 164.

76   Kukrechtová, 'Chicago Edifice', 467.

77 Ibid.

78 Ibid., 469.

79 Ibid.

80 Sheila Hassell Hughes, 'A Prophet Overheard: A Juxtapositional Reading of Gwendolyn Brooks's "in the Mecca"', *African American Review* 38, no. 2 (2004): 274–5.

81 Ortega, 'Black Flaneuse', 146.

82 John Bartlow Martin qtd. in Brooks, *Blacks*, 404.

83 This is the same glow we saw in Maud Martha's glossy magazines and Little Mama's treasured home.

84 Thorsson, 'Black Aesthetic', 163.

85 Jones, 'Community and Voice: Gwendolyn Brooks's "in the Mecca"', 198.

86 Mrs. Sallie's relationship with her home includes frustration. She echoes Maud Martha's thwarted desires to transform her kitchenette. Mrs Sallie's kitchen is 'my soft antagonist' who defeats her wishes: ' "I want to decorate!" But what is that? A / pomade atop a sewage': Brooks, *Blacks*, 410.

87 Thorsson, 'Black Aesthetic', 166.

88 Jones, 'Community and Voice: Gwendolyn Brooks's "in the Mecca" ', 203.

89 Kukrechtová, 'Chicago Edifice', 470.

90 Sheila Hassell Hughes, 'A Prophet Overheard: A Juxtapositional Reading of Gwendolyn Brooks's "in the Mecca"', *African American Review* 38, no. 2 (2004): 274.

91 Thorsson, 'Black Aesthetic', 167; Brooks, *Blacks*, 454.

92 Detloff, *Persistence of Modernism*, 115.

93 Marshall Berman, *All That Is Solid Melts into Air: The Experience of Modernity*, 1982 (London: Verso, 1983), 316–17.

94 Michael Gardiner, *Critique of Everyday Life* (London: Routledge, 2000), 35.

95 Christoph Lindner, *Fictions of Commodity Culture: From the Victorian to the Postmodern* (Aldershot: Ashgate, 2003), 9–10.

96 Heather Walton, *Writing Methods in Theological Reflection* (London: SCM Press, 2014), 34.

97 Heather Walton, *Literature, Theology and Feminism* (Manchester: Manchester University Press, 2007), 166.

98 Jane Bennett, *The Enchantment of Modern Life: Attachments, Crossings, and Ethics* (Princeton, NJ: Princeton University Press, 2001), 128. See also, Walton, *Writing Methods in Theological Reflection*, 38–9.

Bibliography

Adamson, Glen. *The Invention of Craft*. London: Bloomsbury, 2013.

Ahmed, Sara. *Queer Phenomenology: Orientations, Objects, Others*. Durham, NC: Duke University Press, 2006.

Ahmed, Sara. *The Cultural Politics of Emotion*. 2nd ed. 2004. Edinburgh: Edinburgh University Press, 2014.

Alexander, Elizabeth. *The Black Interior*. Saint Paul, MN: Graywolf Press, 2004.

Anderson, Elizabeth. '"The Knight's Move": Fluidity of Identity and Meaning in Mary Butt's *Armed with Madness*'. *Women: A Cultural Review* 18, no. 3 (2007): 245–56.

Anderson, Elizabeth. 'Burnt and Blossoming: Material Mysticism in *Trilogy* and *Four Quartets*'. *Christianity and Literature* 62, no. 1 (2012): 121–42.

Anderson, Elizabeth. *H.D. and Modernist Religious Imagination: Mysticism and Writing*. London: Bloomsbury, 2013.

Anderson, Elizabeth, Andrew Radford and Heather Walton, eds. *Modernist Women Writers and Spirituality: A Piercing Darkness*. London: Palgrave Macmillan, 2016.

Andrews, Larry R. 'The Aliveness of Things: Nature in *Maud Martha*'. In *Gwendolyn Brooks' Maud Martha*, edited by Jacqueline Bryant, 69–87. Chicago, IL: Third World Press, 2002.

Anon. 'Mana'. In *Oxford English Dictionary*. Oxford: Oxford University Press, 2000.

Anon. 'Mauri'. *Māori Dictionary*, 2003–18. www.maoridictionary.co.nz.

Appadurai, Arjun. *The Social Life of Things: Commodities in Cultural Perspective*. Cambridge: Cambridge University Press, 1986.

Appadurai, Arjun. 'The Thing Itself'. *Public Culture* 18, no. 1 (2006): 15–21.

Ardis, Ann L., and Leslie W. Lewis, eds. *Women's Experience of Modernity, 1875–1945*. London: Johns Hopkins University Press, 2003.

Armstrong, Isobel. 'Circumventing the Subject-Object Binary'. In *Bodies and Things*, edited by Katharina Boehm, 17–41. Basingstoke: Palgrave Macmillan, 2012.

Arnold, Matthew. 'Dover Beach'. In *The Norton Anthology of Poetry*, edited by Alexander W. Allison, Herbert Barrows, Caesar R. Blake, Arthur J. Carr, Arthur M. Eastman and Hubert M. English, 794. New York: W. W. Norton, 1983.

Arscott, Caroline. *William Morris and Edward Burne-Jones: Interlacings*. New Haven, CT: Yale University Press, 2008.

Asad, Talal. *Formations of the Secular: Christianity, Islam, Modernity*. Stanford, CA: Stanford University Press, 2003.

Avilez, GerShun. 'Housing the Black Body: Value, Domestic Space, and Segregation Narratives'. *African American Review* 42, no. 1 (2008): 135–47.

Bachelard, Gaston. *The Poetics of Space*. Translated by Maria Jolas. Boston: Beacon Press, [1958] 1994.

Baker, Houston A., Jr. *Modernism and the Harlem Renaissance*. Chicago, IL: Chicago University Press, 1987.

Baker, Houston A., Jr. *Workings of the Spirit: The Poetics of Afro-American Women's Writing*. Chicago, IL: University of Chicago Press, 1991.

Baker-Fletcher, Karen. *Sisters of Dust, Sisters of Spirit*. Minneapolis, MN: Fortress Press, 1998.

Banerjee, Sheela. 'Spectral Poetics in Virginia Woolf's the Waves'. In *Modernist Women Writers and Spirituality: A Piercing Darkness*, edited by Elizabeth Anderson, Andrew Radford and Heather Walton, 153–68. Basingstoke: Palgrave Macmillan, 2016.

Barad, Karen. *Meeting the Universe Halfway: Quantum Physics and the Entanglement of Matter and Meaning*. London: Duke University Press, 2007.

Barad, Karen. ' "Matter Feels, Converses, Suffers, Desires, Yearns and Remembers": Interview with Karen Barad'. In *New Materialism: Interviews and Cartographies*, edited by Rick Dolphijn and Iris van der Tuin. Ann Arbor, MI: Open Humanities Press, 2012. http://dx.doi.org/10.3998/ohp.11515701.0001.001.

Baring, Anne, and Jules Cashford. *The Myth of the Goddess: Evolution of an Image*. London: Penguin, 1993.

Bell, Catherine. *Ritual Theory, Ritual Practice*. Oxford: Oxford University Press, [2002] 2009.

Benjamin, Walter. *One-Way Street and Other Writings*. Translated by Edmund Jephcott and Kingsley Shorter. London: Verso, 2006.

Benko, Stephen. *The Virgin Goddess: Studies in the Pagan and Christian Roots of Mariology*. Leiden: Brill, 2004.

Bennett, Jane. *The Enchantment of Modern Life: Attachments, Crossings, and Ethics*. Princeton, NJ: Princeton University Press, 2001.

Bennett, Jane. *Vibrant Matter: A Political Ecology of Things*. London: Duke University Press, 2010.

Bennett, Phillippa. 'Rejuvenating Our Sense of Wonder: The Last Romances of William Morris'. In *William Morris in the Twenty-First Century*, edited by Phillippa Bennett and Rosie Miles, 209–28. Bern: Peter Lang, 2010.

Benstock, Shari. *Women of the Left Bank: Paris, 1900–1940*. London: Virago, 1986.

Berman, Jessica. *Modernist Fiction, Cosmopolitanism, and the Politics of Community*. Cambridge: Cambridge University Press, 2001.

Berman, Marshall. *All That Is Solid Melts into Air: The Experience of Modernity*. London: Verso, [1982] 1983.

Bird Rose, Deborah. 'Connectivity Thinking, Animism, and the Pursuit of Liveliness'. *Educational Theory* 67, no. 4 (2017): 491–508.

Blakely, Nora Brooks. 'Of Mama and Maud: A Forward'. In *Gwendolyn Brooks' Maud Martha: A Critical Collection*, edited by Jacqueline Bryant, ix–xi. Chicago, IL: Third World Press, 2002.

Blondel, Nathalie. *Mary Butts: Scenes from the Life*. Kingston, NY: McPherson, 1998.

Blondel, Nathalie. 'Introduction'. In *The Journals of Mary Butts*, edited by Nathalie Blondel. New Haven, CT: Yale University Press, 2002.

Boos, Florence Saunders. 'Dystopian Violence: William Morris and the Nineteenth-Century Peace Movement'. *Journal of Pre-Raphaelite Studies* 14 (2005): 15–35.

Boscagli, Maurizia. *Stuff Theory: Everyday Objects, Radical Materialism*. New York: Bloomsbury, 2014.

Bowlby, Rachel. *Feminist Destinations and Further Essays on Virginia Woolf*. Edinburgh: Edinburgh University Press, 1997.

Bowlby, Sophie, Susan Gregory and Linda McKie. ' "Doing Home": Patriarchy, Caring, and Space'. *Women's Studies International Forum* 20, no. 3 (1997): 343–50.

Bowler, Rebecca. *Literary Impressionism: Vision and Memory in Dorothy Richardson, Ford Maddox Ford, H.D. and May Sinclair*. London: Bloomsbury, 2016.

Boyarin, Daniel. *Unheroic Conduct: The Rise of Heterosexuality and the Invention of the Jewish Man*. Berkeley: University of California Press, 1997.

Boyarin, Daniel. *Sparks of the Logos: Essays in Rabbinic Hermeneutics*. Leiden: Brill, 2003.

Braddock, Jeremy. 'Race: Tradition and Archive in the Harlem Renaissance'. In *A Handbook of Modernism Studies*, edited by Jean-Michel Rabaté, 87–106. Hoboken, NJ: John Wiley, 2013.

Bradshaw, David. 'Hyam's Place: *The Years*, the Jews and the British Union of Fascists'. In *Women Writers of the 1930s: Gender, Politics, and History*, edited by Maroula Joannou, 179–91. Edinburgh: Edinburgh University Press, 1999.

Braidotti, Rosi. 'Conclusion: The Residual Spirituality in Critical Theory: A Case for Affirmative Postsecular Politics'. In *Transformation of Religion and the Public Sphere: Postsecular Publics*, edited by Rosi Braidotti, Bolette Blaagaard, Tobijn de Graauw, Eva Midden, 249–70. Basingstoke: Palgrave Macmillan, 2013.

Braidotti, Rosi, Bolette Blaagaard, Tobijn de Graauw, Eva Midden, eds. *Transformation of Religion and the Public Sphere: Postsecular Publics*. Basingstoke: Palgrave Macmillan, 2013.

Bramble, John. *Modernism and the Occult*. Basingstoke: Palgrave Macmillan, 2015.

Brock, Rita Nakashima, and Rebecca Ann Parker. *Saving Paradise: How Christianity Traded Love of This World for Crucifixion and Empire*. Boston, MA: Beacon Press, 2008.

Brooks, Gwendolyn. *Blacks*. Chicago, IL: Third World Press, 1994.

Brooks, Gwendolyn. 'Gladys the Gladiolus'. Bancroft Library, Gwendolyn Brooks Papers, n.d.

Brooks, Gwendolyn. *Report from Part One*. Detroit: Broadside Press, 1972.

Brooks, Gwendolyn. *Maud Martha*. Chicago, IL: Third World Press, [1953] 1993.

Brown, Bill. *Other Things*. London: University of Chicago Press, 2015.

Bryant, Jacqueline. 'Home'. In *Gwendolyn Brooks' Maud Martha: A Critical Collection*, edited by Jacqueline Bryant, 1–12. Chicago, IL: Third World Press, 2002.

Buchli, Victor. 'Households and 'Home Cultures''. In *The Oxford Handbook of Material Culture Studies*, edited by Dan Hicks and Mary C. Beaudry, 502–17. Oxford: Oxford University Press, 2010.

Buck-Morss, Susan. *The Dialectics of Seeing: Walter Benjamin and the Arcades Project*. London: MIT Press, 1999.

Buck-Morss, Susan. 'The Flâneur, the Sandwichman and the Whore: The Politics of Loitering'. In *Walter Benjamin and the Arcades Project*, edited by Beatrice Hanssen, 33–65. London: Bloomsbury, 2006.

Butts, Anthony. 'Letter to Mary Butts'. *Mary Butts Papers*, Beinecke Rare Book and Manuscript Library, Yale University, 1932?

Butts, Mary. 'Progress in the West'. *Mary Butts Papers*, Beinecke Rare Book and Manuscript Library, Yale University, n.d.

Butts, Mary. 'Notebooks'. *Mary Butts Papers*, Beinecke Rare and Manuscript Library, Yale University, 1936.

Butts, Mary. *The Crystal Cabinet: My Childhood at Salterns*. Manchester: Carcanet, 1988.

Butts, Mary. *Armed with Madness*. London: Penguin, [1928] 2001.

Butts, Mary. 'Coda'. In *Papers of Mary Butts, Box 13, Folder 184*: Beinecke Rare Book and Manuscript Library, Yale University, 1929.

Butts, Mary. 'Traps for Unbelievers'. In *Ashe of Rings and Other Writings*. Kingston, NY: McPherson, 1998.

Butts, Mary. *The Journals of Mary Butts*. New Haven, CT: Yale University Press, 2002.

Butts, Mary. *The Complete Stories*. Kingston, NY: McPherson, 2014.

Bynum, Caroline Walker. *Christian Materiality: An Essay on Religion in Late Medieval Europe*. New York: Zone Books, 2015.

Caputo, John D. *The Prayers and Tears of Jacques Derrida: Religion without Religion*. Bloomington: Indiana University Press, 1997.

Carmichael, Adam Burke. 'Post-National Foundation of Judith Butler's and Rosi Braidotti's Relational Subjectivity'. *Atlantis* 37, no. 2 (2016): 134–46.

Carpentier, Martha C. *Ritual, Myth, and the Modernist Text: The Influence of Jane Ellen Harrison on Joyce, Eliot, and Woolf*. Amsterdam: Gordon and Breach, 1998.

Chaudhuri, Nupur. 'Shawls, Jewelry, Curry, and Rice in Victorian Britain'. In *Western Women and Imperialism: Complicity and Resistance*, edited by Nupur Chaudhuri and Margaret Strobel, 231–46. Bloomington: Indiana University Press, 1992.

Cheah, Pheng. 'Introduction Part II: The Cosmoplitical-Today'. In *Cosmopolitics: Thinking and Feeling beyond the Nation*, edited by Bruce Robbins and Pheng Cheah, 21–41. Minneapolis: University of Minnesota Press, 1998.

Cheng, Anne Anlin. *The Melancholy of Race: Psychoanalytic Assimilation, and Hidden Grief*. Oxford: Oxford University Press, 2001.

Cheyette, Bryan. *Constructions of 'the Jew' in English Literature and Society: Racial Representations, 1975-1945*. Cambridge: Cambridge University Press, [1993] 1995.

Chireau, Yvonne Patricia. *Black Magic: Religion and the African-American Conjuring Tradition*. Berkeley: University of California Press, 2003.

Chisholm, Dianne. *H.D.'s Freudian Poetics: Psychoanalysis in Translation*. Ithaca, NY: Cornell University Press, 1992.

Christian, Barbara. 'Nuance and the Novella: A Study of Gwendolyn Brooks's *Maud Martha*'. In *A Life Distilled: Gwendolyn Brooks, Her Poetry and Fiction*, edited by Maria K. Mootry and Gary Smith, 239–53. Urbana: University of Illinois Press, 1987.

Chryssavgis, John. 'The Earth as Sacrament: Insights from Orthodox Christian Theology and Spirituality'. In *The Oxford Handbook of Religion and Ecology*, edited by Roger S. Gottlieb, 92–114. Oxford: Oxford University Press, 2006.

Cixous, Hélène, and Catherine Clément. *The Newly Born Woman*. Translated by Betsy Wing. *La Jeune Née*, Paris: Union Générale d'Editions, 1975 London: I. B. Tauris, 1996.

Coleman, Will. *Tribal Talk: Black Theology, Hermeneutics, and African/American Ways of 'Telling the Story'*. University Park, PA: Pennsylvania State University Press, 2000.

Colesworthy, Rebecca. *Returning the Gift: Modernism and the Thought of Exchange*. Oxford: Oxford University Press, 2018.

Collecott, Diana. *H.D. and Sapphic Modernism, 1910 – 1950*. Cambridge: Cambridge University Press, 1999.

Connolly, William *Why I Am Not a Secularist*. Minneapolis: University of Minnesota Press, 1999.

Connor, Rachel. *H.D. and the Image*. Manchester: Manchester University Press, 2004.

Coward, Harold, ed. *Derrida and Negative Theology*. Albany: State University of New York, 1992.

Cox, Aimee. 'The Body and City Project: Young Black Women Making Space, Community, and Love in Newark, New Jersey'. *Feminist Formations* 26, no. 3 (2014): 1–28.

Crawford, Margo Natalie. '"Perhaps Buddha Is a Woman": Women's Poetry in the Harlem Renaissance'. In *The Cambridge Companion to the Harlem Renaissance*, edited by George Hutchinson. Cambridge: Cambridge University Press, 2007.

Crenshaw, Kimberlé. 'Demarginalizing the Intersection of Race and Sex: A Black Feminist Critique of Antidiscrimination Doctrine, Feminist Theory and Antiracist Politics'. *University of Chicago Legal Forum* 1989, no. 1 (1989): 139–68.

Crockett, Clayton, and Jeffrey W. Robbins, eds. *Religion, Politics, and the Earth: The New Materialism*. New York: Palgrave Macmillan, 2012.

Dalke, Anne. 'Spirit Matters: Re-Possessing the African-American Women's Literary Tradition'. *Legacy: A Journal of American Women Writers* 12, no. 1 (1995): 1–16.

Davis, Thadious M. *Southscapes: Geographies of Race, Region, and Literature*. Chapel Hill: University of North Carolina Press, 2011.

Debo, Annette. *The American H.D.* Iowa City: University of Iowa Press, 2012.

Debo, Annette. 'Introduction'. In *Within the Walls and What Do I Love*, edited by Annette Debo, 1–104. Gainesville: University Press of Florida, 2014.

de Certeau, Michel. *The Practice of Everyday Life*. Translated by Steven Rendall. London: University of California Press, 1988.

de Gay, Jane. *Virginia Woolf and Christian Culture*. Edinburgh: Edinburgh University Press, 2018.

Denisoff, Dennis. 'The Dissipating Nature of Decadent Paganism from Pater to Yeats'. *Modernism/modernity* 15, no. 3 (2008): 431–6.

Derrida, Jacques. *Given Time: 1, Counterfeit Money*. Translated by Peggy Kamuf. Chicago, IL: Chicago University Press, [1991] 1992.

Detloff, Madelyn. *The Persistence of Modernism: Loss and Mourning in the Twentieth Century*. Cambridge: Cambridge University Press, 2010.

Douglas, Mary. *Purity and Danger*. London: Routledge, [1966] 2006.

Duncan, Robert. *The H.D. Book*. Berkeley: University of California Press, 2011.

Duplessis, Rachel Blau. *Writing beyond the Ending: Narrative Strategies of Twentieth-Century Women Writers*. Bloomington: Indiana University Press, 1985.

Eade, John. 'Introduction to the Illinois Paperback'. In *Contesting the Sacred: The Anthropology of Christian Pilgrimage*, edited by John Eade and Michael J. Sallnow, ix–xxvii. Chicago: University of Illinois Press, 2000.

Edmonds, Susan. *Out of Line: History, Psychoanalysis, & Montage in H.D.'s Long Poems*. Stanford, CA: Stanford University Press, 1994.

Elkins, Amy. 'A Stitch in Time: H.D.'s Craft Modernism as Transhistoric Repair'. *The Space Between: Literature and Culture 1914–1945* 12 (2016). http://scalar.usc.edu/works/the-space-between-literature-and-culture-1914-1945/vol12_2016_elkins.

Erkkila, Betsy. *Wicked Sisters: Women Poets, Literary History, and Discord*. Oxford: Oxford University Press, 1992.

Esty, Jed. *A Shrinking Island: Modernism and National Culture in England*. Princeton, NJ: Princeton University Press, 2004.

Evans, David. *A History of Nature Conservation in Britain*. London: Routledge, 1992.

Evans, Elizabeth F., and Sarah E Cornish, eds. *Woolf and the City*. Liverpool: Liverpool University Press, 2010.

Felski, Rita. *The Gender of Modernity*. Cambridge, MA: Harvard University Press, 1995.

Fernald, Anne E. 'Women's Fiction, New Modernist Studies, and Feminism'. *MFS: Modern Fiction Studies* 59, no. 2 (2013): 229–40.

Ferretter, Luke. *The Glyph and the Gramophone: D. H. Lawrence's Religion*. London: Bloomsbury, 2013.

Findlen, Paula, ed. *Early Modern Things: Objects and Their Histories, 1500–1800*. London: Routledge, 2012.

Fisk, Anna. '"To Make, and Make Again": Feminism, Craft and Spirituality'. *Feminist Theology* 20, no. 2 (2012): 160–74.

Floreani, Tracy. *Fifties Ethnicities: The Ethnic Novel and Mass Culture at Midcentury*. New York: State University of New York Press, 2013.

Foster, Thomas. *Transformations of Domesticity in Modern Women's Writing: Homelessness at Home*. Basingstoke: Palgrave Macmillan, 2002.

Foy, Roslyn Reso. *Ritual, Myth, and Mysticism in the Work of Mary Butts: Between Feminism and Modernism*. Fayetteville, NC: University of Arkansas Press, 2000.

Fraiman, Susan. *Extreme Domesticity: A View from the Margins*. New York: Columbia University Press, 2017.

Freedgoode, Elaine. *The Ideas in Things: Fugitive Meaning in the Victorian Novel*. London: University of Chicago Press, 2006.

Freer, Scott. *Modernist Mythopoeia: The Twilight of the Gods*. Basingstoke: Palgrave Macmillan, 2015.

Friedman, Susan . *Penelope's Web: Gender, Modernity, H.D.'s Fiction*. Cambridge: Cambridge University Press, 1990.

Friedman, Susan. *Planetary Modernisms: Provocations on Modernity across Time*. New York: Columbia University Press, 2015.

Friedman, Susan Stanford. *Mappings: Feminism and the Cultural Geographies of Encounter*. Princeton, NJ: Princeton University Press, 1998.

Fuchs, Miriam. *The Text Is Myself: Women's Life Writing and Catastrophe*. Madison: University of Wisconsin Press, 2003.

Fuss, Diana. *The Sense of an Interior: Four Rooms and the Writers that Shaped Them*. London: Routledge, 2004.

Gaipa, Mark. 'An Agnostic's Daughter's Apology: Materialism, Spiritualism and Ancestry in Woolf's *to the Lighthouse*'. *Journal of Modern Literature* 26, no. 2 (2003): 1–41.

Gan, Wendy. 'Solitude and Community: Virginia Woolf, Spatial Privacy and *a Room of One's Own*'. *Literature and History* 18, no. 1 (2009): 68–80.

Gan, Wendy. *Women, Privacy and Modernity in Early Twentieth-Century British Writing*. Basingstoke: Palgrave Macmillan, 2009.

Gardiner, Michael. *Critique of Everyday Life*. London: Routledge, 2000.

Gardner, Clinton. 'Vladimir Solov'ev: From Theism to Panentheism'. In *Vladimir Solov'ev: Reconciler and Polemicist*, edited by Wil van den Bercken, Manon de Courten and Evert van der Zweerde, 107–17. Leuven: University of Nijmegen, 2001.

Garrity, Jane. *Step-Daughters of England: British Women Modernists and the National Imaginary*. Manchester: Manchester University Press, 2003.

Garuba, Harry. 'Explorations in Animist Materialism: Notes on Reading/Writing African Literature, Culture, and Society'. *Public Culture* 15, no. 2 (2003): 261–85.

Gates, Henry Louis, Jr. *Signifying Monkey: A Theory of African-American Literary Criticism*. Oxford: Oxford University Press, [1988] 2014.

Gebara, Ivone. *Longing for Running Water: Ecofeminism and Liberation*. Minneapolis, MN: Fortress Press, 1999.

Gell, Alfred. *Art and Agency: An Anthropological Theory*. Oxford: Oxford University Press, 1998.

Gere, Cathy. *Knossos and the Prophets of Modernism*. Chicago, IL: University of Chicago Press, 2009.

Gilbert, Sandra M., and Susan Gubar. *The Madwoman in the Attic*. New Haven, CT: Yale University Press, 1984.

Goldman, Jane. *The Feminist Aesthetics of Virginia Woolf: Modernism, Post-Impressionism and the Politics of the Visual*. Cambridge: Cambridge University Press, 2001.

Gomez, Michael A. *Exchanging Our Country Marks: The Transformation of African Identities in the Colonial Antebellum South*. Chapel Hill: University of North Carolina Press, 1998.

Gordon, Beverly. *Textiles: The Whole Story*. London: Thames and Hudson, 2011.

Gough, Val. 'With Some Irony in Her Interrogation: Woolf's Ironic Mysticism'. In *Virginia Woolf and the Arts: Selected Papers from the Sixth Annual Conference on Virginia Woolf*, edited by Diane F. Gillespie and Leslie K. Hankins, 85–90. New York: Pace University Press, 1997.

Graham, Sarah H. S. 'Falling Walls: Trauma and Testimony in H.D.'s *Trilogy*'. *English* 56, Autumn (2007): 299–319.

Gregory, Eileen. *H.D. And Hellenism: Classic Lines*. Cambridge: Cambridge University Press, 1997.

Groover, Kristina K. *The Wilderness Within: American Women Writers and Spiritual Quest*. Fayetteville, NC: University of Arkansas Press, 1999.

H.D. 'Letter to Viola Baxter Jordan, April 28, 1942'. *Viola Baxter Jordan Papers*, Yale Collection of American Literature, Beinecke Rare Book and Manuscript Library, Yale University.

H.D. 'Letters to Bryher, 2 January, 10 and 16 February, 8, 10 and 15 November, 1947'. *Bryher Papers*, Beinecke Rare Book and Manuscript Libary, Yale University.

H.D. 'Letter to Bryher, 2 March, 1938.' In *Bryher Papers,* Beinecke Rare Book and Manuscript Library, Yale University.

H.D. 'Letter to Viola Baxter Jordan, 5 September, 1947?' *Viola Baxter Jordan Papers*, Yale Collection of American Literature, Beinecke Rare Book and Manuscript Library.

H.D. *Hermetic Definition*. Oxford: Carcanet Press, 1972.

H.D. *End to Torment: A Memoir of Ezra Pound*. Manchester: Carcanet, 1980.

H.D. *Collected Poems: 1912–1944*. New York: New Directions, 1983.

H.D. 'H.D. by *Delia Alton*'. *Iowa Review* 16, no. 3 (1986): 180–221.

H.D. *The Gift by H.D.: The Complete Text*. Edited by Jane Augustine. Gainesville: University Press of Florida, 1998.

H.D. *Trilogy*. New York: New Directions, 1998.

H.D. *The Sword Went out to Sea: (Synthesis of a Dream), by Delia Alton*. Gainesville: University Press of Florida, 2007.

H.D. *Tribute to Freud*. New York: New Directions, [1956] 2012.

H.D. 'Writing on the Wall'. In *Tribute to Freud*, 3–111. New York: New Directions, 2012.

H.D. *Within the Walls and What Do I Love*. Gainesville: University Press of Florida, 2014.

H.D. *The Hirslanden Notebooks: An Annotated Scholarly Edition*. Victoria: ELS Editions, 2015.

Haar, Sharon, and Christopher Reed. 'Coming Home: A Postscript on Postmodernism'. In *Not at Home: The Suppression of Domesticity in Modern Art and Architecture*, edited by Christopher Reed, 253–73. London: Thames and Hudson, 1996.

Hackney, Fiona. 'Home Craft and Make-Do-and-Mend in British Women's Magazines of the 1920s and 1930s'. *Journal of Design History* 19, no. 1 (2006): 23–38.

Hackney, Fiona. 'Quiet Activism and the New Amateur: The Power of Home and Hobby Crafts'. *Design and Culture* 5, no. 2 (2013): 169–94.

Hadjiafxendi, Kyiaki, and Patricia Zakreski, eds. *Crafting the Woman Professional in the Long Nineteenth Century: Artistry and Industry in Britain*. London: Routledge, 2013.

Halsall, Alison. 'H.D. and the Victorian Spectres of *White Rose and the Red*'. *College Literature* 38, no. 4 (2011): 115–33.

Hanegraaff, Wouter. 'The Emergence of the Academic Science of Magic: The Occult Philosophy in Tylor and Frazer'. In *Religion in the Making*, edited by Arie L. Molendijk and Peter Pels, 253–75. Leiden: Brill, 1998.

Hargreaves, Tracey. 'I Should Explain He Shares My Bath: Art and Politics in *the Years*'. *English* 50, no. Autumn (2001): 183–98.

Harris, Jennifer. 'William Morris and the Middle Ages'. In *William Morris and the Middle Ages*, edited by Joanna Banham and Jennifer Harris, 1–17. Manchester: Manchester University Press, 1984.

Harrison, Jane Ellen. *Themis: A Study of the Social Origins of Greek Religion*. 2nd ed. Cambridge: Cambridge University Press, [1912] 1927.

Hart, Imogen. *Arts and Crafts Objects*. Manchester: Manchester University Press, 2010.

Harvey, Graham. *Animism: Respecting the Living World*. London: Hurst, 2005.

Haughton, Hugh. 'Introduction'. In *Sigmund Freud: The Uncanny*, vii–lx. London: Penguin, 2003.

Hawkes, Joel. 'Inside *the Crystal Cabinet*: Truth, Lies and Vision in Mary Butts's Autobiography of Place'. *Creative Spaces* 1 (2010): 31–49.

Heath, Stephen. 'Introduction: Chances of the Sacred Game'. In *Armed with Madness*, edited by Mary Butts, vii–xxiv. London: Penguin, 2001.

Hoberman, Ruth. *Gendering Classicism: The Ancient World in Twentieth-Century Women's Historical Fiction*. Albany: State University of New York, 1997.

Hobson, Suzanne. *Angels of Modernism: Religion, Culture, Aesthetics 1910–1960*. Basingstoke: Palgrave Macmillan, 2011.

Hogan, Linda. *Dwellings: A Spiritual History of the Living World*. New York: W. W. Norton, 2007.

Hogan, Linda. 'We Call It *Tradition*'. In *The Handbook of Contemporary Animism*, edited by Graham Harvey, 17–26. London: Routledge, 2015.

Hogue, Cynthia, and Julie Vandivere. 'Introduction'. In *The Sword Went out to Sea: (Synthesis of a Dream), by Delia Alton*, xv–liii. Gainesville: University Press of Florida, 2007.

Hollenberg, Donna Krolik, ed. *Between History & Poetry: The Letters of H.D. & Norman Holmes Pearson*. Iowa City: University of Iowa Press, 1997.

Hollywood, Amy. *The Soul as Virgin Wife: Mechthild of Magdeburg, Marguerite Porete and Meister Eckhart*. Notre Dame: University of Notre Dame Press, 1995.

hooks, bell. *Yearning: Race, Gender, and Cultural Politics*. Boston, MA: South End Press, 1990.

hooks, bell. *Wounds of Passion: A Writing Life*. London: Women's Press, 1998.

hooks, bell. *Belonging: A Culture of Place*. New York: Routledge, 2009.

Hopkins, Dwight N. *Down, Up, and Over: Slave Religion and Black Theology*. Minneapolis, MN: Fortress Press, 2000.

Hopkins, Gerard Manley. *The Major Works*. Oxford: Oxford University Press, 2002.

Howard, Constance. *Twentieth-Century Embroidery in Great Britain to 1939*. London: Batsford, 1981.

Howard, Constance. *Twentieth-Century Embroidery in Great Britain 1940–1963*. London: Batsford, 1983.

Howe, Nicholas. *Landscapes of the Secular: Law, Religion, and American Sacred Space*. Chicago, IL: University of Chicago Press, 2016.

Hughes, Gertrude Reif. 'Making It Really New: Hilda Doolittle, Gwendolyn Brooks, and the Feminist Potential of Modern Poetry'. *American Quarterly* 42, no. 3 (1990): 375–401.

Hughes, Sheila Hassell. 'A Prophet Overheard: A Juxtapositional Reading of Gwendolyn Brooks's "In the Mecca" '. *African American Review* 38, no. 2 (2004): 257–80.

Hurston, Zora Neale. *Their Eyes Were Watching God*. London: Virago Press, [1937] 2018.

Hyest, Jenny. 'Anne Spencer's Feminist Modernist Poetics'. *Journal of Modern Literature* 38, no. 3 (2015): 129–47.

Hyest, Jenny. ' "Born with God in the House": Feminist Vision and Religious Revision in the Works of Zora Neale Hurston'. *Legacy* 35, no. 1 (2018): 25–47.

Ingman, Heather. *Women's Spirituality in the Twentieth Century: An Exploration through Fiction*. Bern: Peter Lang, 2004.

Ingold, Tim. *Being Alive: Essays on Movement, Knowledge and Description*. Abingdon: Routledge, 2011.

Ingold, Tim. *Making: Anthropology, Archaeology, Art and Architecture*. New York: Routledge, 2013.

Ingold, Tim. 'Being Alive to a World without Objects'. In *The Handbook of Contemporary Animism*, edited by Graham Harvey, 213–25. London: Routledge, 2014.

Iovino, Serenella, and Serpil Oppermann. 'Introduction: Stories Come to Matter'. In *Material Ecocriticism*, edited by Serenella Iovino and Serpil Oppermann, 1–17. Bloomington: Indiana University Press, 2014.

Jacobus, Mary. *Romantic Things: A Tree, a Rock, a Cloud*. Chicago, IL: University of Chicago Press, 2012.

James, William. *Some Problems of Philosophy*. 1911. Cambridge, MA: Harvard University Press, 1979.

Jantzen, Grace. *Power, Gender and Christian Mysticism*. Cambridge: Cambridge University Press, 1995.

Jantzen, Grace. *Becoming Divine: Towards a Feminist Philosophy of Religion*. Manchester: Manchester University Press, 1998.

Jimoh, A. Yemisi. 'Double Consciousness, Modernism, and Womanist Themes in Gwendolyn Brooks's "The Anniad"'. *MELUS* 23, no. 3 (1998): 167–86.

Johnson, Barbara. *Persons and Things*. Cambridge, MA: Harvard University Press, 2008.

Jones, Feminista. *Reclaiming Our Space: How Black Feminists Are Changing the World from the Tweets to the Streets*. Boston, MA: Beacon Press, 2019.

Jones, Gayle. 'Community and Voice: Gwendolyn Brooks's "in the Mecca"'. In *A Life Distilled: Gwendolyn Brooks, Her Poetry and Fiction*, edited by Maria K. Mootry and Gary Smith, 193–204. Urbana: University of Illinois Press, 1987.

Kane, Julie. 'Varieties of Mystical Experience in the Writings of Virginia Woolf'. *Twentieth Century Literature* 41 (1995): 328–49.

Kearney, Richard. 'Epiphanies of the Everyday: Toward a Micro-Eschatology'. In *After God: Richard Kearney and the Continental Turn in Contemporary Philosophy*, edited by John Panteleimon Manoussakis, 3–20. New York: Fordham University Press, 2006.

Keller, Catherine. *Apocalypse Now and Then: A Feminist Guide to the End of the World*. Minneapolis, MN: Fortress Press, [1996] 2005.

Keller, Catherine. *Face of the Deep: A Theology of Becoming*. London: Routledge, 2003.

Keller, Catherine. *God and Power: Counter-Apocalyptic Journeys*. Minneapolis, MN: Fortress Press, 2005.

Keller, Catherine. 'The Apophasis of Gender: A Fourfold Unsaying of Feminist Theology'. *Journal of the American Academy of Religion* 76, no. 4 (2008): 905–33.

Keller, Catherine. *Cloud of the Impossible: Negative Theology and Planetary Entanglement*. New York: Columbia, 2015.

Keller, Catherine, and Mary-Jane Rubenstein, eds. *Entangled Worlds: Religion, Science, and New Materialisms*. New York: Fordham University Press, 2017.

Keller, Catherine, and Mary-Jane Rubenstein. 'Introduction: Tangled Matters'. In *Entangled Worlds: Religion, Science, and New Materialisms*, edited by Catherine Keller and Mary-Jane Rubenstein, 1–14. New York: Fordham University Press, 2017.

Kimmerer, Robin Wall. *Braiding Sweetgrass*. Minneapolis, MN: Milkweed Editions, 2013.

King, Kathryn R. 'Of Needles and Pens and Women's Work'. *Tulsa Studies in Women's Literature* 14, no. 1 (1995): 77–93.

Kontou, Tatiana. *Spiritualism and Women's Writing: From the Fin De Siècle to the Neo-Victorian*. Basingstoke: Palgrave Macmillan, 2009.

Kukrechtová, Daniela. 'The Death and Life of a Chicago Edifice: Gwendolyn Brooks's "In the Mecca"'. *African American Review* 43, no. 2–3 (2009): 457–72.

Kwok, Pui-lan. *Postcolonial Imagination & Feminist Theology*. London: SCM Press, 2005.

Laity, Cassandra. *H.D. and the Victorian Fin De Siècle: Gender, Modernism, Decadence*. Cambridge: Cambridge University Press, 1996.

Laity, Cassandra. 'Editor's Introduction: Toward Feminist Modernisms'. *Feminist Modernist Studies* 1, no. 1–2 (2018): 1–7.

Lanzetta, Beverly J. *The Other Side of Nothingness: Toward a Theology of Radical Openness*. Albany: State University of New York Press, 2001.

Larsen, Nella. *Quicksand and Passing*. 1928–29. New Brunswick, NJ: Rutgers University Press, 1998.

Larsson, Lisbeth. *Walking Virginia Woolf's London*. Palgrave, 2017. doi:10.1007/978-3-319-55672-7_1.

Lassner, Phyllis. '"The Milk of Our Mother's Kindness Has Ceased to Flow": Virginia Woolf, Stevie Smith, and the Representation of the Jew'. In *Between 'Race' and Culture: Representations of 'the Jew' in English and American Literature*, edited by Bryan Cheyette, 129–44. Stanford, CA: Stanford University Press, 1996.

Lassner, Phyllis, and Mia Spiro. 'A Tale of Two Cities: Virginia Woolf's Imagined Jewish Spaces and London's East End Jewish Culture'. *Woolf Studies Annual* 19 (2013): 58–82.

Latour, Bruno. *We Have Never Been Modern*. Translated by Catherine Porter. Cambridge, MA: Harvard University Press, 1993.

Lattin, Patricia H., and Vernon E. Lattin. 'Dual Vision in Gwendolyn Brooks's *Maud Martha*'. *Critique* 25, no. 4 (1984): 180–8.

Lazenby, Donna. *A Mystical Philosophy: Transcendence and Immanence in the Works of Virginia Woolf and Iris Murdoch*. London: Bloomsbury, 2014.

Lewis, Pericles. *Religious Experience and the Modernist Novel*. Cambridge: Cambridge University Press, 2010.

Lindner, Christoph. *Fictions of Commodity Culture: From the Victorian to the Postmodern*. Aldershot: Ashgate, 2003.

Linett, Maren. 'Introduction: Modernism's Jews/Jewish Modernism'. *MFS: Modern Fiction Studies* 51, no. 2 (2005): 249–57.

Linett, Maren Tova. *Modernism, Feminism, and Jewishness*. Cambridge: Cambridge University Press, 2007.

Louis, Margot K. 'Gods and Mysteries: The Revival of Paganism and the Remaking of Mythography through the Nineteenth Century'. *Victorian Studies* 47, no. 3 (2005): 329–61.

Louis, Margot K. *Persephone Rises, 1860–1927: Mythography, Gender, and the Creation of a New Spirituality*. Farnham: Ashgate, 2009.

Lowney, John. *History, Memory, and the Literary Left: Modern American Poetry, 1935–1968*. Iowa City: University of Iowa Press, 2006.

Lynch, Gordon. *The Sacred in the Modern World: A Cultural Sociological Approach*. Oxford: Oxford University Press, 2012.

Lysack, Krista. *Come Buy, Come Buy: Shopping and the Culture of Consumption in Victorian Women's Writing*. Athens: Ohio University Press, 2008.

MacCarthy, Fiona. *William Morris: A Life for Our Time*. London: Faber and Faber, 1994.

Mahmood, Saba. 'Sexuality and Secularism'. In *Religion, the Secular, and the Politics of Sexual Difference*, edited by Linell E. Cady and Tracy Fessenden, 47–58. New York: Columbia University Press, 2013.

Mance, Ajuan Maria. *Inventing Black Women: African American Women Poets and Self-Representation, 1877–2000*. Knoxville: University of Tennessee Press, 2007.

Mansfield, Katherine. *Selected Stories*. Edited by Angela Smith. Oxford: Oxford University Press, 2008.

Mao, Douglas. *Solid Objects: Modernism and the Test of Production*. Princeton, NJ: Princeton University Press, 1998.

Mao, Douglas, and Rebecca L. Walkowitz. 'The New Modernist Studies'. *PMLA* (2008): 737–48.

Marcus, Jane. *Virginia Woolf and the Languages of Patriarchy*. Bloomington: Indiana University Press, 1987.

Marsh, Jan. *Dante Gabriel Rossetti: Painter and Poet*. London: Phoenix, 2005.

Maskiell, Michelle. 'Consuming Kashmir: Shawls and Empires, 1500–2000'. *Journal of World History* 13, no. 1 (2002): 27–65.

Massey, Doreen. *For Space*. London: Sage, 2005.

Mataira, Peter J. '*Mana* and *Tapu*: Sacred Knowledge, Sacred Boundaries'. In *Indigenous Religions: A Companion*, edited by Graham Harvey, 99–112. London: Bloomsbury, 2000.

Materer, Timothy. *Modernist Alchemy: Poetry and the Occult*. Ithaca, NY: Cornell University Press, 1995.

Mauss, Marcel. *The Gift; Forms and Functions of Exchange in Archaic Societies*. Translated by Ian Cunnison. London: Cohen & West, 1954.

McDannell, Colleen. *Material Christianity: Religion and Popular Culture in America*. London: Yale University Press, 1995.

McDowell, Linda. *Gender, Identity and Place: Understanding Feminist Geographies*. Cambridge: Polity Press, 1999.

McFague, Sallie. *The Body of God: An Ecology Theology*. London: SCM Press, 1993.

McGinn, Bernard. *The Presence of God: A History of Western Christian Mysticism:*. New York: Crossroads, 1992–2006.

Mendes-Flohr, Paul R., and Jehuda Reinharz, eds. *The Jew in the Modern World: A Documentary History*. 2nd ed. Oxford: Oxford University Press, 1995.

Middleton, Angela. *Te Puna – a New Zealand Mission Station: Historical Archaeology in New Zealand*. New York: Springer, 2008.

Miller, Daniel. *The Comfort of Things*. London: Polity Press, 2009.

Miller, Elizabeth. *Slow Print: Literary Radicalism and Late Victorian Print Culture*. Stanford, CA: Stanford University Press, 2013.

Mitchell, W. J. T. 'Romanticism and the Life of Things'. *Critical Inquiry* 28, no. 1 (2001): 167–84.

Mootry, Maria K. '"Tell It Slant": Disguise and Discovery as Revisionist Poetic Discourse in *The Bean Eaters*'. In *A Life Distilled: Gwendolyn Brooks, Her Poetry and Fiction*, edited by Maria K. Mootry and Gary Smith, 167–92. Chicago: University of Illinois Press, 1987.

Moran, Joe. 'Houses, Habit and Memory'. In *Our House: The Representation of Domestic Space in Modern Culture*, edited by Gerry Smyth and Jo Croft, 27–42. Amsterdam: Rodopi, 2006.

Morgan, David. 'Introduction: The Matter of Belief'. In *Religion and Material Culture: The Matter of Belief*, edited by David Morgan, 1–18. London: Routledge, 2010.

Morris, Adalaide. *How to Live/What to Do: H.D.'s Cultural Poetics*. Chicago: University of Illinois Press, 2003.

Morris, William. *The Defense of Guinevere, and Other Poems*. London: Bell and Daldy, 1858.

Morrison, Toni. *Beloved*. New York: Alfred A. Knopf, [1987] 2006.

Morrison, Toni. *Mouth Full of Blood: Essays, Speeches, Meditations*. London: Chatto & Windus, 2019.

Mullen, Bill V. *Popular Fronts: Chicago and African-American Cultural Politics, 1935–56*. Urbana: University of Illinois Press, 1999.

Mullholland, Terri. *British Boarding Houses in Interwar Women's Literature: Alternative Domestic Spaces*. London: Routledge, 2017.

Olsson, Tord. 'Animate Objects: Ritual Perception and Practice among the Bambara in Mali'. In *The Handbook of Contemporary Animism*, edited by Graham Harvey, 226–43. London: Routledge, 2015.

Orr, Emma Restall. *The Wakeful World: Animism, Mind and the Self in Nature*. Winchester: Moon Books, 2012.

Ortega, Kirsten Bartholomew. 'The Black Flaneuse: Gwendolyn Brooks's "In the Mecca"'. *Journal of Modern Literature* 30, no. 4 (2007): 139–55.

Ortega, Mariana. 'Gift of Being, Gift of Self'. In *Women and the Gift: Beyond the Given and the All-Giving*, edited by Morny Joy, 111–15. Bloomington: Indiana University Press, 2013.

Ostriker, Alicia. *Writing Like a Woman*. Ann Arbor: University of Michigan Press, 1983.

Owen, Alex. *The Place of Enchantment: British Occultism and the Culture of the Modern*. Chicago: University of Chicago Press, 2004.

Park, Julie. *The Self and It: Novel Objects and Mimetic Subjects in Eighteenth-Century England*. Stanford, CA: Stanford University Press, 2009.

Parker, Rozsika. *The Subversive Stitch*. London: I. B. Tauris, 2010.

Parkins, Wendy. 'Jane Morris's Art of Everyday Life at Kelmscott'. In *William Morris and the Art of Everyday Life*, edited by Wendy Parkins, 133–54. Newcastle: Cambridge Scholars, 2010.

Parsons, Deborah L. *Streetwalking the Metropolis: Women, the City and Modernity*. Oxford: Oxford University Press, 2000.

Pattison, Stephen, and John Swinton. 'Moving Beyond Clarity: Towards a Thin, Vague, and Useful Understanding of Spirituality in Nursing Care'. *Nursing Philosophy* 11 (2010): 226–37.

Peat, Alexandra. *Travel and Modernist Literature: Sacred and Ethical Journeys*. London: Routledge, 2011.

Pedersen, Ann. 'Creativity, Christology and Science: A Process of Composition and Improvisation'. In *Creating Women's Theology: A Movement Engaging Process Thought*, edited by Monica A. Coleman, Nancy R. Howell and Helene Tallon Russell, 160–75. Eugene, OR: Pickwick, 2011.

Pels, Peter. 'The Spirit of Matter: On Fetish, Rarity, Fact, and Fancy'. In *Border Fetishisms: Material Objects in Unstable Spaces*, edited by Patricia Spyer. New York: Routledge, 1998.

Pietz, William. 'The Problem of the Fetish, I'. *RES: Anthropology and Aesthetics* 9 (1985): 5–17.

Radford, Andrew. *Mary Butts and British Neo-Romanticism: The Enchantment of Place*. London: Bloomsbury, 2014.

Radford, Andrew. 'A 'Fine, Mysterious, Almost Sacred Fable'? Retelling the Grail Quest in Mary Butts' *Armed with Madness*'. *Literature and Theology* 29, no. 3 (2015): 298–322.

Ramazani, Jahan. *A Transnational Poetics*. Chicago, IL: University of Chicago Press, 2009.

Randall, Bryony. "Funny, but No Hybrid': H.D., Tea and Expatriate Identity'. *Symbiosis* 13, no. 2 (2009): 189–210.

Reek, Jennifer. *A Poetics of Church: Reading and Writing Sacred Spaces of Poetic Dwelling*. Abingdon: Routledge, 2018.

Renshaw, Sal. 'Graceful Gifts: Hélène Cixous and the Radical Gifts of Other Love'. In *Women and the Gift: Beyond the Given and the All-Giving*, edited by Morny Joy, 131–49. Bloomington: Indiana University Press, 2013.

Rich, Adrienne. *The Dream of a Common Language: Poems 1974–1977*. London and New York: W. W. Norton, 1978.

Rieger, Joerg, and Edward Waggoner, eds. *Religious Experience and New Materialism: Movement Matters*. New York: Palgrave Macmillan, 2016.

Rivera, Mayra. *The Touch of Transcendence: A Postcolonial Theology of God*. London: Westminster John Knox Press, 2007.

Rivera, Mayra. *Poetics of the Flesh*. Durham, NC: Duke University Press, 2015.

Rives, Rochelle. 'Problem Space: Mary Butts, Modernism, and the Etiquette of Placement'. *Modernism/modernity* 12, no. 4 (2005): 607–27.

Robinson, Matte. *The Astral H.D.: Occult and Religious Sources and Contexts for H.D.'s Poetry and Prose*. London: Bloomsbury, 2016.

Rosner, Victoria. *Modernism and the Architecture of Private Life*. New York: Columbia University Press, 2005.

Rossetti, Dante Gabriel. *The Correspondence of Dante Gabriel Rossetti*. Vol. IV, Cambridge: Brewer, 2004.

Rubenstein, Mary-Jane. 'The Matter with Pantheism: On Shepherds and Goat-Gods and Mountains and Monsters'. In *Entangled Worlds: Religions, Science, and New Materialisms*, edited by Catherine Keller and Mary-Jane Rubenstein, 157–74. New York: Fordham University Press, 2017.

Rubenstein, Roberta. *Home Matters: Longing and Belonging, Nostalgia and Mourning in Women's Fiction*. New York: Palgrave, 2001.

Ruether, Rosemary Radford. *Gaia and God: An Ecofeminist Theology of Earth Healing*. London: SCM Press, 1992.

Ryan, Judylyn. *Spirituality as Ideology in Black Women's Film and Literature*. Charlottesville: University of Virginia Press, 2005.

Saber, Yomna Mohamed. *Brave to Be Involved: Shifting Positions in the Poetry of Gwendolyn Brooks*. Oxford: Peter Lang, 2010.

Sandercock, Leonie. *Cosmopolis II: Mongrel Cities of the 21st Century*. New York: Continuum, 2003.

Sanders, Mark A. 'African American Folk Roots and Harlem Renaissance Poetry'. In *The Cambridge Companion to the Harlem Renaissance*, edited by George Hutchinson, 96–111. Cambridge: Cambridge University Press, 2007.

Saunders, Corrine. 'Religion and Magic'. In *The Cambridge Companion to the Arthurian Legend*, edited by Elizabeth Archibald and Ad Putter, 201–27. Cambridge: Cambridge University Press, 2009.

Schaffer, Talia. *Novel Craft: Victorian Domestic Handicraft and Nineteenth-Century Fiction*. Oxford: Oxford University Press, 2011.

Schaffer, Talia, and Kathy Alexis Psomiades. 'Introduction'. In *Women and British Aestheticism*, edited by Talia Schaffer and Kathy Alexis Psomiades, 1–15. Charlottesville: University Press of Virginia, 1999.

Schaffner, Perdita. 'Running'. *The Iowa Review* 16, no. 3 (1986): 7–13.

Schmidt, Leigh Eric. *Hearing Things: Religion, Illusion and the American Enlightenment*. Cambridge, MA: Harvard University Press, 2000.

Schmidt, Leigh Eric. 'The Making of Modern "Mysticism"'. *Journal of the American Academy of Religion* 71, no. 2 (2003): 273–302.

Schröder, Leena Kore. 'Tales of Abjection and Miscegenation: Virginia Woolf's and Leonard Woolf's "Jewish" Stories'. *Twentieth Century Literature* 49, no. 3 (2003): 298–327.

Schweik, Susan. *A Gulf So Deeply Cut: American Women Poets and the Second World War*. Madison: University of Wisconsin Press, 1991.

Scott, Bonnie Kime, ed. *The Gender of Modernism: A Critical Anthology*. Bloomington: Indiana University Press, 1990.

Scott, Bonnie Kime, ed. *Gender in Modernism: New Geographies, Complex Intersections*. Urbana: University of Illinois Press, 2007.

Scott, Bonnie Kime. *In the Hollow of the Wave: Virginia Woolf and the Modernist Uses of Nature*. Charlottesville: University of Virginia Press, 2012.

Scott, Joan Wallach. 'Secularism and Gender Equality'. In *Religion, the Secular, and the Politics of Sexual Difference*, edited by Linell E. Cady and Tracy Fessenden, 25–45. New York: Columbia University Press, 2013.

Seshagiri, Urmila. *Race and the Modernist Imagination*. Ithaca, NY: Cornell University Press, 2010.

Seshagiri, Urmila. 'Mind the Gap! Modernism and Feminist Praxis'. *Modernism/ modernity Print Plus Forum* 2, no. 2 (2017). doi: https://doi.org/10.26597/mod.0022, https://doi.org/10.26597/mod.0022.

Shakespeare, William. 'The Winter's Tale'. In *The Norton Shakespeare: Based on the Oxford Edition*, edited by Stephen Greenblatt, Walter Cohen, Jean E. Howard and Katherine Eisaman Maus, 2873–953. New York: W. W. Norton, 1997.

Sheail, John. *Rural Conservation in Interwar Britain*. Oxford: Oxford University Press, 1981.

Sherry, Vincent. *Modernism and the Reinvention of Decadence*. Cambridge: Cambridge University Press, 2015.

Shiach, Morag. 'Modernism, the City and the "Domestic Interior"'. *Home Cultures* 2, no. 3 (2005): 251–67.

Sim, Lorraine. *Virginia Woolf: The Patterns of Ordinary Experience*. Abingdon: Routledge, 2010.

Simpson, Kathryn. *Gifts, Markets and Economies of Desire in Virginia Woolf*. Basingstoke: Palgrave Macmillan, 2008.

Simpson, Kathryn. '"Street Haunting," Commodity Culture, and the Woman Artist'. In *Woolf and the City*, edited by Elizabeth F. Evans and Sarah E. Cornish, 47–53. Liverpool: Liverpool University Press, 2010.

Sitwell, Edith. 'Letter to H.D., Undated, 1942–44?' In *H.D. Papers, Yale Collection of American Literature*. New Haven, CT: Beinecke Rare Book and Manuscript Library, Yale University.

Sizemore, Christine W. 'Cosmopolitanism from Below in *Mrs. Dalloway* and "Street Haunting"'. In *Woolf and the City*, edited by Sarah E. Cornish and Elizabeth F. Evans. Liverpool: Liverpool University Press, 2016.

Smethurst, James. *The African American Roots of Modernism: From Reconstruction to the Harlem Renaissance*. Chapel Hill: University of North Carolina Press, 2011.

Smith, Gary. 'Paradise Regained: The Children of Gwedolyn Brooks's Bronzeville'. In *A Life Distilled: Gwendolyn Brooks, Her Poetry and Fiction*, edited by Maria K. Mootry and Gary Smith, 128–39. Chicago: University of Illinois Press, 1987.

Smith, Mick. 'Lost for Words? Gadamer and Benjamin on the Nature of Language and the 'Language' of Nature'. *Environmental Values* 10 (2001): 59–75.

Smith, Oliver. *Vladimir Soloviev and the Spiritualization of Matter*. Brighton, MA: Academic Studies Press, 2011.

Smith, Preston H. *Racial Democracy and the Black Metropolis: Housing Policy in Postwar Chicago*. Minneapolis: University of Minnesota Press, 2012.

Smith, Theophus H. *Conjuring Culture: Biblical Formations of Black America*. New York: Oxford University Press, 1994.

Snaith, Anna. *Virginia Woolf: Public and Private Negotiations*. New York: Palgrave Macmillan, 2003.

Snyder, Jean E. *Harry T Burleigh: From the Spiritual to the Harlem Renaissance*. Champaigne: University of Illinois Press, 2016.

Spillers, Hortense J. ' "An Order of Constance" ': Notes on Brooks and the Feminine'. In *Reading Black, Reading Feminist*, edited by Jr. Gates, Henry Louis, 244–71. New York: Penguin, 1999.

Spiro, Mia. *Anti-Nazi Modernism: The Challenges of Resistance in 1930s Fiction*. Evanston, IL: Northwestern University Press, 2013.

Stewart, Kathleen. 'Afterword: Worlding Refrains'. In *The Affect Theory Reader*, edited by Melissa Gregg and Gregory J. Seigworth, 239–53. Durham, NCDuke University Press, 2010.

Stocking, George W., Jr. *Race, Culture, and Evolution: Essays in the History of Anthropology*. Chicago, IL: University of Chicago Press, [1968] 1982.

Stringer, Martin D. 'Building on Belief: Defining Animism in Tylor and Contemporary Society'. In *The Handbook of Contemporary Animism*, edited by Graham Harvey, 63–72. Abingdon: Routledge, 2015.

Sundberg, Juanita. 'Decolonizing Posthumanist Geographies'. *Cultural Geography* 21, no. 1 (2014): 33–47.

Surette, Leon. *The Birth of Modernism: Ezra Pound, T.S. Eliot, W.B. Yeats, and the Occult*. Montreal: McGill-Queens University Press, 1994.

Sword, Helen. *Ghostwriting Modernism*. Ithaca, NY: Cornell University Press, 2002.

Tally, Robert T. *Spatiality*. London: Routledge, 2013.

Taussig, Michael. 'Crossing the Face'. In *Border Fetishisms: Material Objects in Unstable Spaces*, edited by Patricia Spyer, 224–44. New York: Routledge, 1998.

Tawhai, T. P. 'Maori Religion'. In *Readings in Indigenous Religons*. Edited by Graham Harvey, 237–49. London: Continuum, 2002.

Thacker, Andrew. *Moving through Modernity: Space and Geography in Modernism*. 2003. Manchester: Manchester University Press, 2009.

Thorsson, Courtney. 'Gwendolyn Brooks's Black Aesthetic of the Domestic'. *MELUS* 40, no. 1 (2015): 149–76.

Thurswell, Pamela. *Literature, Technology and Magical Thinking, 1880–1920*. Cambridge: Cambridge University Press, 2001.

Todd, Zoe. 'An Indigenous Feminist's Take on the Ontological Turn: "Ontology" Is Just another Word for Colonialism', *Journal of Historical Sociology* 29, no. 1 (2016): 4–22

Tompkins, Kyla Wazana. 'New Materialisms'. *Lateral* 5, no. 1 (2016). https://doi.org/10.25158/L5.1.8.

Torgovnick, Marianna. *Primitive Passions: Men, Women and the Quest for Ecstasy.* Chicago, IL: University of Chicago Press, 1996.

Tracy, Steven. 'Introduction'. In *Writers of the Black Chicago Renaissance*, edited by Steven Tracy, 1–14. Chicago: University of Illinois Press, 2011.

Tryphonopoulos, Demetres P. *The Celestial Tradition: A Study of Ezra Pound's the Cantos.* Waterloo: Wilfred Laurier University Press, 1992.

Tryphonopoulos, Demetres P. 'Introduction'. In *Majic Ring*, edited by Demtres Tryphonopoulos, xxi-xxxix. Gainesville: University Press of Florida, 2009.

Turner, Denys. *The Darkness of God: Negativity in Christian Mysticism.* Cambridge: Cambridge University Press, 1995.

Turney, Joanne. *The Culture of Knitting.* Oxford: Berg, 2009.

Tuveson, Ernest Lee. *The Avatars of Thrice Great Hermes.* London: Associated University Presses, 1982.

Tylor, Edward B. *Primitive Culture: Researches into the Development of Mythology, Philosophy, Religion, Art, and Custom.* Vol. 2. London: John Murray, 1871.

Tylor, Edward B. *Primitive Culture: Researches into the Development of Mythology, Philosophy, Religion, Art, and Custom.* Vol. 1, London: John Murray, 1871.

Vaninskaya, Anna. *William Morris and the Idea of Community: Romance, History and Propaganda 1880–1914.* Edinburgh: Edinburgh University Press, 2010.

Vásquez, Manuel A. *More than Belief: A Materialist Theory of Religion.* Oxford: Oxford University Press, 2011.

Vetter, Lara. 'Afterword: Modernist Women Writers and Spirituality'. In *Modernist Women Writers and Spirituality: A Piercing Darkness*, edited by Elizabeth Anderson, Andrew Radford and Heather Walton, 237–46. London: Palgrave Macmillan, 2016.

Vetter, Lara. *Modernist Writings and Religio-Scientific Discourse: H.D., Loy and Toomer.* Basingstoke: Palgrave Macmillan, 2010.

Vetter, Lara. *A Curious Peril: H.D.'s Late Modernist Prose.* Gainesville: University Press of Florida, 2017.

Walker, Alice. *In Search of Our Mother's Gardens: Womanist Prose.* New York: Harcourt Brace Jovanovich, [1967] 1983.

Walter, Hilary Laucks. 'Another Stitch to the Legacy of William Morris: May Morris's Designs and Writings on Embroidery'. In *William Morris in the Twenty-First Century*, edited by Phillippa Bennett and Rosie Miles, 73–90. Bern: Peter Lang, 2010.

Walton, Heather. *Literature, Theology and Feminism.* Manchester: Manchester University Press, 2007.

Walton, Heather. *Writing Methods in Theological Reflection.* London: SCM Press, 2014.

Walton, Heather. *Not Eden: Spiritual Life-Writing for This World.* London: SCM Press, 2015.

Washington, Mary Helen. '"Taming All That Anger Down" Rage and Silence in Gwendolyn Brooks' *Maud Martha'. Massachusetts Review* 24, no. 2 (1983): 453–66.

Watts, Vanessa. 'Indigenous Place-Thought & Agency amongst Humans and Non-Humans (First Woman and Sky Woman Go on a European World Tour!)'. *Decolonization: Indigeneity, Education & Society* 2, no. 1 (2013): 20–34.

West, Elizabeth J. *African Spirituality in Black Women's Fiction: Threaded Visions of Memory, Community, Nature, and Being*. 2011. Plymouth: Lexington Books, 2013.

Weston, Jessie L. *From Ritual to Romance*. 1920. Princeton, NJ: Princeton University Press, 1993.

Wilson, Leigh. *Modernism and Magic: Experiments with Spiritualism, Theosophy and the Occult*. Edinburgh: Edinburgh University Press, 2012.

Winick, Mimi. 'Modernist Feminist Witchcraft: Margaret Murray's Fantastic Scholarship and Sylvia Townsend Warner's Realist Fantasy'. *Modernism/modernity* 22, no. 3 (2015): 565–92.

Winick, Mimi. 'Scholarly Enchantment'. *Nineteenth-Century Literature* 73, no. 2 (2018): 187–226.

Wiseman, Sam. 'Cosmopolitanism and Environmental Ethics in Mary Butts's Dorset'. *Twentieth Century Literature* 61, no. 3 (2015): 373–91.

Wiseman, Sam. *The Reimagining of Place in English Modernism*. Clemson, SC: Clemson University Press, 2015.

Wolfson, Elliot R. 'Circumcision and the Divine Name: A Study in the Transmission of Esoteric Doctrine'. *Jewish Quarterly Review* 78, no. 1–2 (1987): 77–112.

Woolf, Virginia. *The Essays of Virginia Woolf*. Vol. VI 1933–1941 & Additional Essays 1906–1924. London: Hogarth Press, 2011.

Woolf, Virginia. *Three Guineas*. New York: Harcourt, [1938] 1966.

Woolf, Virginia. *Moments of Being*. San Diego, CA: Harcourt, 1985.

Woolf, Virginia. 'Street Haunting'. In *The Crowded Dance of Modern Life: Selected Essays: Volume Two*, edited by Rachel Bowlby, 70–81. London: Penguin, 1993.

Woolf, Virginia. *A Room of One's Own*. London: Penguin, [1929] 2004.

Woolf, Virginia. *The Mark on the Wall and Other Short Fiction*. Oxford: Oxford University Press, 2008.

Woolf, Virginia. *To the Lighthouse*. Oxford: Oxford University Press, [1927] 2008.

Woolf, Virginia. *The Years*. The Cambridge Edition of the Works of Virginia Woolf. Cambridge: Cambridge University Press, [1937] 2012.

Woolf, Virginia. *Mrs Dalloway*. The Cambridge Edition of the Works of Virginia Woolf. Cambridge: Cambridge University Press, [1925] 2015.

Wright, Patrick. 'Coming Back to the Shores of Albion: The Secret England of Mary Butts (1890–1937)'. In *On Living in an Old Country*, edited by Patrick Wright, 93–134. London: Verso, 1985.

Wright, Steven Caldwell. 'Gwendolyn Brooks'. In *Writers of the Black Chicago Renaissance*, edited by Steven Tracy, 96–120. Chicago: University of Illinois Press, 2011.

Wright, Tamra, Peter Hughes and Alison Ainley. 'The Paradox of Morality: An Interview with Emmanuel Levinas'. In *The Provocation of Levinas: Rethinking*

the Other, edited by Robert Bernasconi and David Woods, 168–80.
London: Routledge, 1988.

Wynne, Deborah. "Charlote Brontë's Frocks and Shirley's Queer Textiles". In *Literary Bric-À-Brac and the Victorians*, edited by Jen Harrison and Jonathan Shears, 147–62. Farnham: Ashgate, 2013.

Yates, Frances. *Giordano Bruno and the Hermetic Tradition*. 1964. London: Routledge and Kegan Paul, 1971.

Zakreski, Patricia. 'The Victorian Christmas Card as Aesthetic Object'. *Journal of Design History* 29, no. 2 (2015): 120–36.

Zilboorg, Caroline, ed. *Richard Aldington & H.D.: Their Lives in Letters 1918–61*. Manchester: Manchester University Press, 2003.

Index

Printed in Great Britain
by Amazon

57539358R00123